Global Economic Prospects

*A World Bank Group
Flagship Report*

JUNE 2022

Global
Economic
Prospects

WORLD BANK GROUP

ISBN (paper): 978-1-4648-1843-1
ISBN (electronic): 978-1-4648-1844-8
DOI: 10.1596/978-1-4648-1843-1

Cover design: Bill Pragluski (Critical Stages).

The Library of Congress Control Number has been requested.

The cutoff date for the data used in this report was May 31, 2022.

Summary of Contents

Contents

Acknowledgments

This World Bank Group Flagship Report is a product of the Prospects Group in the Equitable Growth, Finance and Institutions (EFI) Vice Presidency. The project was managed by M. Ayhan Kose and Franziska Ohnsorge, under the general guidance of Indermit Gill.

Global and regional surveillance work was led by Carlos Arteta. The report was prepared by a team that included John Baffes, Justin-Damien Guénette, Jongrim Ha, Osamu Inami, Sergiy Kasyanenko, Philip Kenworthy, Jeetendra Khadan, Sinem Kilic Celik, Patrick Kirby, Peter Nagle, Lucia Quaglietti, Franz Ulrich Ruch, Naotaka Sugawara, Ekaterine Vashakmadze, Collette Wheeler, and Takefumi Yamazaki.

Research assistance was provided by Lule Bahtiri, Hrisyana Doytchinova, Jiayue Fan, Dhruv Gandhi, Arika Kayastha, Maria Hazel Macadangdang, Muneeb Ahmad Naseem, Julia Roseman Norfleet, Vasiliki Papagianni, Lorëz Qehaja, Juan Felipe Serrano, Shijie Shi, Kaltrina Temaj, Jingran Wang, and Juncheng Zhou. Modeling and data work were provided by Rajesh Kumar Danda and Shijie Shi.

Online products were produced by Graeme Littler. Alejandra Viveros managed communications and media outreach with a team that included Joe Rebello and Nandita Roy and extensive support from the World Bank's media and digital communications teams. Graeme Littler provided editorial support, with contributions from Adriana Maximiliano.

The print publication was produced by Adriana Maximiliano, in collaboration with Andrew Berghauser, Cindy Fisher, Michael Harrup, Maria Hazel Macadangdang, and Jewel McFadden.

Regional projections and write-ups were produced in coordination with country teams, country directors, and the offices of the regional chief economists.

Many reviewers provided extensive advice and comments. The analysis also benefited from comments and suggestions by staff members from World Bank Group country teams and other World Bank Group Vice Presidencies as well as Executive Directors in their discussion of the report on May 31, 2022. However, both forecasts and analysis are those of the World Bank Group staff and should not be attributed to Executive Directors or their national authorities.

Foreword

Just over two years after COVID-19 caused the deepest global recession since World War II, the world economy is again in danger. This time it is facing high inflation and slow growth at the same time. Even if a global recession is averted, the pain of stagflation could persist for several years—unless major supply increases are set in motion.

Amid the war in Ukraine, surging inflation, and rising interest rates, global economic growth is expected to slump in 2022. Several years of above-average inflation and below-average growth are now likely, with potentially destabilizing consequences for low- and middle-income economies. It's a phenomenon—stagflation—that the world has not seen since the 1970s.

Our forecasts reflect a sizable downgrade to the outlook: global growth is expected to slow sharply from 5.7 percent in 2021 to 2.9 percent this year. This also reflects a nearly one-third cut to our January 2022 forecast for this year of 4.1 percent. The surge in energy and food prices, along with the supply and trade disruptions triggered by the war in Ukraine and the necessary interest rate normalization now underway, account for most of the downgrade.

COVID-19 already dealt a major setback to income growth and poverty reduction in developing economies. The fallout from the war in Ukraine compounds the challenges for many of them. They are expected to grow 3.4 percent in 2022—barely half the rate in 2021 and well below the average from 2011 through 2019. Middle-income countries will see a sharp downgrade to growth in 2022, losing 1.3 percentage points relative to the January forecast. Because of the adverse shocks of the past two years, real income per capita in 2023 will remain below pre-COVID-19 levels in about 40 percent of developing economies. For many countries, recession will be hard to avoid. With the supply of natural gas constrained, especially for use in fertilizer and electricity grids in poorer countries, announcements of major production increases worldwide will be essential for breaking out of stagflation and restoring noninflationary growth.

This edition of the *Global Economic Prospects* report offers the first systematic assessment of how current global economic conditions compare with the era of stagflation of the 1970s—with a particular emphasis on how stagflation could affect developing economies. The insights are sobering: the interest rate increases that were required to control inflation at the end of the 1970s were so steep that they touched off a global recession, along with a string of debt crises in developing economies, ushering in a "lost decade" in some of them.

The danger of stagflation is considerable today. Between 2021 and 2024, global growth is projected to have slowed by 2.7 percentage points—more than twice the deceleration between 1976 and 1979. Subdued growth will likely persist throughout the decade because of weak investment in most of the world. With inflation now running at multidecade highs in many countries and supply expected to grow slowly, there is a risk that inflation will remain higher for longer than currently anticipated.

External public debt in developing economies is at record levels today. Most of it is owed to private creditors, and much of it involves variable interest rates that could spike suddenly. As global financing conditions tighten and currencies depreciate, debt distress—previously confined to low-income economies—is spreading to middle-income countries.

The removal of monetary accommodation in the United States and other advanced economies, along with the ensuing increase in global borrowing costs, represents another significant headwind for the developing world. In addition, over the next two years, most of the fiscal support provided in 2020 to fight the pandemic will have been unwound. Despite this consolidation, debt levels will remain elevated.

Yet the analysis shows that the current conditions differ from those in the 1970s in multiple dimensions. The dollar is strong, a sharp contrast with its severe weakness in the 1970s. Oil prices quadrupled in 1973-1974 and doubled in 1979-1980. Today, in inflation-adjusted terms, oil prices are only two-thirds of what they were in 1980. The balance sheets of major financial institutions were a risk in the 1970s; today, they are generally strong. Economies across the world are also more flexible than they were in the 1970s, with fewer structural rigidities involving wages and labor markets. Importantly, policy makers are in a better position today to stave off stagflationary headwinds. Monetary policy frameworks are more credible—with clear price stability mandates for central banks in advanced and many developing economies alike. Long-term inflation expectations are also better anchored. Existing technology and capital have the capacity to provide massive increases in supply, holding down price expectations.

Reducing the risk of stagflation will require targeted and impactful measures by policy makers across the world. This report spells out what they can do to avoid the worst outcomes—and why that work must begin immediately. In an extraordinary era of overlapping global crises, policy makers across the world will need to focus their efforts in five key areas:

- *First, limit the harm to people affected by the war in Ukraine* by coordinating the crisis response, including delivery of emergency food, medical, and financial aid to war-torn areas. It will also be necessary to share the burden of housing, supporting, and possibly relocating refugees and internally displaced people.

- *Second, counter the spike in oil and food prices.* It's essential to boost the supply of key food

and energy commodities. Markets look forward, so even mere *announcements* of future supply would help reduce prices and inflation expectations. In the poorest nations at greatest risk of a food crisis, social safety nets should be buttressed. It's also crucial to avoid export and import restrictions that magnify the rise in prices.

- *Third, step up debt relief efforts.* Debt vulnerabilities were acute for low-income countries even before the pandemic. As debt distress spreads to middle-income countries, the risk for the global economy is growing. Debt relief needs to be rapid, comprehensive, and sizable in order to minimize debt overhang and risks to future growth.

- *Fourth, strengthen health preparedness and efforts to contain COVID-19.* Expanding vaccination coverage in low-income countries, including that for COVID-19 vaccinations, must be a global priority.

- *Fifth, speed the transition to low-carbon energy sources.* Reducing dependency on fossil fuels will need more investments in electricity grids, cleaner energy sources, and greater energy efficiency. National policy makers should create climate-smart regulatory frameworks, adjust incentive structures, and strengthen land use regulations.

After multiple crises, long-term prosperity will depend on returning to faster growth and a more stable, rules-based policy environment. There is good reason to expect that, once the war in Ukraine stops, efforts will redouble—including by the World Bank Group—to rebuild the Ukrainian economy and revive global growth. In the meantime, policy makers everywhere must fight the world's other development crises: the catastrophe of higher food and energy prices, the threat of stagflation, the rise in inequality and instability, climate change, and the growing overhang of debt.

David Malpass
President
World Bank Group

Executive Summary

The world economy continues to suffer from a series of destabilizing shocks. After more than two years of pandemic, the Russian Federation's invasion of Ukraine and its global effects on commodity markets, supply chains, inflation, and financial conditions have steepened the slowdown in global growth. In particular, the war in Ukraine is leading to soaring prices and volatility in energy markets, with improvements in activity in energy exporters more than offset by headwinds in most other economies. The invasion of Ukraine has also led to a significant increase in agricultural commodity prices, which is exacerbating food insecurity and extreme poverty in many emerging market and developing economies (EMDEs). Numerous risks could further derail what is now a precarious recovery. Among them is, in particular, the possibility of stubbornly high global inflation accompanied by tepid growth, reminiscent of the stagflation of the 1970s. This could eventually result in a sharp tightening of monetary policy in advanced economies to rein in inflation, lead to surging borrowing costs, and possibly culminate in financial stress in some EMDEs. A forceful and wide-ranging policy response is required by EMDE authorities and the global community to boost growth, bolster macroeconomic frameworks, reduce financial vulnerabilities, provide support to vulnerable population groups, and attenuate the long-term impacts of the global shocks of recent years.

Global outlook: Following more than two years of pandemic, spillovers from the Russian Federation's invasion of Ukraine are set to sharply hasten the deceleration of global economic activity, which is now expected to slow to 2.9 percent in 2022. The war in Ukraine is leading to high commodity prices, adding to supply disruptions, increasing food insecurity and poverty, exacerbating inflation, contributing to tighter financial conditions, magnifying financial vulnerability, and heightening policy uncertainty. Growth in emerging market and developing economies (EMDEs) this year has been downgraded to 3.4 percent, as negative spillovers from the invasion of Ukraine more than offset any near-term boost to some commodity exporters from higher energy prices. Despite the negative shock to global activity in 2022, there is essentially no rebound projected next year: global growth is forecast to edge up only slightly to a still-subdued 3 percent in 2023, as many headwinds—in particular, high commodity prices and continued monetary tightening—are expected to persist. Moreover, the outlook is subject to various downside risks, including intensifying geopolitical tensions, growing stagflationary headwinds, rising financial instability, continuing supply strains, and worsening food insecurity.

These risks underscore the importance of a forceful policy response. The global community needs to ramp up efforts to mitigate humanitarian crises caused by the war in Ukraine and conflict elsewhere and alleviate food insecurity, as well as expand vaccine access to ensure a durable end of the pandemic. Meanwhile, EMDE policy makers need to refrain from implementing export restrictions or price controls, which could end up magnifying the increase in commodity prices. With rising inflation, tightening financial conditions, and elevated debt levels sharply limiting policy space, spending can be reprioritized toward targeted relief for vulnerable households. Over the long run, policies will be required to reverse the damage inflicted by the dual shocks of the pandemic and the war on growth prospects, including preventing fragmentation in trade networks, improving education, and raising labor force participation.

Regional prospects: Russia's invasion of Ukraine is affecting EMDE regions to different degrees via impacts on global trade and output, commodity prices, inflation, and interest rates. The adverse spillovers from the war will be most severe for Europe and Central Asia, where output is forecast to sharply contract this year. Output growth is projected to slow this year in all other regions except the Middle East and North Africa, where the benefits of higher energy prices for energy exporters are expected to outweigh those prices' negative impacts for other economies in the region. Risks for all EMDE regions are tilted to the downside and include intensifying geopolitical tensions, rising inflation and food shortages, financial stress and rising borrowing costs, renewed outbreaks of COVID-19, and disruptions from disasters.

This edition of *Global Economic Prospects* also includes short analytical pieces on the risk of global stagflation and the impact of Russia's invasion of Ukraine on the global economy through global energy markets.

Global stagflation. Global inflation has risen sharply from its lows in mid-2020, on rebounding global demand, supply bottlenecks, and soaring food and energy prices, especially since Russia's invasion of Ukraine. Markets expect inflation to peak in mid-2022 and then decline, but to remain elevated even after these shocks subside and monetary policies are tightened further. Global growth has been moving in the opposite direction: it has declined sharply since the beginning of the year and, for the remainder of this decade, is expected to remain below the average of the 2010s. In light of these developments, the risk of stagflation—a combination of high inflation and sluggish growth—has risen. The recovery from the stagflation of the 1970s required steep increases

in interest rates by major advanced-economy central banks to quell inflation, which triggered a global recession and a string of financial crises in EMDEs. If current stagflationary pressures intensify, EMDEs would likely face severe challenges again because of their less well-anchored inflation expectations, elevated financial vulnerabilities, and weakening growth fundamentals. This makes it urgent for EMDEs to shore up their fiscal and external buffers, strengthen their monetary policy frameworks, and implement reforms to reinvigorate growth.

Russia's invasion of Ukraine: Implications for energy markets and activity. Russia's invasion of Ukraine has disrupted global energy markets and damaged the global economy. Compared with what took place in the 1970s, the shock has led to a surge in prices across a broader set of energy-related commodities. In energy-importing economies, higher prices will reduce real disposable incomes, raise production costs, tighten financial conditions, and constrain policy space. Some energy exporters may benefit from improved terms of trade and higher commodities production. However, on net, model-based estimates suggest that the war-driven surge in energy prices could reduce global output by 0.8 percent after two years. The experience of previous oil price shocks has shown that these shocks can provide an important catalyst for policies to encourage demand reduction, substitution to other fuels, and development of new sources of energy supply.

Abbreviations

CPI	consumer price index
EAP	East Asia and Pacific
ECA	Europe and Central Asia
EMDE	emerging market and developing economy
EU	European Union
FAVAR	factor-augmented vector autoregression
G7	Group of Seven: Canada, France, Germany, Italy, Japan, the United Kingdom, and the United States
GCC	Gulf Cooperation Council
GDP	gross domestic product
GEP	*Global Economic Prospects*
GNFS	goods and nonfactor services
IEA	International Energy Agency
ILO	International Labour Organization
IMF	International Monetary Fund
LAC	Latin America and the Caribbean
LIC	low-income country
MNA/MENA	Middle East and North Africa
OECD	Organisation for Economic Co-operation and Development
OPEC	Organization of the Petroleum Exporting Countries
OPEC+	OPEC and Azerbaijan, Bahrain, Brunei Darussalam, Kazakhstan, Malaysia, Mexico, Oman, the Russian Federation, South Sudan, and Sudan
PMI	Purchasing Managers' Index
PPP	purchasing power parity
RHS	right-hand scale
SAR	South Asia
SSA	Sub-Saharan Africa
UN	United Nations
WAEMU	West African Economic and Monetary Union

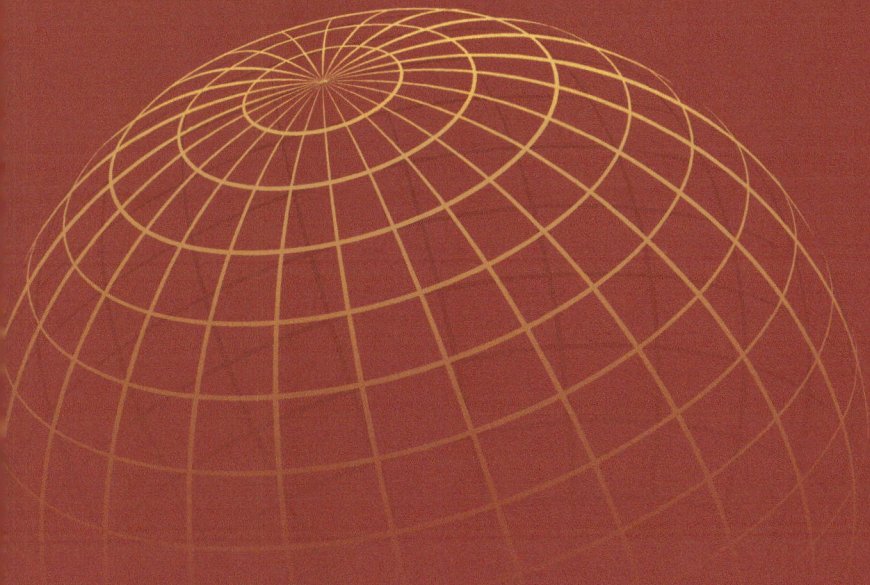

CHAPTER 1

GLOBAL OUTLOOK

Following more than two years of pandemic, spillovers from the Russian Federation's invasion of Ukraine are set to sharply hasten the deceleration of global economic activity, which is now expected to slow to 2.9 percent in 2022. The war in Ukraine is leading to high commodity prices, adding to supply disruptions, increasing food insecurity and poverty, exacerbating inflation, contributing to tighter financial conditions, magnifying financial vulnerability, and heightening policy uncertainty. Growth in emerging market and developing economies (EMDEs) this year has been downgraded to 3.4 percent, as negative spillovers from the invasion of Ukraine more than offset any near-term boost to some commodity exporters from higher energy prices. Despite the negative shock to global activity in 2022, there is essentially no rebound projected next year: global growth is forecast to edge up only slightly to a still-subdued 3 percent in 2023, as many headwinds—in particular, high commodity prices and continued monetary tightening—are expected to persist. Moreover, the outlook is subject to various downside risks, including intensifying geopolitical tensions, growing stagflationary headwinds, rising financial instability, continuing supply strains, and worsening food insecurity. These risks underscore the importance of a forceful policy response. The global community needs to ramp up efforts to mitigate humanitarian crises caused by the war in Ukraine and conflict elsewhere, alleviate food insecurity, and expand vaccine access to ensure a durable end of the pandemic. Meanwhile, EMDE policy makers need to refrain from implementing export restrictions or price controls, which could end up magnifying the increase in commodity prices. With rising inflation, tightening financial conditions, and elevated debt levels sharply limiting policy space, spending can be reprioritized toward targeted relief for vulnerable households. Over the long run, policies will be required to reverse the damage inflicted by the dual shocks of the pandemic and the war on growth prospects, including preventing fragmentation in trade networks, improving education, and raising labor force participation.

Summary

Still suffering from the effects of more than two years of pandemic, the global economy is experiencing yet another major negative shock. Russia's invasion of Ukraine has not only precipitated a humanitarian catastrophe—with thousands of civilians killed and millions more displaced—but also resulted in a deep regional slowdown and substantial negative global spillovers. These spillovers are magnifying pre-existing strains from the pandemic, such as bottlenecks in global supply chains and significant increases in the price of many commodities.

The effects of the invasion have also caused a further reduction in policy space, which is now much more limited than at the onset of the pandemic. Amid surging commodity prices and supply disruptions, inflation has soared across the world, exacerbating the exceedingly difficult tradeoffs policy makers face between supporting

growth and controlling price pressures. Global financial conditions have tightened and borrowing costs have increased, particularly in emerging market and developing economies (EMDEs), reflecting reduced policy accommodation in response to inflationary pressures, elevated uncertainty, and heightened geopolitical risks. In addition, the unwinding of fiscal support measures has continued to weigh on global activity.

Against the backdrop of this significantly more challenging context, the world economy is expected to experience its sharpest deceleration following an initial recovery from global recession in more than 80 years. Global growth is projected to slow from 5.7 percent in 2021 to 2.9 percent in 2022 and average 3 percent in 2023-24, as Russia's invasion of Ukraine significantly disrupts activity and trade in the near term, pent-up demand fades, and policy support is withdrawn amid high inflation (figures 1.1.A and 1.1.B). The effects of the war—including more acute inflationary pressures and a faster pace of monetary tightening than previously assumed—account for most of the 1.2 percentage points downward revision to this year's growth forecast. Growth projections for 2022 have been downgraded for most economies—including for

Note: This chapter was prepared by Carlos Arteta, Justin-Damien Guénette, Patrick Kirby, Lucia Quaglietti, and Collette Wheeler, with contributions from Jongrim Ha, Osamu Inami, Sergiy Kasyanenko, Phil Kenworthy, Peter Nagle, and Ekaterine Vashakmadze.

TABLE 1.1 Real GDP[1]

(Percent change from previous year)

	2019	2020	2021e	2022f	2023f	2024f	Percentage point differences from January 2022 projections 2022f	2023f
World	**2.6**	**-3.3**	**5.7**	**2.9**	**3.0**	**3.0**	**-1.2**	**-0.2**
Advanced economies	**1.7**	**-4.6**	**5.1**	**2.6**	**2.2**	**1.9**	**-1.2**	**-0.1**
United States	2.3	-3.4	5.7	2.5	2.4	2.0	-1.2	-0.2
Euro area	1.6	-6.4	5.4	2.5	1.9	1.9	-1.7	-0.2
Japan	-0.2	-4.6	1.7	1.7	1.3	0.6	-1.2	0.1
Emerging market and developing economies	**3.8**	**-1.6**	**6.6**	**3.4**	**4.2**	**4.4**	**-1.2**	**-0.2**
East Asia and Pacific	5.8	1.2	7.2	4.4	5.2	5.1	-0.7	0.0
China	6.0	2.2	8.1	4.3	5.2	5.1	-0.8	-0.1
Indonesia	5.0	-2.1	3.7	5.1	5.3	5.3	-0.1	0.2
Thailand	2.2	-6.2	1.6	2.9	4.3	3.9	-1.0	0.0
Europe and Central Asia	2.7	-1.9	6.5	-2.9	1.5	3.3	-5.9	-1.4
Russian Federation	2.2	-2.7	4.7	-8.9	-2.0	2.2	-11.3	-3.8
Turkey	0.9	1.8	11.0	2.3	3.2	4.0	0.3	0.2
Poland	4.7	-2.2	5.9	3.9	3.6	3.7	-0.8	0.2
Latin America and the Caribbean	0.8	-6.4	6.7	2.5	1.9	2.4	-0.1	-0.8
Brazil	1.2	-3.9	4.6	1.5	0.8	2.0	0.1	-1.9
Mexico	-0.2	-8.2	4.8	1.7	1.9	2.0	-1.3	-0.3
Argentina	-2.0	-9.9	10.3	4.5	2.5	2.5	1.9	0.4
Middle East and North Africa	0.9	-3.7	3.4	5.3	3.6	3.2	0.9	0.2
Saudi Arabia	0.3	-4.1	3.2	7.0	3.8	3.0	2.1	1.5
Iran, Islamic Rep. [3]	-6.8	3.4	4.1	3.7	2.7	2.3	1.3	0.5
Egypt, Arab Rep. [2]	5.6	3.6	3.3	6.1	4.8	5.0	0.6	-0.7
South Asia	4.1	-4.5	7.6	6.8	5.8	6.5	-0.8	-0.2
India [3]	3.7	-6.6	8.7	7.5	7.1	6.5	-1.2	0.3
Pakistan [2]	3.1	-0.9	5.7	4.3	4.0	4.2	0.9	0.0
Bangladesh [2]	7.9	3.4	6.9	6.4	6.7	6.9	0.0	-0.2
Sub-Saharan Africa	2.6	-2.0	4.2	3.7	3.8	4.0	0.1	0.0
Nigeria	2.2	-1.8	3.6	3.4	3.2	3.2	0.9	0.4
South Africa	0.1	-6.4	4.9	2.1	1.5	1.8	0.0	0.0
Angola	-0.7	-5.2	0.7	3.1	3.3	3.2	0.0	0.5
Memorandum items:								
Real GDP[1]								
High-income countries	1.7	-4.6	5.1	2.7	2.2	2.0	-1.1	-0.2
Middle-income countries	4.0	-1.3	6.8	3.3	4.2	4.5	-1.3	-0.3
Low-income countries	4.8	1.9	3.9	4.1	5.3	5.7	-0.8	-0.6
EMDEs excl. Russian Federation and Ukraine	3.9	-1.5	6.7	4.2	4.5	4.5	-0.5	0.0
EMDEs excl. China	2.5	-4.0	5.6	2.7	3.4	4.0	-1.5	-0.4
Commodity-exporting EMDEs	1.8	-3.8	4.8	1.2	2.6	3.2	-2.1	-0.5
Commodity-exporting EMDEs excl. Russian Federation and Ukraine	1.8	-4.0	4.8	3.7	3.3	3.4	0.3	-0.1
Commodity-importing EMDEs	4.9	-0.4	7.5	4.4	4.9	5.0	-0.8	-0.1
Commodity-importing EMDEs excl. China	3.2	-4.2	6.6	4.6	4.5	4.9	-0.7	-0.1
EM7	4.5	-0.5	7.3	3.3	4.3	4.7	-1.5	-0.4
World (PPP weights) [4]	2.9	-3.0	6.0	3.1	3.4	3.5	-1.3	-0.2
World trade volume [5]	**1.4**	**-8.0**	**10.3**	**4.0**	**4.3**	**3.8**	**-1.8**	**-0.4**
Commodity prices [6]								
Oil price	-9.9	-33.9	66.5	42.0	-8.0	-13.0	35.0	3.8
Non-energy commodity price index	-4.2	3.3	32.7	17.9	-8.1	-3.1	19.9	-4.1

Source: World Bank.

1. Headline aggregate growth rates are calculated using GDP weights at average 2010-19 prices and market exchange rates. The aggregate growth rates may differ from the previously published numbers that were calculated using GDP weights at average 2010 prices and market exchange rates. Data for Afghanistan and Lebanon are excluded.

2. GDP growth rates are on a fiscal year basis. Aggregates that include these countries are calculated using data compiled on a calendar year basis. Pakistan's growth rates are based on GDP at factor cost. The column labeled 2022 refers to FY2021/22.

3. GDP growth rates are on a fiscal year basis. Aggregates that include these countries are calculated using data compiled on a calendar year basis. The column labeled 2022 refers to FY2022/23.

4. World growth rates are calculated using average 2010-19 purchasing power parity (PPP) weights, which attribute a greater share of global GDP to emerging market and developing economies (EMDEs) than market exchange rates.

5. World trade volume of goods and nonfactor services.

6. Oil price refers to the Brent crude oil benchmark. The non-energy index is the weighted average of 39 commodity prices (7 metals, 5 fertilizers, and 27 agricultural commodities). For additional details, please see https://www.worldbank.org/commodities.

Note: e = estimate; f = forecast. World Bank forecasts are frequently updated based on new information. Consequently, projections presented here may differ from those contained in other World Bank documents, even if basic assessments of countries' prospects do not differ at any given date. For the definition of EMDEs, commodity exporters, and commodity importers, please refer to table 1.2. EM7 includes Brazil, China, India, Indonesia, Mexico, the Russian Federation, and Turkey. The World Bank is currently not publishing economic output, income, or growth data for Turkmenistan and República Bolivariana de Venezuela owning to lack of reliable data of adequate quality. Turkmenistan and República Bolivariana de Venezuela are excluded from cross-country macroeconomic aggregates.

the majority of commodity exporters despite improved terms of trade, partly due to higher input costs in non-energy exporters (figure 1.1.C). The cumulative losses to global activity relative to its pre-pandemic trend are expected to continue mounting over the forecast horizon, especially among EMDE commodity importers, as a result of lasting damage inflicted by more than two years of negative shocks (figure 1.1.D).

In advanced economies, activity is being dampened by rising energy prices, less favorable financial conditions, and supply chain disruptions, all of which have been exacerbated by the war in Ukraine. As a result, growth in these economies is projected to decelerate from 5.1 percent in 2021 to 2.6 percent in 2022—1.2 percentage points below previous projections. Growth is expected to further moderate to 2.2 percent in 2023, largely reflecting the further unwinding of the fiscal and monetary policy support provided during the pandemic.

EMDE growth is projected to roughly halve this year, slowing from 6.6 percent in 2021 to 3.4 percent in 2022—well below its annual average of 4.8 percent over 2011-19, despite a still-incomplete recovery from the pandemic. The slowdown in part reflects the spillovers from the war in Ukraine, which have led to commodity price volatility, higher input costs, trade disruptions, and weaker confidence. These spillovers are also magnifying the effects of pre-existing headwinds to growth, including rising inflationary pressures, tightening financial conditions, continued withdrawal of macro-economic policy support, and softening external demand. And since EMDE households devote a relatively large proportion of their spending to basic necessities, the war's impact on food and energy prices is also weighing markedly on consumption. This is especially true among commodity importers, whereas energy exporters are benefitting from higher global energy prices and easing oil production cuts.

The forecast for EMDE growth in 2022 has been downgraded by 1.2 percentage points, largely on account of the adverse effects of the war. Excluding Russia and Ukraine, growth in EMDEs

FIGURE 1.1 Global prospects

The Russian Federation's invasion of Ukraine has significantly accelerated the projected slowdown in global growth. Forecasts for most economies have been downgraded for this year. Headwinds from the war are adding to large cumulative losses in output since the onset of the pandemic, particularly for commodity-importing emerging market and developing economies (EMDEs). Surging commodity prices have contributed to broadening price pressures, pushing inflation above central bank targets in the vast majority of inflation-targeting countries. For many EMDEs, adverse shocks from the pandemic and war have reversed the catch-up of per capita income with advanced economies.

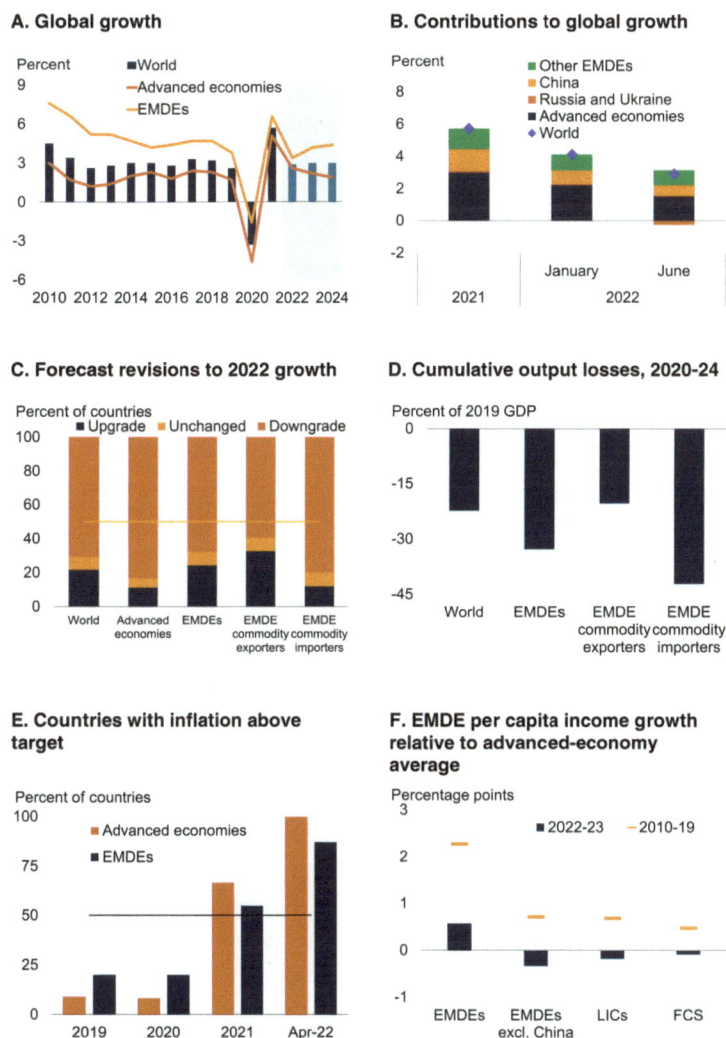

A. Global growth

B. Contributions to global growth

C. Forecast revisions to 2022 growth

D. Cumulative output losses, 2020-24

E. Countries with inflation above target

F. EMDE per capita income growth relative to advanced-economy average

Sources: Consensus Economics; International Monetary Fund; World Bank.
Note: EMDEs = emerging market and developing economies; FCS = fragile and conflict-affected situations; LICs = low-income countries. Unless otherwise indicated, aggregate growth rates are calculated using real U.S. dollar GDP weights at average 2010-19 prices and market exchange rates.
A. Shaded area indicates forecasts.
B. Figure shows the contributions to global growth forecasts in the January 2022 and June 2022 editions of *Global Economic Prospects*.
C. Forecast revisions are the change in 2022 growth forecasts between January 2022 and June 2022 editions of *Global Economic Prospects*.
D. Bars show cumulative output losses over 2020-24, which are computed as deviations from trend, expressed as a share of GDP in 2019. Output is measured in U.S. dollars at 2010-19 prices and market exchange rates. Trend is assumed to grow at the regression-estimated trend growth rate of 2010-19. EMDE commodity exporters exclude the Russian Federation and Ukraine.
E. Bars show the share of inflation-targeting economies with average inflation during the course of the year (or month) above the target range. Sample includes 12 advanced economies and 31 EMDEs.
F. Relative per capita income growth is computed as the difference in per capita GDP growth between each respective EMDE group and the advanced-economy average.

in 2022 has been revised down by 0.5 percentage point, as improved prospects in energy exporters are more than offset by downgrades to most other EMDEs. Indeed, forecasts for 2022 growth have been revised down in nearly 70 percent of EMDEs, including most commodity-importing countries. EMDE growth is anticipated to firm to an average of 4.3 percent in 2023-24, as the lingering effects of the war abate.

Global consumer price inflation has climbed higher around the world and is above central bank targets in almost all countries which have them (figure 1.1.E). Inflation is envisioned to remain elevated for longer and at higher levels than previously assumed. It is expected to peak around mid-2022 and then decline only gradually as global growth moderates, demand shifts further from goods toward services, supply chain bottlenecks abate, and commodity prices edge down, including for energy. Whereas wage pressures remain generally contained in EMDEs, they are likely to persist in several advanced economies in the near term. Despite new headwinds to growth, monetary policy across the world is expected to be further tightened as central banks seek to contain inflationary pressures. Pandemic-related fiscal support will also continue to be withdrawn in advanced economies and EMDEs.

The abrupt growth slowdown in EMDEs implies a pronounced deceleration in per capita income growth, from 5.4 percent in 2021 to 2.3 percent in 2022. As a result of the damage from the pandemic and the war in Ukraine, the level of EMDE per capita income this year will be nearly 5 percent below its pre-pandemic trend. EMDE catch-up with advanced-economy income levels is expected to be markedly slower over the next few years than in the pre-pandemic period, with progress reversing in EMDEs excluding China (figure 1.1.F). Higher food prices are likely to lower real per capita incomes in many EMDEs reliant on food imports and substantially worsen global food insecurity and poverty. The lingering effects of the pandemic, the war, and the surge in food prices are combining to make the external environment far more challenging for many countries, and are expected to lead to a net increase of 75 million people in extreme poverty by the end of this year relative to pre-pandemic projections.

The global outlook is subject to various interlinked downside risks. Intensifying geopolitical tensions could further disrupt economic activity, generate policy uncertainty and, if persistent, lead to fragmentation in global trade, investment, and financial systems. Supply disruptions from the pandemic and the war in Ukraine have led to a spike in commodity prices comparable to the oil shocks of 1973 and 1979-80 (figure 1.2.A). Additional adverse shocks would increase the possibility that the global economy will experience a period of stagflation reminiscent of the 1970s, with low growth and high inflation (Special Focus 1).

Central banks may be forced to tighten monetary policy more rapidly than currently expected to bring rising price pressures under control. Historically, EMDE financial crises have been more likely when U.S. monetary policy pivots toward a more aggressive tightening stance, as it is currently doing to rein in elevated inflation (figure 1.2.B). Financial stress could spread across countries. The production and shipping of food and fertilizer could be further disrupted, leading to widespread food shortages, pushing millions of people into food insecurity and extreme poverty. The pandemic could worsen due to the appearance of new, more virulent variants and lead to the reintroduction of disruptive control measures. The simultaneous materialization of several downside risks could result in a much sharper and more prolonged global slowdown. Specifically, if faster tightening of U.S. monetary policy were to cause acute financial stress in EMDEs, European Union (EU) member countries were to face a sudden ban on their energy imports, and China were to experience renewed pandemic-related lockdowns, global growth could fall to 2.1 percent and 1.5 percent in 2022 and 2023, respectively (figure 1.2.C).

The more subdued global economic prospects and the risks clouding the outlook underscore the major challenges policy makers face at the global and national levels. Global efforts are urgently required to alleviate the mounting human suffering caused by Russia's invasion of Ukraine and conflict elsewhere, including forced displacement, as well as acute food shortages. Regional cooperation will also be needed to house refugees and meet their basic needs. Once hostilities in Ukraine subside, large-scale coordinated support will be necessary to accelerate reconstruction efforts. The war also underscores the need to enhance global energy security, including by accelerating the transition toward low-carbon energy sources. At the same time, global cooperation is still needed to achieve a durable end to the COVID-19 pandemic, particularly in fostering vaccination in the poorest countries.

Policy interest rates in many economies have been increasing at a far slower pace than headline inflation, as central banks have generally attempted to look through fluctuations driven by commodity prices. As a result, despite recent nominal policy hikes, monetary conditions—including in major economies such as the United States and the euro area—continue to be accommodative (figure 1.2.D). The surge in oil and other commodity prices has created additional monetary policy challenges, as the ensuing rise in inflationary pressures heightens the possibility of a de-anchoring of inflation expectations. Addressing these new pressures without unduly impairing the recovery will require clear communication and a steadfast commitment to credible monetary frameworks. Maintaining the resilience of financial institutions through effective macroprudential regulation is also critical.

The ability of EMDE fiscal authorities to provide support will be severely limited by tighter financing conditions and higher borrowing costs amid elevated debt loads and depleted policy space. Debt was already on an unsustainable path for many EMDEs prior to the war, and fiscal sustainability is likely to be eroded further by weaker growth prospects and higher borrowing costs. Balancing the need to ensure fiscal sustainability against that of mitigating the war's adverse effects on vulnerable populations may require reprioritizing existing spending, especially in commodity importers. Recent global developments underscore the urgency for EMDEs

FIGURE 1.2 Global risks and policy challenges

Surging energy and food prices heighten the risk of a prolonged period of global stagflation reminiscent of the 1970s. Broad-based inflationary pressures in the United States may precipitate more aggressive monetary tightening, potentially triggering financial stress in emerging market and developing economies (EMDEs). Global growth could be substantially weaker if key downside risks were to materialize. Despite central bank rate hikes, real rates remain low amid high inflation, suggesting that further policy tightening may be needed. To address rising food insecurity, EMDE policy makers can deploy targeted support rather than distortionary price controls, which are already widespread.

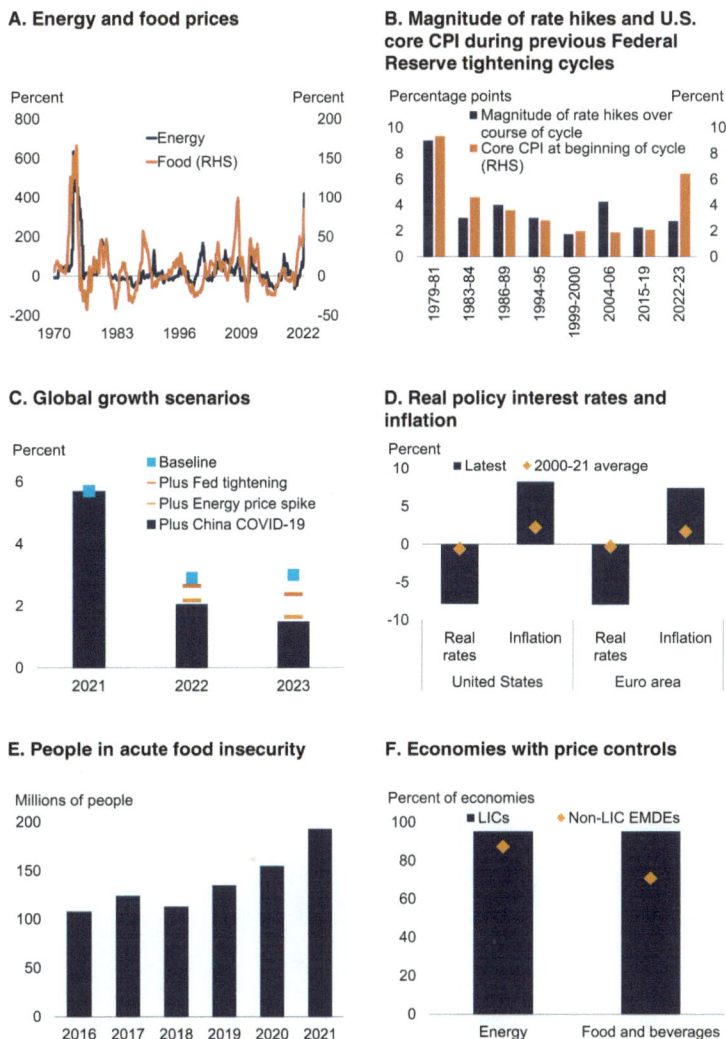

Sources: Eurostat (database); Federal Reserve Economic Data; FSIN and GNAFC (2022); Guénette (2020); Haver Analytics; Oxford Economics; World Bank; World Trade Organization (WTO).
Note: EMDEs = emerging market and developing economies; LICs = low-income countries.
A. Figure shows percent change in monthly energy and food price indexes over a 24-month period. This facilitates a comparison of the April 2020 trough with the most recent data (April 2022). Due to data limitations, prior to 1979, the energy price change is proxied using the oil price change.
B. Blue bars show the extent of policy rate increases during previous tightening cycles. The value for 2023 is an estimate based on market expectations for the level of the Fed Funds rate in mid-2023. U.S. core CPI for 2023 shows latest data associated with tightening cycle.
C. Scenario outcomes produced using the Oxford Economics Global Economic Model. Scenarios are linearly additive.
D. "Real rates" are policy interest rates minus consumer price index inflation. "Latest" refers to the last available data, which are for April 2022.
E. Data from the Food Security Information Network's *Global Report on Food Crises* 2022.
F. Listed price control policies are retrieved from WTO *Trade Policy Review* publications. Sample includes 21 low-income countries and 56 other EMDEs.

to redirect expenditures from inefficient and costly items, such as fossil fuel subsidies, toward targeted fiscal relief for vulnerable households, and thus mitigate additional spikes in poverty and food insecurity. EMDEs also need to emphasize spending on growth-enhancing investments and social protection. For some energy exporters, higher commodity prices represent an opportunity to invest windfall gains in measures that yield long-term growth dividends and promote diversification, which will help these economies adapt to the green transition.

EMDEs continue to be confronted with significant long-term challenges. Enhancing resilience to food crises remains a key priority in light of worsening food insecurity (figure 1.2.E). To this end, policy makers in EMDEs should refrain from putting in place controls on food and energy prices, which are already widespread and have been shown to be ineffective and costly (figure 1.2.F). Instead, they need to strengthen targeted social safety nets and enhance the resilience of food systems, including by investing in public infrastructure that can improve the efficiency of food production and trade. Over the long run, reversing the damage inflicted by the dual shocks of the pandemic and the war in Ukraine on growth prospects will require measures to prevent fragmentation in trade networks, effective investment in education and digital technologies, and the promotion of labor force participation—especially female participation—through active labor market policies.

Global context

Russia's invasion of Ukraine—the second major global shock in just over two years—is exacerbating the global economic slowdown. It has worsened the strains in global supply chains and caused significant additional increases in the prices of many commodities, particularly those exported by Russia and Ukraine. This has contributed to a further acceleration of inflation in both advanced economies and EMDEs. Global financial conditions have tightened considerably, reflecting increases in monetary policy rates, greater volatility, and waning risk appetite.

Russia's invasion of Ukraine represents not only an enormous humanitarian crisis but also a significant negative shock for a world economy still struggling to recover from the pandemic. Global activity was already slowing as pent-up demand was being depleted and supportive macroeconomic policies were being unwound, while inflation was mounting owing to supply disruptions and rising prices for food and energy. The war has aggravated these strains on the global economy, with particularly large costs for poor and vulnerable populations.

Global trade

Goods trade slowed in the first half of 2022 as supply chains continued to be affected by the lingering effects of the pandemic, including disruptions in major Asian ports and lockdowns in key cities in China. In addition, Russia's invasion of Ukraine and its repercussions have led to severe physical and logistical dislocations that have magnified pre-existing bottlenecks (figure 1.3.A).

Russia and Ukraine account for a small share—under 3 percent—of global exports. However, many global industries rely on supplies of key commodities produced in the two countries, especially in Russia. Shortages and unprecedented increases in the prices of these inputs have rippled through global value chains (GVCs), leading to production standstills and elevated producer prices. At the same time, transport costs have increased, including in the wake of the war in Ukraine. Navigation and trade in the Black Sea have been materially disrupted, negatively affecting the transport of food and crude oil. Cargos and shipments held at Russian and Ukrainian ports have been rerouted through longer and more expensive routes (Ruta 2022).

Services trade has regained its pre-pandemic level, driven by a rebound in non-tourism services. While tourism activity has started to recover in advanced economies with high vaccination levels, it remains generally subdued in EMDEs, especially in tourism-reliant countries and in small states. The invasion is also weighing on tourism activity in countries that rely on tourists from Russia and Ukraine.

Global trade growth is anticipated to slow to 4 percent in 2022 as the war in Ukraine further disrupts global value chains, global activity gradually shifts back toward the less trade-intensive services sector, and international mobility moves toward pre-pandemic levels only gradually. This is a substantial downward revision relative to previous forecasts, largely because of higher transport costs and significant global value chain disruptions associated with the war (figure 1.3.B). Global trade growth is expected to moderate to an average of 4.1 percent in 2023-24 as global demand for tradable goods continues to decelerate.

Prolonged closures of factories and key ports in China as a result of COVID-19 lockdowns pose a significant downside risk to the near-term trade outlook. Delivery times could lengthen further, leading to new trade disruptions and global supply shortages, which could in turn severely affect production and activity in other countries. In addition, although some of the effects of the invasion of Ukraine could be mitigated by new trade linkages, a more protracted war and its long-lasting repercussions, such as persistent uncertainty, represent a substantial downside risk to the longer-term trade outlook, as it could lead to fragmentation in the global trade system.

Commodity markets

Commodity prices surged in the first half of 2022, in part reflecting the effects of Russia's invasion of Ukraine, and following a broad-based rise that began in mid-2020 spurred by a rebound in demand amid constrained production for several commodities. The increase in prices was particularly pronounced for commodities of which Russia and Ukraine are large exporters, including energy and wheat, as the war resulted in major disruptions to production and trade (figures 1.4.A and 1.4.B). Prices of oil products, notably diesel and gasoline, rose much more than crude oil prices as a result of insufficient refining capacity and disruption to Russia's exports of refined oil products. The G7 and the EU announced they would ban or gradually phase out their imports of Russian oil, with similar measures taken for coal and natural gas. Several oil companies also

FIGURE 1.3 Global trade

Supply chains continue to be under strain amid new COVID-19 lockdowns affecting major Asian ports and logistical disruptions associated with Russia's invasion of Ukraine. Global trade growth has been substantially revised down, in part reflecting significant value chain disruptions associated with the war.

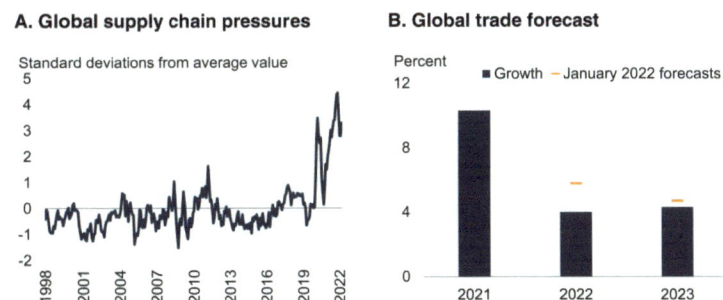

A. Global supply chain pressures

B. Global trade forecast

Sources: Benigno et al. (2022); Federal Reserve Bank of New York; World Bank.
A. Figure shows the Global Supply Chain Pressure Index on a monthly basis since 1998. The index is normalized such that zero indicates the average value and positive/negative values represent how many standard deviations the index is above/below this average value.
B. Trade measured as the average of export and import volumes. January 2022 forecasts are from the January 2022 edition of *Global Economic Prospects* report.

announced they would cease operations in Russia, while many traders chose to boycott Russian oil.

The ultimate impact of the war on energy markets—and commodity markets more broadly—will depend on its duration and the extent of sanctions as a result of Russia's invasion. The International Energy Agency estimates that, under current sanctions, Russia's oil exports could be temporarily reduced by 2.5 million barrels per day, about 30 percent of its current exports and about 3 percent of global supply (IEA 2022). A combination of diversion of oil to other countries, use of strategic petroleum reserves, and potentially some additional production from OPEC would likely be sufficient to fill this shortfall (figure 1.4.C; World Bank 2022a). While some energy commodities are already being redirected to other countries, this process is constrained by the availability of physical transportation infrastructure. This is particularly the case for Russian natural gas, which depends on pipelines largely oriented toward Europe.

Against this backdrop, energy prices are forecast to rise 52 percent in 2022, 47 percentage points higher than previously projected (Special Focus 2). Brent crude oil prices are forecast to average $100/bbl—an upward revision of $24/bbl. Sanc-

FIGURE 1.4 Commodity markets

Commodity prices surged in the first half of 2022, especially for those commodities of which the Russian Federation and Ukraine are major global exporters. Further disruption to Russia's exports of crude oil could be offset by inventory releases or the scaling up of production among other major exporters; however, increasing production would take time. The increase in energy prices this year is unusual compared with previous episodes since price increases have been broad-based across all fuels, reducing the possibilities for substitution.

A. Commodity price changes

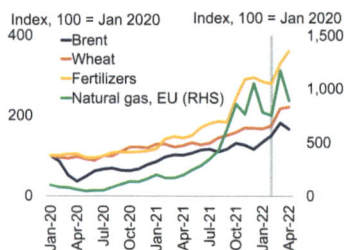

B. Russian Federation's and Ukraine's commodity exports

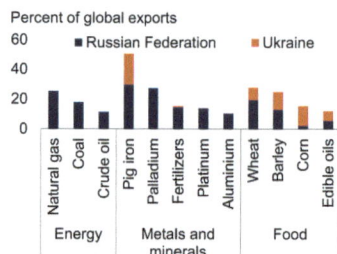

C. Alternative sources of oil

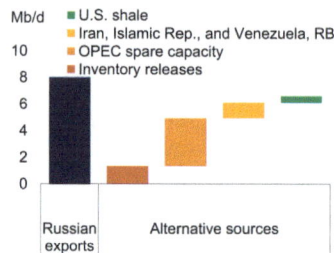

D. Real energy prices during price spikes

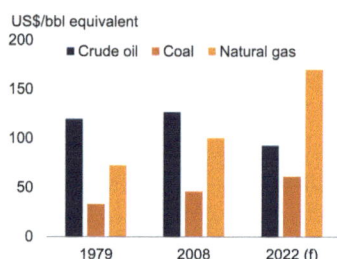

Sources: Bloomberg; Comtrade (database); IEA (2022); World Bank.
A. Monthly data, last observation is April 2022. Gray line denotes the onset of the Russian Federation's invasion of Ukraine.
B. Data for energy and food is trade volume; data for metals and minerals is trade values. Fertilizers include phosphate rock and potash minerals, and ammonia-based non-minerals. Data are for 2020.
C. Figure shows exports of Russian oil and oil products prior to the war in Ukraine and alternative sources of supply. "Inventory releases" refer to the current announced release of oil by IEA members, including the United States. Estimates for production are author calculations based on IEA's "Oil Market Report—April 2022." Production from OPEC refers to Iraq, Saudi Arabia, and United Arab Emirates only.
D. Figure shows the annual price of coal, Brent crude oil, and European natural gas, deflated using U.S. CPI. 2022 shows the current price forecast.

tions imposed on Russia in response to the invasion are expected to have a lasting negative effect on the country's crude oil and natural gas production on account of the exit of foreign oil companies, lower investment, and reduced access to foreign technology. Prices are projected to moderate in 2023 as production rises elsewhere, including in the United States; however, they will remain much higher than previously forecast, and well above the average of the past five years.

There is a material risk that energy prices could increase much more than expected. Disruption to

Russia's energy exports, particularly natural gas, could be more severe than expected if bans are implemented more rapidly, or if there is less diversion of exports to other countries.[1] For example, as a result of the invasion of Ukraine, the EU and the United States have proposed restricting the provision of shipping and insurance services related to the transport of Russian oil, which could materially reduce the scope for redirection of oil to other countries. In addition, inventories have fallen (and are set to decline further) and there are concerns that OPEC spare capacity may be lower than currently estimated, as evidenced by a sluggish supply response. U.S. shale faces several constraints on significantly increasing output, including shortages of labor and other inputs, as well as demands on the industry to focus on returning cash to shareholders. Furthermore, in contrast to previous oil price spikes when plentiful coal and natural gas enabled substitution away from oil, the prices of all fossil fuel energy sources are currently very high, which reduces the possibility of easing price pressures by substituting to cheaper fuels (figure 1.4.D).

Agricultural prices are forecast to rise 18 percent this year, above previous projections, reflecting weaker grain production in Ukraine as well as much higher input costs, including for fuel, chemicals, and fertilizers. Fertilizer prices are expected to increase by nearly 70 percent in 2022, due to soaring input costs, reduced production, and trade disruptions (World Bank 2022a). Russia and Ukraine are key exporters of wheat, together accounting for about one-quarter of global wheat exports. Russia is also the world's largest exporter of fertilizers and has instituted new quotas and restrictions on exports. About 90 percent of Ukraine's grain exports flow through Black Sea ports, which are not currently operational. Some wheat may be transported through road and railway corridors, but volumes will be sharply reduced because of infrastructure bottlenecks and safety concerns. Russia's invasion is likely to partially disrupt agricultural production in

---

[1] The "Global outlook and risks" section presents a quantification of this risk as part of downside scenarios for global growth.

Ukraine for 2022—including for corn, barley, and sunflowers, which are typically planted during spring. In addition, there is a risk that Russian production of grains could be reduced by more limited access to imported agricultural inputs, such as seeds and pesticides (FAO 2022). Accordingly, the projected 2022 price increase reflects a surge in wheat and corn prices that is partially offset by modest declines in the price of other major staples, including rice and soybeans, for which global supplies are currently adequate.

Agricultural prices are forecast to moderate in 2023, reflecting increased supplies from the rest of the world, particularly for wheat in Canada and the EU. Nonetheless, agricultural commodity prices are expected to remain much higher than earlier projections, and well above their average over the previous five years. Prices could rise further if input costs are higher than expected; for example, an extended disruption to Russian fertilizer exports could impede future agricultural production in other large EMDE producers. Export bans are a further risk to agricultural prices, as exemplified by the fact that several countries have already implemented export bans on food commodities (Chavez 2022). These measures can have harmful consequences; for example, measures undertaken during the 2007-08 and 2010-11 food price spikes resulted in higher price volatility and were not effective in protecting vulnerable populations (Laborde, Lakatos, and Martin 2019; World Bank 2019a).

Metal prices have continued to increase in 2022, adding to last year's substantial gains. Aluminum and nickel prices rose by about 30 percent due to the importance of Russia as an exporter, as well as a "short squeeze" on the nickel market (World Bank 2022a). Metal prices are now expected to rise 12 percent in 2022, a significant upward revision from previous forecasts. Most prices are expected to moderate in 2023, reflecting increasing supply—for example, nickel production is expected to increase in Indonesia. The effects of the war in Ukraine are assumed to have less of a lasting impact on metal prices than on energy prices given that, with the exception of palladium and nickel, Russia has a more modest role as a global exporter.

Global inflation

Inflation has accelerated in both advanced economies and EMDEs, reflecting firming demand; persistent supply disruptions; tight labor markets in some countries; and, especially, surging commodity prices, which have been pushed up further by the invasion. Global median headline CPI inflation rose to 7.8 percent (y/y) in April 2022, its highest level since 2008. Aggregate EMDE inflation reached over 9.4 percent—its highest level since 2008—while inflation in advanced economies, at 6.9 percent, is the highest since 1982 (figure 1.5.A). The energy component of global consumer price inflation has risen sharply and is at its highest level since the early 1980s. In two-fifths of EMDEs and most low-income countries (LICs), consumer food price inflation is expected to remain in double-digits this year.

While increases in food and energy prices have mainly driven the sharp rise in headline inflation, core inflation has also risen globally. In the first half of 2022, the housing, fuel, transport, and furnishing sectors contributed about two-thirds and two-fifths to total headline inflation in advanced economies and EMDEs, respectively. In particular, housing price inflation has been pronounced in advanced economies.

Inflation is above target in the vast majority of advanced economies and EMDEs that have adopted inflation targeting (figure 1.5.B). In most countries, both market- and survey-based inflation expectations have risen further since Russia's invasion of Ukraine (figures 1.5.C and 1.5.D). Although inflation expectations have generally been well contained, in about one-third of EMDEs (particularly in ECA, LAC, and SAR) survey-based long-term inflation expectations have increased by more than ¼ percentage point from pre-pandemic levels.

Financial developments

Rising inflation has led to expectations of faster monetary policy tightening across the world. Advanced-economy bond yields have risen markedly, and measures of equity volatility have seen a sustained increase, weighing on valuations

FIGURE 1.5 Global inflation and financial developments

The invasion of Ukraine is intensifying inflationary pressures. Inflation in many countries is reaching multidecade highs and is now above target in most advanced economies and emerging market and developing economies (EMDEs). Inflation expectations have also risen further. The war triggered an initial appreciation of the U.S. dollar that was larger than those following the taper tantrum and previous geopolitical events. Sovereign spreads have increased across EMDEs, but by substantially more among commodity importers relative to commodity exporters.

A. Monthly CPI inflation, year-on-year

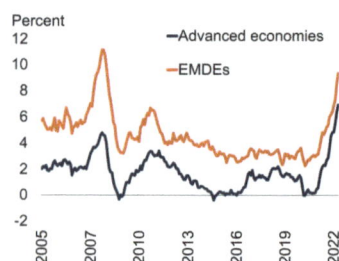

B. Countries with inflation above target

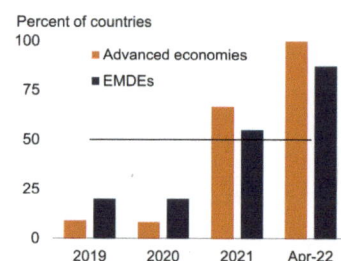

C. Survey-based EMDE inflation expectations

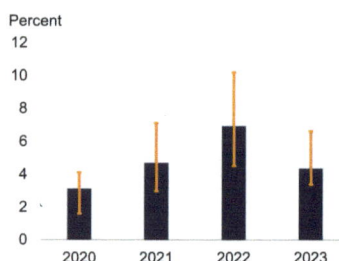

D. Market-based five-year inflation expectations

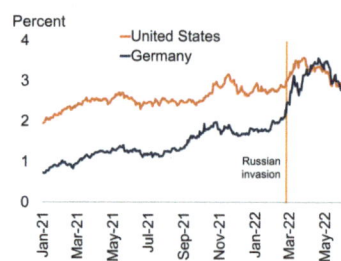

E. Evolution of the U.S. dollar against EMDE currencies during select events

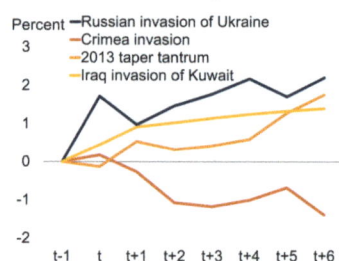

F. Change in EMDE sovereign spreads by commodity exporter status

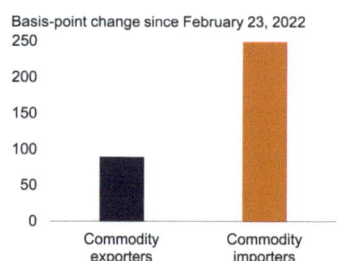

Sources: BIS (database); Consensus Economics; Haver Analytics; International Monetary Fund; J.P. Morgan; World Bank.
Note: EMDEs = emerging market and developing economies.
A. CPI refers to consumer price index. Lines show group median inflation for 81 countries, of which 31 are advanced economies and 50 are EMDEs. Last observation is April 2022.
B. Bars show the share of inflation-targeting economies with average inflation during the course of the year (or month) above the target range. Sample includes 12 advanced economies and 31 EMDEs.
C. Consensus forecast for median headline CPI inflation for 2022-23 based on May 2022 surveys of 50 EMDEs. 2020-2021 numbers are based on actual inflation.
D. Implied breakeven inflation, measured as the spreads between nominal and real five-year treasury bond yields in Germany and the United States. Last observation is May 30, 2022.
E. Figure shows cumulative daily percentage change in a GDP-weighted index of exchange rates between the U.S. dollar and EMDE currencies from the trading day before an event (t-1) to six trading days afterwards (t+6). The EMDEs in the index are Brazil, India, Indonesia, Mexico, Poland, South Africa, and Turkey.
F. Figure shows the difference in bond spreads between the latest available data and February 23, 2022 (day prior to the invasion of Ukraine). Last observation is May 23, 2022.

of risky assets. Since the beginning of the year, U.S. and euro area stocks have fallen about 13 percent and 12 percent, respectively. The invasion triggered an initial appreciation of the U.S. dollar against EMDE currencies that was larger than appreciations related to the 2013 taper tantrum and previous conflict-related events involving oil exporters (figure 1.5.E). It has since strengthened further, increasing the cost of servicing dollar-denominated liabilities globally.

In Russia, financial markets initially suffered significant dislocations following the invasion of Ukraine. Russian financial asset prices have since stabilized, though yields on Russia's dollar-denominated sovereign debt continue to indicate a prominent risk of default. Negative effects on global banks appear largely contained, however, reflecting limited balance-sheet exposures. Credit default swap spreads on the sovereign debt of countries neighboring Ukraine have also increased notably.

Overall, EMDE financial conditions have reached their tightest level since the start of the pandemic, as investor risk appetite has been sapped by the war in Ukraine, lockdowns in China, a weaker growth outlook, and higher interest rates in advanced economies. Equity and debt flows to EMDEs turned sharply negative in March, while bond issuance in the first quarter of 2022 across EMDEs was weaker than in any first quarter since 2016. Whereas ECA and regions with substantial numbers of commodity importers (such as EAP and SAR) have experienced sizable short-term debt and equity outflows, regions with large numbers of commodity exporters (such as LAC and MENA) have seen more resilient flows. Since the invasion, sovereign spreads have increased on average across EMDEs, but by considerably more among commodity importers relative to commodity exporters (figure 1.5.F).

Major economies: Recent developments and outlook

The recovery in advanced economies is being dampened by surging energy prices and supply chain disruptions, which have been aggravated by Russia's invasion of Ukraine. Growth is expected to decline markedly in 2022—especially in the euro area, which has closer economic links with Russia. Monetary policy support is expected to be withdrawn at a notably faster pace than previously anticipated, especially in the United States. Authorities in China have significantly eased macroeconomic policy to cushion the ongoing slowdown.

Advanced economies

Growth in advanced economies slowed during the first half of 2022, reflecting the war in Ukraine, pandemic resurgences at the turn of the year, persistent supply chain disruptions, reduced fiscal support, and tightening financial conditions. Russia's invasion of Ukraine has increased financial market volatility, policy uncertainty, and supply chain strains, especially in the euro area. Moreover, its effect on energy prices is weighing significantly on disposable income and profit margins, and thus on activity, and is raising inflation to multidecade highs (figure 1.6.A). Given rapid increases in energy and food prices and a broadening of inflation across components, major central banks are expected to tighten monetary policy at a faster pace than previously anticipated (figure 1.6.B). The effects of the invasion and of policy tightening are likely to exert a significant drag on output.

Growth in advanced economies is projected to slow markedly in 2022, to 2.6 percent, as spillovers associated with the war weigh on near-term activity, especially in the euro area. Growth is then expected to continue to moderate, averaging 2.1 percent in 2023-24, as macroeconomic policy support is unwound further and pent-up demand is exhausted. A worsening war in Ukraine is the major risk clouding the outlook, as it could destabilize an already fraught geopolitical situation, trigger additional increases in energy and food prices, exacerbate inflationary pressures, further tighten financial conditions, and prolong policy uncertainty.

In the **United States**, activity lost momentum in the first half of this year, owing to the short-lived hit from the Omicron wave, tighter financing conditions, and the economic effects of Russia's invasion of Ukraine. Although the direct impact of

FIGURE 1.6 Major economies: Recent developments and outlook

In advanced economies, surges in commodity prices are weighing significantly on activity. To respond to rising inflation, major central banks are expected to tighten monetary policy at a faster pace than previously anticipated. Given its large reliance on Russian oil and natural gas, the euro area is particularly vulnerable to spillovers from the war in Ukraine. In China, fiscal policy is envisioned to be more supportive than previously expected to cushion the slowdown.

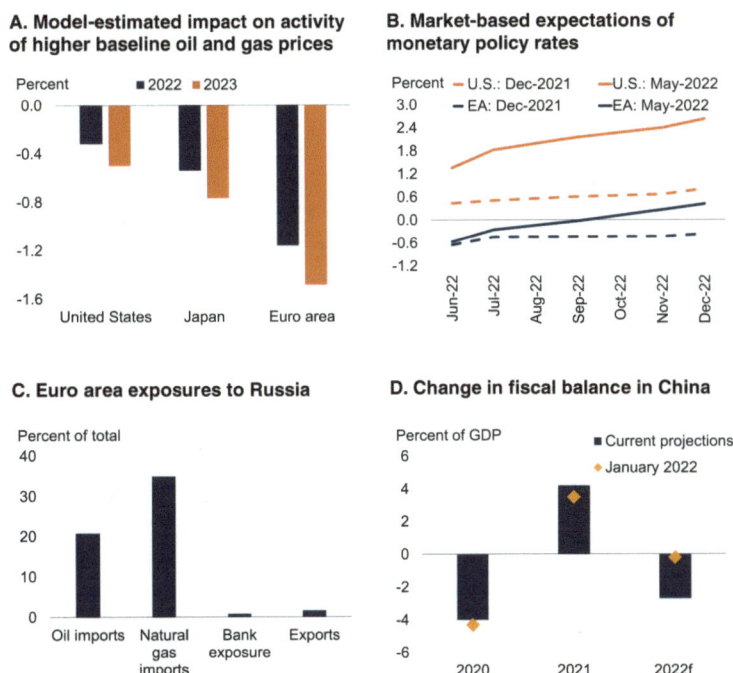

A. Model-estimated impact on activity of higher baseline oil and gas prices

B. Market-based expectations of monetary policy rates

C. Euro area exposures to Russia

D. Change in fiscal balance in China

Sources: BIS (database); Bloomberg; Comtrade (database); Eurostat (database); Oxford Economics; World Bank.
Note: EA = Euro area.
A. Simulation prepared using the Oxford Economics Global Economic Model. It combines the impacts on global output of supply-driven increases in Brent oil prices and natural gas prices over a two-year period (2022-2023). Brent oil prices average 40 percent above baseline while natural gas prices average 70 percent above baseline. Upward revision to natural gas prices is average of revisions to U.S. prices (+33 percent), European prices (+115 percent), and Japanese prices (+61 percent). These revisions are scaled to match the upward revision to energy price projections from January 2022 to June 2022.
B. Figure shows changes in market-based expectations of monetary policy rates over time.
C. Bank exposure shows claims of BIS foreign banks on Russian residents on a consolidated basis. Claims are expressed as shares of total outstanding cross-border claims. Bank exposure data is for quarter ending September 2021. Oil imports, natural gas imports, and exports data are for 2020, shown in percent of total oil and gas imports.
D. f = forecast. World Bank staff calculations. "January 2022" refers to the January 2022 edition of the *Global Economic Prospects* report. The augmented fiscal balance is a sum of the general public (excluding adjustment from the stabilization fund), government fund, state capital operation, and the social security fund budget balances.

the invasion has been contained so far, owing to limited trade and financial linkages, it is heightening inflationary pressures, which have already been more pronounced than in other advanced economies. With inflation well above target, the Federal Reserve began to raise policy rates in March; in all, markets expect policy rates to reach 2.5 percent by end-2022—an increase of almost 170 basis point from December market expectations.

U.S. growth is forecast to slow to 2.5 percent in 2022, 1.2 percentage points below previous projections, reflecting sharply higher energy prices, tighter financial conditions, and additional supply disruptions caused by the invasion of Ukraine. Growth is expected to moderate further to an average of 2.2 percent in 2023-24, as continued withdrawal of fiscal support and monetary policy tightening weighs further on activity. Although inflation is expected to peak around mid-2022 and gradually decline thereafter, it is envisioned to remain above its 2 percent target over the forecast horizon owing to persistent wage pressures from a tight labor market.

Activity in the **euro area** decelerated in the first half of 2022, mainly on account of Russia's invasion of Ukraine and an earlier resurgence of COVID-19. Key members of the euro area are particularly dependent on energy imports from Russia—including imports of gas, which account for about 35 percent of total gas imports into the area (figure 1.6.C). Beyond energy, direct trade exposures to Russia are small, which limits the direct impact of sanctions. However, indirect effects through distressed supply chains, increased financial strains, and declines in consumer and business confidence have dented activity. Surging energy and food prices have contributed to a sharp rise in inflation, which reached a record-high of 5.8 percent in February 2022.

Euro area growth is projected to slow to 2.5 percent in 2022, as additional supply shocks caused by the invasion of Ukraine weigh on activity. The outlook has been revised down by 1.7 percentage points this year, as the war leads to higher energy prices, continued supply disruptions, and tighter financial conditions. Energy subsidies in several major euro area members, albeit distortive, are expected to slightly cushion the impact of high energy costs on household consumption. Growth is projected to moderate further to an average of 1.9 percent in 2023-24, as the European Central Bank tightens

monetary policy and lingering repercussions of the war continue to weigh on activity.

Activity in **Japan** has slowed in the first half of 2022, amid subdued domestic demand and unfavorable external conditions. Growth is expected to be 1.7 percent this year, 1.2 percentage points below previous forecasts, reflecting a larger-than-expected drag from COVID-19, a deterioration in the terms of trade caused by the war in Ukraine, and weaker exports. Growth is forecast to slow over 2023-24, as pent-up demand is exhausted.

China

Activity has slowed sharply due mainly to COVID-19 outbreaks and strict lockdowns, with growth in consumer spending particularly subdued. Trade and manufacturing investment have lost momentum, owing to supply disruptions and the negative impact of the war in Ukraine. While the contraction of real estate investment moderated at the start of the year, it has deepened again due to pandemic-related restrictions.

Policy action has been pursued to cushion the slowdown. The People's Bank of China has implemented policy rate and reserve requirement cuts, relaxed regulations on bank loans for low-cost rental housing, and allowed commercial banks to lower mortgage rates. Following last year's sharp fiscal consolidation, policy has eased and infrastructure investment has rebounded.

China is expected to grow 4.3 percent in 2022 and 5.2 percent in 2023. The forecast for this year has been downgraded 0.8 percentage point, reflecting larger-than-expected damage from COVID-19 and related lockdowns. Higher commodity prices will reduce the current account surplus and push up inflation toward target. To mitigate the impact of the lingering pandemic and worsening terms of trade, fiscal, monetary, and regulatory policies are envisioned to be more supportive than previously expected (figure 1.6.D).

The outlook is subject to significant risks. Repeated COVID-19 outbreaks and strict lockdowns across major cities would curtail the recovery of consumption and services activity, disrupt supply chains, and weigh on investor confidence.[2] In addition, renewed stress in the housing sector would further reduce real estate investment and government revenues, affect the solvency of developers and local government financing vehicles, and weigh on house prices and consumer spending.

Emerging market and developing economies

The effects of Russia's invasion of Ukraine are weighing on growth across many EMDEs and resulting in a deep downturn in the ECA region. Activity in most EMDEs is expected to decelerate as negative spillovers from the war add to rising inflationary pressures and lead to tighter financial conditions, fiscal and monetary policy support continues to be unwound, and external demand weakens further. The effects may be somewhat cushioned by higher commodity prices in some EMDE commodity exporters. High inflation and disruptions to global food markets are worsening food insecurity in many EMDEs, especially LICs. EMDE per capita income growth is anticipated to slow markedly in 2022, as real household income is dampened by high food and fuel prices.

Recent developments

The war in Ukraine has delivered another major shock to EMDEs, well before their recovery from the pandemic is complete (box 1.1; chapter 2). Prior to the invasion, EMDE output, which expanded 6.6 percent in 2021, was already slowing across many countries. The war has exacerbated this deceleration, made the external environment markedly less supportive, and caused a devasting economic contraction in Ukraine and deep recession in Russia (chapter 2). To varying degrees, the war is also having significant economic spillovers in many other EMDEs, including through commodity and trade linkages (figure 1.7.A). Trade disruptions are feeding through value chains, as many EMDEs heavily depend on both Russia and Ukraine for key

---

[2] The "Global outlook and risks" section presents a quantification of this risk as part of downside scenarios for global growth.

FIGURE 1.7 Recent developments in emerging market and developing economies

The Russian Federation's invasion of Ukraine is adversely affecting activity in emerging market and developing economies (EMDEs), to varying degrees, through multiple channels such as commodity markets and trade. Trade disruptions are affecting value chains, as many EMDEs are heavily dependent on Russia and Ukraine for key commodity imports. Surges in commodity prices are weighing on private consumption, especially in low-income countries due to high food and fuel shares in the consumption basket. Rising energy and fertilizer costs are offsetting the benefits of higher prices for agricultural exporters.

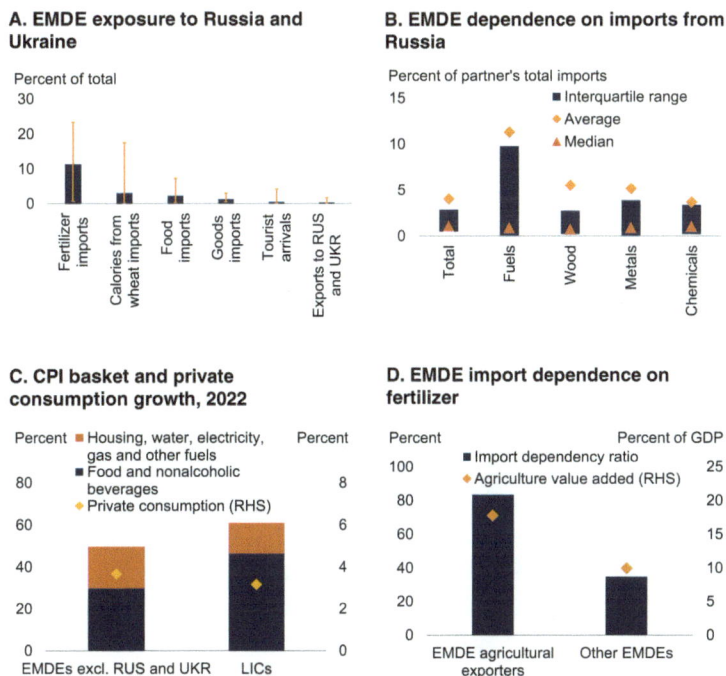

A. EMDE exposure to Russia and Ukraine

B. EMDE dependence on imports from Russia

C. CPI basket and private consumption growth, 2022

D. EMDE import dependence on fertilizer

Sources: Comtrade (database); International Monetary Fund; Ministry of Economy of the Republic of Armenia; United Nations World Food Programme; UNWTO (2021); Winkler, Wuester, and Knight (2022); World Bank.

Note: EMDEs = emerging market and developing economies; LICs = low-income countries; RUS = the Russian Federation; UKR = Ukraine.

A. Bars show the EMDE median. Trade data show goods exports/imports to/from the Russian Federation and Ukraine as a share of the total goods exports/imports in 2019-20. Tourist arrivals refer to nonresident tourists at national borders by nationality. For countries where this data series is not available, estimates use number of non-resident visitors at national borders by nationality. Orange whiskers show the interquartile range.

B. Figure shows 2018-20 average from Winkler, Wuester, and Knight (2022). Sample includes 94 EMDEs.

C. Includes CPI basket data for 126 EMDEs and 20 LICs and private consumption data for 100 EMDEs and 17 LICs. Aggregate growth rates are calculated using real U.S. dollar GDP weights at average 2010-19 prices and market exchange rates. Data for 2022 are forecasts.

D. Import dependency ratio is defined as imports / (production + imports – exports). Sample includes 103 EMDEs. Aggregates are calculated using simple averages. Data as of 2019 for imports and 2020 for agriculture value added.

commodity imports and intermediate goods (figure 1.7.B). As a result, the aggregate EMDE manufacturing PMI and new export orders subcomponent have fallen to their lowest readings since mid-2020 and point to a contraction of activity. Business confidence has also slipped in a broad set of countries.

BOX 1.1 Regional perspectives: Outlook and risks

The Russian Federation's invasion of Ukraine is affecting emerging market and developing economy (EMDE) regions to different degrees via impacts on global trade and output, commodity prices, inflation, and interest rates. The adverse spillovers from the invasion will be most severe for Europe and Central Asia, where output is forecast to sharply contract this year. Output growth is projected to slow this year in all other regions except the Middle East and North Africa, where the benefits of higher energy prices for energy exporters are expected to outweigh those prices' negative impacts for other economies in the region. Risks for all EMDE regions are tilted to the downside and include intensifying geopolitical tensions, rising inflation and food shortages, financial stress and rising borrowing costs, renewed outbreaks of COVID-19, and disruptions from disasters.

Introduction

The economic rebound in emerging market and developing economies (EMDEs) following the pandemic-induced recession of 2020 was already fading prior to Russia's invasion of Ukraine. Spillovers from the invasion will slow the recovery further and exacerbate inflationary pressures through higher commodity prices and renewed supply chain disruptions. EMDE regions are at different stages in their recovery and will be affected by the war in Ukraine in different ways. The war is expected to cause a major recession in Europe and Central Asia (ECA), while its global spillovers will weigh particularly heavily on regions with many commodity importers. Regions with many commodity exporters, by contrast, will benefit from higher commodity prices, but new investment in extractive sectors is expected to be limited because of policy uncertainty, price volatility, and higher input costs. Downside risks to regional baseline forecasts—such as worsening geopolitical tensions, financial stress, and severe food insecurity—have increased because of the war in Ukraine, while disasters or renewed outbreaks of COVID-19 still have the potential to weaken activity.

This box considers two questions:

- What are the cross-regional differences in the outlook for growth?

- What are the key risks to the outlook for each region?

Outlook

The cyclical rebound from the global recession of 2020 was already waning prior to Russia's invasion of Ukraine as macroeconomic support was being withdrawn amid rising inflation. The invasion and its repercussions are expected to exacerbate the global slowdown and add to inflation pressures. Despite the fact that the recovery from the 2020 recession remains incomplete, activity in most EMDE regions is forecast to slow sharply this year (figure B1.1.1.A).

The invasion and its spillovers are having substantially different effects across EMDE regions. They are weighing particularly heavily on regions with a large number of commodity importers, as well as in those with countries especially vulnerable to the increases in global inflation and investor risk aversion (figure B1.1.1.B).

The worst affected region is ECA. In addition to its tragic human toll, the invasion is expected to cause a devastating economic contraction in Ukraine this year, a sharp recession in Russia, and a significant slowdown in the rest of the ECA region through direct trade and financial linkages. Spillovers from the invasion in the form of higher prices for energy and food are reducing incomes and increasing input costs, with particularly negative impacts on the terms of trade of South Asia (SAR). Forecasts for activity have also been downgraded this year in East Asia and the Pacific (EAP) a result of lockdowns in China and recent commodity price movements, while the forecast for Sub-Saharan Africa (SSA) has been downgraded if major energy exporters such as Nigeria are excluded.

By contrast, some regions with large numbers of commodity exporters, especially in Middle East and North Africa (MNA), are expected to benefit from the significant increases in the prices of energy, some agricultural commodities, and several metals. However, increased policy uncertainty, price volatility, higher input costs, and weaker global demand are all expected to reduce new investment, including in extractive sectors.

Note: This box was prepared by Patrick Kirby.

BOX 1.1 Regional perspectives: Outlook and risks (*continued*)

FIGURE B1.1.1 Regional outlooks

Growth in most emerging market and developing economy regions is expected to slow sharply this year, despite the fact that the recovery from the pandemic is far from complete. The Russian Federation's invasion of Ukraine has led to a substantial downgrade in the forecast for Europe and Central Asia, and is also weighing on regions with large numbers of commodity importers. Per capita income is expected to be lower in 2023 than in 2019 in about half of the countries in East Asia and the Pacific, the Middle East and North Africa, Latin America and the Caribbean, and Sub-Saharan Africa.

A. Output growth

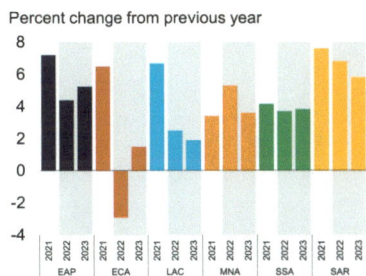

B. Revisions to 2022 forecast since January

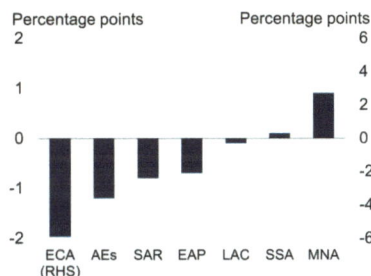

C. First year in which 2019 per capita income is surpassed

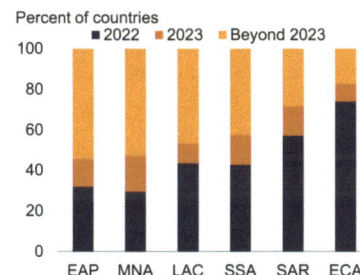

Source: World Bank.
Note: AEs = advanced economies; EAP = East Asia and Pacific, ECA = Europe and Central Asia, LAC = Latin America and the Caribbean, SAR = South Asia, SSA = Sub-Saharan Africa.
A.B. Aggregates are calculated using constant GDP weights at average 2010-19 prices and market exchange rates.
A. Shaded areas indicate forecasts.
C. Sample includes 22 EAP, 23 ECA, 30 LAC, 17 MNA, 7 SAR, and 47 SSA economies.

The combined effects of the pandemic, increased inflation, the war in Ukraine, and country-specific factors are expected to lead to a net increase of 75 million people in extreme poverty by the end of this year relative to pre-pandemic projections, primarily in regions where poverty is already elevated. Per capita income is expected to be lower in 2023 than its pre-pandemic level in about half of the countries in EAP (predominantly small island economies), MNA, Latin America and the Caribbean (LAC), and SSA (figure B1.1.1.C). Within regions, the recovery in per capita incomes is expected to be slowest low-income countries and island economies dependent on tourism, where incomes remain deeply depressed relative to pre-pandemic levels. In tourism dependent EMDE small states (countries with populations under 1.5 million), most of which are in EAP and LAC, per capita income is expected to remain 7 percent below its pre-pandemic level in 2022.

Risks

Downside risks to the baseline forecast, many of which have increased since Russia's invasion of Ukraine, dominate all regional outlooks. Intensifying geopolitical

tensions could result from the use of weapons of mass destruction, the spread of the war in Ukraine to a larger region, a prolongation of the war, or widespread state-sponsored cyberattacks on public infrastructure or financial systems. This could result in lower global demand, renewed trade disruptions, greater policy uncertainty, further damage to business and consumer confidence, and refugee crises. Although these risks are especially pronounced in the ECA region, spillovers would also cast a shadow over activity in other regions, especially those that are most dependent on integration into global supply chains and foreign demand, notably EAP. Shortages of vital inputs due to production disruptions or trade barriers—such as those related to sanctions in response to Russia's invasion of Ukraine—could disrupt supply chains already struggling with bottlenecks and elevated costs.

Food imports have become notably more expensive, increasing the risk of widespread food insecurity and social unrest (figure B1.1.2.A). Food accounts for an average of about one-third of the consumption basket in EMDEs, but considerably more in SAR and SSA (44 and 37 percent of average consumption baskets, respectively; figure B1.1.2.B). Russia and Ukraine are

BOX 1.1 Regional perspectives: Outlook and risks *(continued)*

FIGURE B1.1.2 Regional risks

The war in Ukraine has increased downside risks. Elevated food prices increase the risk of widespread food insecurity, especially in regions where food is a large share of the consumption basket. Higher costs in some regions from supply chain disruptions and persistently elevated commodity prices could add to already-high inflationary pressures and de-anchor inflation expectations. Renewed outbreaks of COVID-19 remain a risk in all regions, particularly those with lower vaccination coverage.

A. Number of people in acute food insecurity

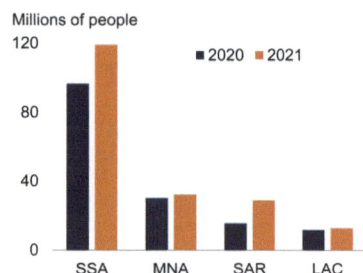

B. Food share in consumption basket and food inflation

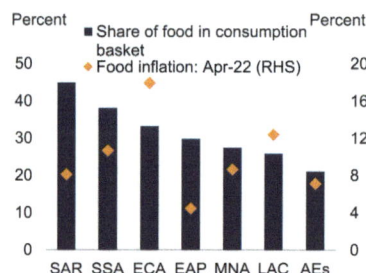

C. CPI inflation

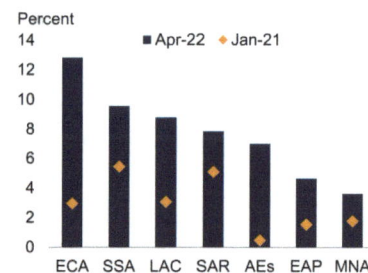

D. Five-year ahead inflation expectations

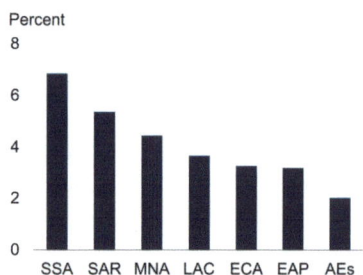

E. Vaccinations against COVID-19

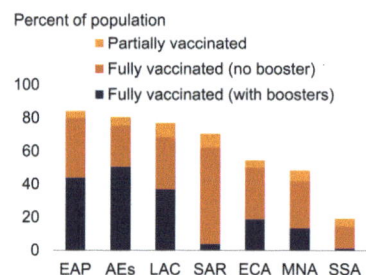

F. Shipping intensity of GDP

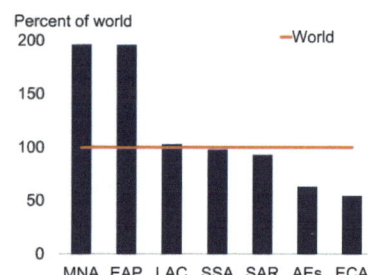

Sources: Consensus Economics; FSIN and GNAFC (2022); Haver Analytics; Our World in Data (database); Ritchie et al. (2022); World Bank.

Note: AEs = advanced economies; EAP = East Asia and Pacific, ECA = Europe and Central Asia, LAC = Latin America and the Caribbean, MNA = Middle East and North Africa, SAR = South Asia, SSA = Sub-Saharan Africa.

A. Bars represent the sum of people in high levels of food insecurity, measured here as phase 3 or above of the Integrated Food Security Phase Classification (IPC) for 2020 and 2021. Sample size includes 3 SAR, 36 SSA, 9 MNA, and 5 LAC economies.

B. Blue bars show median food share in consumption basket. Sample includes 8 advanced economies, 10 EAP, 13 ECA, 19 LAC, 11 MNA, 6 SAR, and 25 SSA economies. Orange diamonds show median food inflation. Sample includes 33 advanced economies, 8 EAP, 19 ECA, 18 LAC, 9 MNA, 3 SAR, and 22 SSA economies.

C. CPI refers to consumer price index. Bars show median 12-month inflation for latest data available (March 2022), while diamonds show inflation data for January 2021. Sample includes 34 advanced economies, 5 EAP, 20 ECA, 18 LAC, 6 MNA, 3 SAR, and 9 SSA economies.

D. Chart shows the median inflation expectations for 2027 based on Consensus Economics April 2022 Survey data. Sample includes 33 AEs, 7 EAP, 19 ECA, 18 LAC, 2 MNA, 3 SAR, and 2 SSA economies.

E. Sample includes 37 advanced economies, 24 EAP, 31 ECA, 39 LAC, 19 MNA, 8 SAR, and 47 SSA economies. Last observation is May 25, 2022.

F. Data are for 2019. Values are ratios of port container traffic (20-foot equivalent units) to real 2019 GDP, normalized to the world ratio.

both major exporters of agricultural commodities, and global food prices could increase further in the face of additional disruptions to planting, harvesting, and transportation. Food shortages would squeeze budgets for both households and governments—particularly in net food-importing countries concentrated in ECA, MNA, and SSA—with urban consumers and vulnerable groups suffering the most. In the past, food shortages have also contributed to rising social unrest. Food production is also at risk of further disruption through lack of access to critical agricultural inputs. The sharp increases in the prices of fuel, chemicals, and fertilizers may be especially damaging in regions where agriculture accounts for a large share of the economy, such as SSA and SAR (19 and 18 percent of value added in 2020, respectively).

BOX 1.1 Regional perspectives: Outlook and risks (*continued*)

Elevated levels of inflation, combined with sharply slowing growth, raise concerns that the global economy is entering a period of stagflation reminiscent of the 1970s. Higher costs from supply chain disruptions and persistently elevated commodity prices could add to already-high inflationary pressures (figure B1.1.2.C). Monetary authorities may tighten monetary policy at a faster-than-expected pace to avoid a de-anchoring of inflation expectations, particularly in regions where inflation is rising at a faster pace and long-term inflation expectations are higher (SSA, LAC, ECA; figure B1.1.2.D). In regions with many commodity-importing countries, the rising cost of food and energy subsidies are adding to the strain on governments' budgets.

Elevated inflation and rising interest rates could combine with high debt and weak growth to produce financial stress in some regions. The recession and financial turmoil in ECA could spill over to other regions directly through balance sheet effects, or through a more general increase in investor risk aversion. A disorderly tightening of financial conditions could stem from capital outflows and currency depreciations, which would further worsen inflationary pressures, macroeconomic instability, and debt burdens. This is more likely given existing debt sustainability problems (SSA), elevated sovereign debt (LAC) and corporate debt (EAP), and substantial hidden public debt and contingent liabilities (Melecky 2021; SAR).

Renewed outbreaks of COVID-19 remain a risk in all regions, particularly those with lower vaccination coverage (SSA, MNA; figure B1.1.2.E). Persistent or worsening disruptions from the pandemic to activity at critical infrastructure, such as ports in China, could cause further disruptions to supply chains, with larger spillovers for regions that are more heavily embedded in global value chains or particularly dependent on shipping (figure B1.1.2.F). A new wave of COVID-19 could also interrupt the rebound in global tourism, as was the case during the spread of the Omicron variant in early 2022, with especially important consequences for tourism-dependent small states concentrated in LAC and EAP.

Disruptions from disasters are a persistent source of downside risk. Island countries face rising sea levels and increasingly extreme storms that can wipe out years of economic development. About half of the population of SAR lives in areas where changing weather patterns risk permanently lowering living standards, for example through increasingly frequent heatwaves (Mani et al. 2018). In about one-quarter of countries in EAP and LAC, more than 10 percent of the population lives in areas 5 meters or less above sea level and is at serious risk from more frequent storms. In MNA, SAR and SSA, more severe heatwaves and floods threaten to reduce agricultural yields and exacerbate water-scarcity, undermining food security and raising the likelihood of conflict. By one estimate, crop yields in MNA could decrease by up to 30 percent if temperatures rise 1.5-2 degrees Celsius above pre-industrial levels (World Bank 2014).

Across EMDEs, the spillovers from the war are magnifying the pre-existing drag from lingering COVID-19 disruptions, persistent supply-chain bottlenecks, and continued withdrawal of macroeconomic policy support. Financing conditions have tightened further, as mounting inflationary pressures in major advanced economies has led to expectations of faster withdrawal of monetary support. In EMDEs, inflation has also increased as the war has put additional pressure on commodity prices and supply chains. Higher prices have eroded real incomes and dampened private consumption, especially in economies with high shares of food and energy in their consumption baskets (figure 1.7.C). Investment has weakened further in many EMDEs, particularly in those facing tighter financial conditions amid marked increases in policy uncertainty, an erosion in confidence, and subdued growth prospects. External demand is also softening as global growth decelerates, particularly for countries that rely on Russia and Ukraine as destinations for exports or as sources of tourists.

The impact of the war differs across EMDEs. For commodity importers, the negative spillovers from the war are particularly significant as they face a large shock to their terms of trade. In contrast, higher energy prices are cushioning some of the adverse effects of the war in energy exporters. In other commodity exporters, however, the beneficial effects of higher metal and agricultural prices have been dampened by a sharp increase in input costs. To a large extent, this reflects these economies' reliance on energy and fertilizer imports for domestic activity—including industrial and agricultural production—as well as their limited ability to substitute these imports with domestically produced sources (figure 1.7.D).

Growth in LICs—which reached a modest 3.9 percent in 2021, far slower than the pace of recovery in EMDEs as a whole and well below the rate of potential growth—is mainly being adversely affected by the war's impact on food prices. More than half of the population in LICs are experiencing food shortages, with food availability already stressed by the prevalence of conflict in some countries and vulnerabilities to climate change (FSIN and GNAFC 2021). Import disruptions and higher prices are worsening food insecurity and reducing access to proper nutrition (FAO 2022). Even in LICs with low food insecurity, price increases and disruptions to the food supply are tipping many more people into extreme poverty (Wang et al. 2020).

Outlook

EMDE outlook

The war in Ukraine is weighing on aggregate EMDE growth prospects owing to higher inflation and input costs, disruptions to trade, weaker confidence, and a steep rise in policy uncertainty. These will add to pre-existing headwinds to growth, including rising inflationary pressures and tightening financial conditions, the ongoing removal of fiscal and monetary policy support, and softening external demand. EMDE growth is expected to roughly halve in 2022, to 3.4 percent—far weaker than its annual average of 4.8 percent over 2011-19—a downgrade of 1.2 percentage points relative to previous projections

(figure 1.8.A). This downward revision reflects, to a significant degree, deep recessions in Russia and Ukraine. Excluding these two countries, the EMDE growth forecast for 2022 has been downgraded by 0.5 percentage point, as improved growth prospects in energy exporters partly offset broad-based downgrades in other EMDEs (figure 1.8.B). Forecasts for 2022 growth have been lowered in nearly 70 percent of EMDEs, including most commodity-importing economies (figure 1.8.C). EMDE growth is anticipated to firm to an average of 4.3 percent in 2023-24, as the lingering effects of the war abate.

The near-term outlook for EMDE private consumption has weakened, driven in part by higher prices and the erosion of real incomes. EMDE households' exposure to commodity price shocks has risen in recent years, as an increasing proportion of spending is on basic necessities, including food and energy (figure 1.8.D; FAO 2021). The weakness in private consumption also reflects job losses in economies affected by the war, as well as those highly dependent on remittances from Russia.

Investment, which was already expected to be subdued, is likely to be further weakened by soft investor confidence, higher interest rates, and heightened uncertainty about growth prospects and policy, especially in economies perceived as less creditworthy. Increases in extractive investment are expected to be limited by investor concerns regarding the significant volatility in commodity prices and heightened geopolitical uncertainty.

EMDE exports are expected to be dampened by a sharp slowdown in growth in advanced economies and continued strains on global supply chains. The spike in commodity prices and disruption to exports from Russia and Ukraine are anticipated to hinder production in some large manufacturing economies, as their value chains are especially exposed to intermediate goods and services from these countries (Winkler, Wuester, and Knight 2022).

On balance, recent increases in commodity prices are a drag on aggregate EMDE activity. On the one hand, the increase in energy prices will improve fiscal space, current account positions, and incomes of some commodity exporters. On the other hand, the increase in commodity prices will raise production costs for firms and weaken purchasing power among households in commodity importers, which account for more than two-thirds of EMDE GDP. For agricultural and metal commodity exporters, sharply higher input costs—including fuel as well as fertilizers, for which Russia is a key exporter—are expected to limit the gains from higher commodity prices.

Although the pandemic is weighing less heavily on the near-term outlook, it is still expected to have lasting effects on long-term growth across EMDEs, and many of these effects will be compounded by the war. The adverse impact on human capital, investor confidence, fixed capital formation, and supply chains from these two crises will weigh on long-term growth prospects. As a result, EMDE potential growth is expected to be below 4 percent over 2022-30—a sharp slowdown from about 5 percent in the 2010s.

LICs outlook

Growth in LICs is anticipated at 4.1 percent in 2022 and 5.3 percent in 2023 (box 1.2). Despite improving terms of trade in commodity exporters, the forecast for this year has been downgraded 0.8 percentage point, in part reflecting sharp increases in global food and fuel prices due to the invasion of Ukraine—growth in more than four-fifths of LICs has been revised down. In many LICs, where households on average spend over 40 percent of their budget on staple foods, food price inflation remains stubbornly high, eroding real incomes and weighing on consumption. Higher fertilizer prices are expected to make agricultural production even more costly, which will lower agricultural output for many LICs. Elevated levels of conflict and violence are also dampening growth and investment in some LICs.

The outlook for LICs is clouded by various risks. Median inflation in LICs is approaching 11 percent—its highest reading in five years—and is expected to continue to rise in the near term (figure 1.8.E). Many LICs are at risk of worsening food insecurity and malnutrition if grain imports from Russia and Ukraine are further disrupted

FIGURE 1.8 Outlook in emerging market and developing economies

Growth in emerging market and developing economies (EMDEs) is forecast to slow to 3.4 percent in 2022—1.2 percentage points below previous projections, largely on account of the effects of the war. Excluding the Russian Federation and Ukraine, the deterioration is more modest, as an improvement in energy exporters partly offsets broad-based downgrades in most other EMDEs. Surging food and energy prices are fueling inflation and eroding real incomes, particularly for low-income households and countries, which devote a large share of their expenditures to these goods. Continued disruptions to Russian and Ukrainian wheat exports would worsen food insecurity and increase malnutrition in some countries, including many low-income countries.

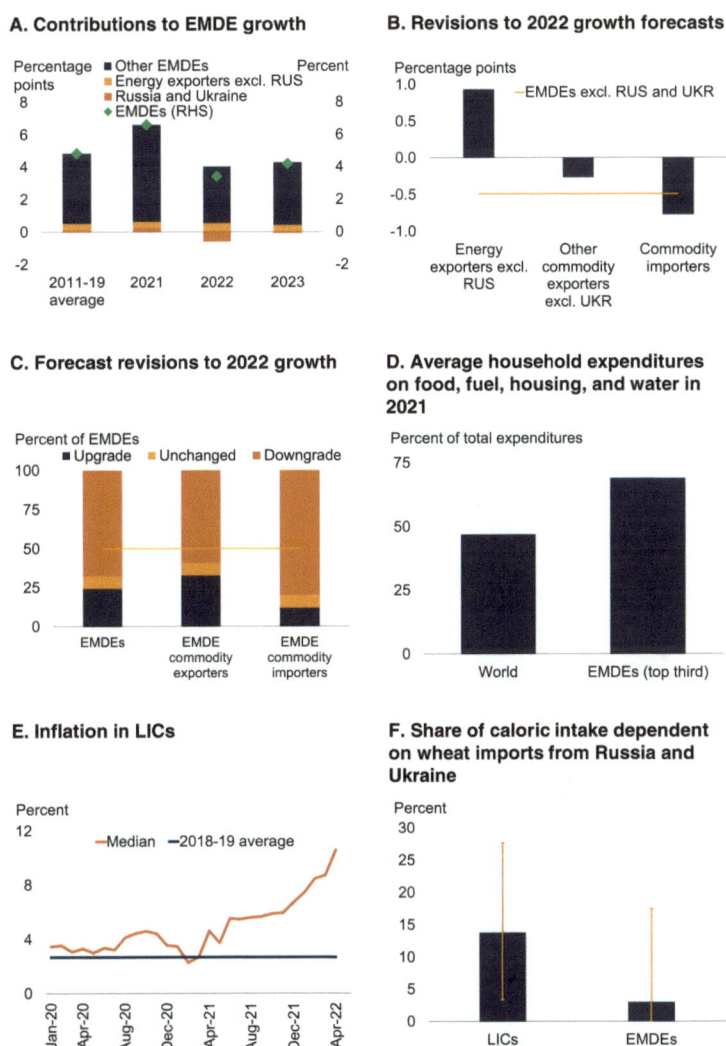

A. Contributions to EMDE growth

B. Revisions to 2022 growth forecasts

C. Forecast revisions to 2022 growth

D. Average household expenditures on food, fuel, housing, and water in 2021

E. Inflation in LICs

F. Share of caloric intake dependent on wheat imports from Russia and Ukraine

Sources: Comtrade (database); FAO (2021); Haver Analytics; U.S. Department of Agriculture; World Bank.
Note: EMDEs = emerging market and developing economies; LICs = low-income countries; RUS = the Russian Federation; UKR = Ukraine. Data for 2022-23 are forecasts.
A.B. Aggregates are calculated using real U.S. dollar GDP weights at average 2010-19 prices and market exchange rates.
B.C. Figures show the change in 2022 growth forecasts between the January 2022 and June 2022 editions of *Global Economic Prospects.*
D. Figure shows share of energy, water, housing, and food based on FAO (2021) calculations. "World" includes 176 countries and "EMDEs (top third)" includes the 53 countries with the highest expenditure shares on these categories.
E. Sample includes seven LICs. Last observation is April 2022.
F. Figure shows the share of wheat imports from the Russian Federation and Ukraine (as percent of total wheat imports in 2020) multiplied by the share of dietary energy supply derived from cereals, roots, and tubers multiplied by the share of wheat imports to wheat consumption. Sample includes 85 EMDEs and 15 LICs. Blue bars are medians and orange whiskers are the interquartile ranges.

FIGURE 1.9 Per capita income in emerging market and developing economies

Per capita income growth forecasts have been revised down in about 70 percent of emerging market and developing economies (EMDEs) in 2022. EMDEs are expected to make little headway toward catching up with advanced-economy per capita income levels over the next couple of years; if China is excluded, catch-up progress is forecast to reverse.

A. Forecast revisions to EMDE per capita income growth, 2022

B. EMDE per capita income growth relative to advanced-economy average

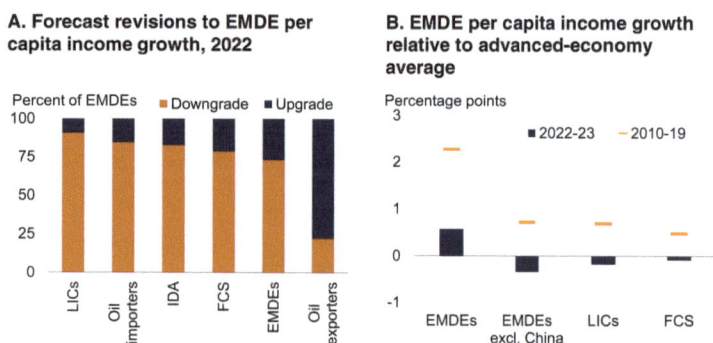

Source: World Bank.
Note: EMDEs = emerging market and developing economies; FCS = fragile and conflict-affected situations; IDA = International Development Association; LICs = low-income countries. Per capita GDP levels calculated using the total GDP for each subgroup divided by its total population. Data for 2022-23 are forecasts. Sample includes 145 EMDEs, 22 LICs, and 28 FCS.
A. FCS excludes oil exporters; oil importers excludes China. Figure shows the change in 2022 per capita income growth forecasts between the January 2022 and June 2022 editions of *Global Economic Prospects*.
B. Aggregates calculated using GDP weights at average 2010-19 prices and market exchange rates. Relative per capita income growth is computed as the difference in per capita GDP growth between each respective EMDE group and the advanced-economy average.

(figure 1.8.F; WFP 2022). Food price surges of the same magnitude have been associated with tens of millions more people falling into extreme poverty in LICs (de Hoyos and Medvedev 2011; Ivanic, Martin, Zaman 2011). In addition, debt distress, slowing activity in major export markets, violence, and social unrest could substantially weigh on growth in many LICs.

Per capita income growth

Per capita income growth in EMDEs is expected to decelerate sharply, from 5.4 percent in 2021 to 2.3 percent in 2022. Excluding Russia and Ukraine, EMDE per capita income growth is still anticipated to slow markedly in 2022, to 3 percent, as high food and fuel prices weigh on real household incomes, constrained fiscal space limits government support, and labor market recoveries decelerate. After remarkable resilience over the past two years, growth in remittances to EMDEs is likely to moderate, as mounting inflationary pressures erode real wages and pandemic-related income support programs subside in advanced economies. A steep recession in Russia is also

expected to trigger a sharp decline in transfers to neighboring countries, where remittances from Russia can account for as much as 30 percent of GDP.

Aggregate EMDE measures mask differing near-term prospects across countries. In energy exporters excluding Russia, per capita income growth is forecast to firm from 1.8 percent in 2021 to 3.3 percent this year, as higher energy prices help cushion the negative impact from the war. In contrast, in commodity importers, where inflation is rising at a faster pace than in most energy exporters, per capita income growth is projected to soften, as weaker terms of trade fuel further price increases and diminish household purchasing power.

Per capita income growth forecasts for 2022 have been revised down in about 70 percent of EMDEs, primarily reflecting the adverse effects of the war, with particularly pronounced downward revisions in countries in fragile and conflict-affected situations (figure 1.9.A). Weaker growth will also slow the pace of catch-up with advanced-economy per capita income for many EMDEs—especially in LICs, where per capita income is projected to grow at only half the pace of advanced economies. Over the next few years, EMDEs are expected to make little progress toward catching up with advanced-economy income levels—and, if China is excluded, progress is expected to reverse, undoing some of the gains made over 2010-19 (figure 1.9.B).

Together, and in the absence of policies that alleviate their scarring effects, the pandemic and the war will have long-lasting adverse impacts on per capita incomes. Even by 2023, per capita incomes are projected to be below 2019 levels in about two fifths of EMDEs. The rising cost of food is likely to have particularly adverse near-term effects, especially in countries reliant on importing staple foods like wheat and corn. Attempts to safeguard domestic food supplies could further increase global prices, as has been the case in the past (Ivanic and Martin 2014; World Bank 2019b). Taken together, the lingering effects of the pandemic, the war, and the surge in food prices are expected to lead to a net increase of 75 million people in extreme poverty by the end of this year relative to pre-pandemic projections (World Bank 2022a).

Global outlook and risks

The effects of Russia's invasion of Ukraine—particularly, sharply higher commodity prices—coupled with the anticipated policy response to higher global inflation, are expected to accentuate the near-term slowdown in advanced economies and most EMDEs. The war is also exacerbating various risks, including intensifying geopolitical tensions, acute financial stress, stagflation, and widespread food shortages. The simultaneous materialization of several downside risks could result in substantially weaker growth.

Global outlook

The war in Ukraine has steepened the projected slowdown in global activity (figure 1.10.A). In addition to causing a deep recession in the ECA region, the economic effects of the war are spilling over across the globe through commodity prices, financial conditions, trade patterns, migration flows, and confidence.

The invasion of Ukraine represents an additional supply shock to a global economy still recovering from the pandemic. The associated physical and logistical disruptions and the ensuing sharp rise in commodity prices are driving inflation higher and weighing on activity, exacerbating the pre-existing strains from the pandemic on the global economy. The war has also eroded confidence and heightened risk aversion, contributing to weaker trade and investment as firms seek to hedge against adverse outcomes.

Global growth is expected to slow sharply from 5.7 percent in 2021 to 2.9 percent in 2022 as a result of deep recessions in Russia and Ukraine, adverse global spillovers from the war in Ukraine, the fading of pent-up demand, and the withdrawal of policy support amid high inflation. Despite the negative shock to global activity in 2022, there is essentially no rebound projected next year. Global growth is forecast to edge up only slightly, to a still-subdued 3 percent in 2023, as many headwinds—in particular, high commodity prices and continued monetary tightening—are expected

FIGURE 1.10 Global outlook

The war in Ukraine has steepened the projected slowdown in global economic activity, adding to the cumulative output losses since the onset of the pandemic. Global inflation is set to peak around mid-2022 before declining gradually, aided by a projected moderation in energy prices. The global growth outlook is subject to significant uncertainty, and risks are markedly tilted to the downside in the near term.

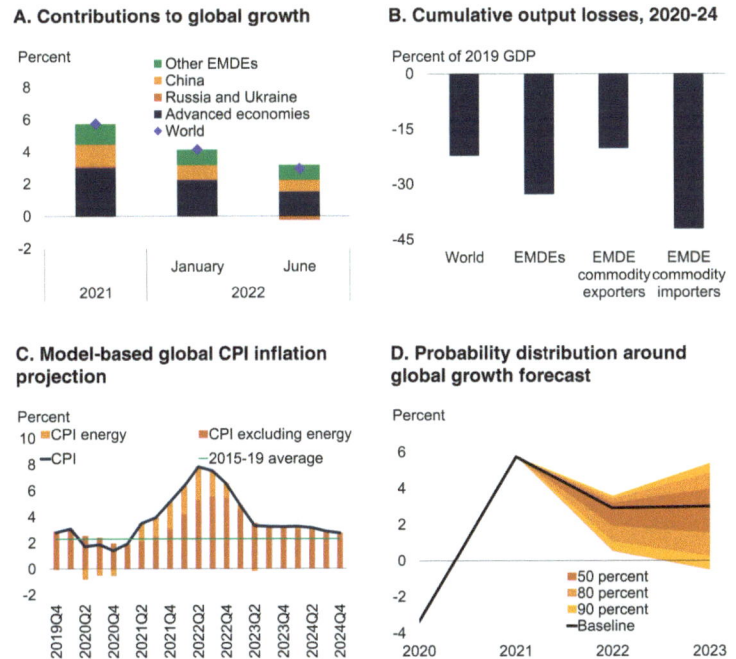

Sources: Bloomberg; Consensus Economics; Haver Analytics; Ohnsorge, Stocker, and Some (2016); Oxford Economics; World Bank.
Note: EMDEs = emerging market and developing economies. Aggregate growth rates calculated using real U.S. dollar GDP weights at average 2010-19 prices and market exchange rates. Data for 2022-24 are forecasts.
A. Figure shows the contributions to global growth forecasts in the January 2022 and June 2022 editions of *Global Economic Prospects*.
B. Bars show cumulative output losses over 2020-24, which are computed as deviations from trend, expressed as a share of GDP in 2019. Output is measured in U.S. dollars at 2010-19 prices and market exchange rates. Trend is assumed to grow at the regression-estimated trend growth rate of 2010-19. EMDE commodity exporters exclude the Russian Federation and Ukraine.
C. Model-based projection of quarterly global year-over-year CPI inflation using Oxford Economics Global Economic Model. Projection embeds global oil price forecast presented in table 1.1.
D. Probabilities for the forecast distribution of global growth are generated using time-varying estimates of the standard deviation and skewness extracted from the forecast distribution of oil price futures, S&P 500 equity price futures, and term spread forecasts, as described in Ohnsorge, Stocker, and Some (2016). Values for 2022 and 2023 are based on 6-month-ahead and 18-month-ahead forecast distributions, respectively. Last observation for S&P 500 and oil price futures is May 31, 2022, whereas term spread forecasts are from May 2022.

to persist. In 2024, global growth is projected to remain at 3 percent, as activity converges to its long-run potential pace. The cumulative losses to global activity relative to its pre-pandemic trend are expected to continue mounting, especially among EMDE commodity importers (figure 1.10.B).

High global consumer price inflation is envisioned to persist for longer than previously assumed as a result of surging commodity prices and lingering

BOX 1.2 Recent developments and outlook for low-income countries

The economic recovery in low-income countries (LICs) is anticipated to remain weak this year, with growth expected at 4.1 percent—almost a full percentage point below previous projections. Growth forecasts for 2022 have been downgraded in more than 80 percent of LICs, largely reflecting a sharp surge in food prices due to the Russian Federation's invasion of Ukraine. The ensuing increase in the cost of living across LICs is offsetting the benefit to commodity exporters from high industrial metal and energy prices. The disruption of global food supplies caused by the war in Ukraine has led to food shortages and a rapid deterioration of food security in many LICs. A sustained increase in food prices could further deepen poverty, stoke social unrest, and dampen economic recoveries, especially in LICs already experiencing high incidence of extreme poverty and acute food insecurity.

Introduction

Russia's invasion of Ukraine has pushed global food prices to all-time highs, sharply lifting inflation and eroding food affordability across many low-income countries (LICs). Although elevated global commodity prices benefit some exporters of metals and energy, millions of people across LICs are experiencing deepening poverty and worsening food insecurity. As a result, the economic recovery stemming from a gradual waning of the pandemic and increased export earnings is being muted, as rapidly rising costs of living are weakening domestic demand. In some countries, debt distress, policy uncertainty, social unrest, and violence still hamper recoveries, especially in fragile and conflict-affected LICs.

This box explores recent developments in, and the outlook for, LICs by examining the following questions.

- What have been the main recent economic developments in LICs?

- What is the outlook for LICs, and what are the associated risks?

The economic outlook for LICs comprises subdued per capita income growth, and remains highly uncertain, as a predominance of downside risks surrounds baseline projections. Higher-than-expected food prices could cause a growing number of people to fall into extreme poverty and experience acute food insecurity, considerably dampening growth prospects. A further slowdown in global growth amid a protracted war in Ukraine, as well as renewed lockdowns in China, could have sizable adverse effects on many LICs.

Recent developments

After growing 3.9 percent in 2021, the tepid economic recovery in LICs continued in the first half of this year, albeit at a much slower pace than previously envisaged. Disruptions to global commodity markets, considerably amplified by Russia's invasion of Ukraine, have led to food and fuel shortages and surging prices of staple consumer goods, eroding real incomes and weakening domestic demand. Rapid food price inflation, preceding the war in Ukraine in many economies (Burkina Faso, Ethiopia, Togo) has accelerated further, contributing to LIC median inflation rising to a five-year high (figure B1.2.1.A). Surging food and energy prices are also pushing many vulnerable people into acute food insecurity, especially in those LICs that rely heavily on imports of wheat from Russia and Ukraine (figure B1.2.1.B). High food prices and food shortages are causing severe hardship for tens of millions of people in LICs, adding to the protracted humanitarian crisis caused by fragility, conflict, and large population displacements in some countries (Afghanistan, Somalia, Syrian Arab Republic, Republic of Yemen).

In many LIC commodity exporters, increasing living costs have also tempered gains from higher global prices of energy and metals. Industrial metals (mostly copper), energy, and gold account for about one half of all LIC exports. Prices of these commodities were already elevated amid persistent supply bottlenecks and firming global demand, before war-induced supply shocks pushed them even higher. This favorable price environment is supporting increased mining activity along with positive spillovers to nonresource sectors in some LICs (Chad, Democratic Republic of Congo, Mozambique). In a few countries, higher export revenues also helped partly offset increased fiscal and external financing needs due to rising costs of imported food and fuel.

Note: This box was prepared by Sergiy Kasyanenko.

BOX 1.2 Recent developments and outlook for low-income countries (*continued*)

FIGURE B1.2.1 LICs: Recent developments

Inflation in LICs—which was already rising before Russia's invasion of Ukraine—has accelerated, as the war has pushed global food prices to very high levels. Rapidly rising living costs are weighing on growth, especially in LICs reliant on wheat imports from the Russian Federation and Ukraine. Following a surge in COVID-19 cases in LICs earlier this year, new infections have trended down, facilitating a further easing of social restrictions.

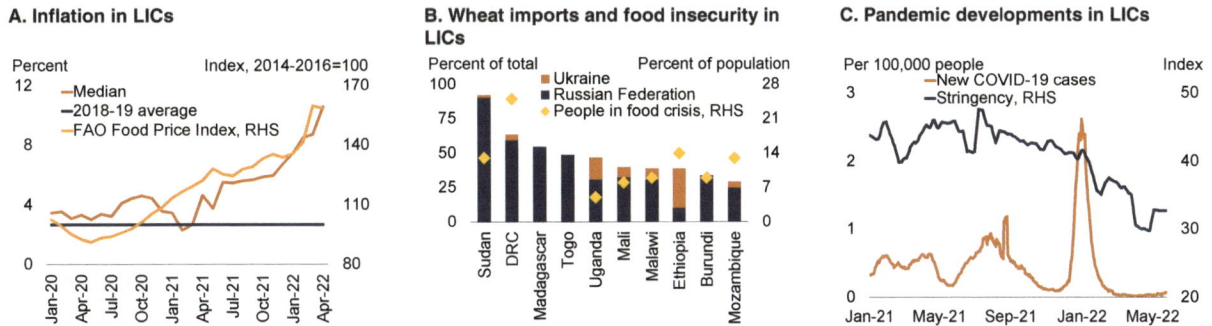

A. Inflation in LICs

B. Wheat imports and food insecurity in LICs

C. Pandemic developments in LICs

Sources: Blavatnik School of Government, University of Oxford; Comtrade (database); Global Network Against Food Crises; Haver Analytics; Johns Hopkins University; World Bank.

Note: LICs = low-income countries; DRC = Democratic Republic of Congo.

A. "Median" line shows median percentage increase in consumer prices from 12 months earlier, for a sample of seven LICs. Last observation April 2022.

B. Wheat imports shares are averages for 2019-2020; wheat imports data for Sudan are available only for 2018. "People in food crisis" indicates the estimated percentage of population being in phase 3 or above of the Integrated Food Security Phase Classification (IPC) for 2022; estimates are not available for Madagascar and Togo.

C. New case count shows the seven-day moving average of daily new infections. "Stringency" indicates the COVID-19 Government Response Stringency Index—a simple average of nine response indicators including school closures, workplace closures, and travel bans, rescaled to a value from 0 to 100 (100 = strictest). Last observation May 31, 2022.

Pandemic developments have been broadly favorable across LICs following a short-lived surge in COVID-19 cases earlier this year, supporting activity as mobility restrictions have eased and borders have reopened (figure B1.2.1.C). Yet, the boon to growth from eased pandemic restrictions remains fragile amid extremely low vaccination rates in many countries.

Outlook

Although most LICs have very small direct trade and financial exposures to Russia and Ukraine, the war's indirect adverse effects will weigh substantially on LICs activity this year. Reflecting these effects, growth forecasts for 2022 have been downgraded in more than 80 percent of LICs. In particular, a number of countries—such as the Democratic Republic of Congo, Madagascar, Rwanda, and Uganda—that rely heavily on wheat imports from Russia and Ukraine are expected to experience persistently elevated food inflation as the war disrupts global cereals trade and worsens food shortages. In addition to the adverse impact of surging living costs, the growth outlook for LICs is anticipated to be further weakened by the global economic

slowdown. Aggregate growth in LICs is forecast at only 4.1 percent in 2022 and 5.3 percent in 2023 – 0.8 and 0.6 percentage points below the January projections (figure B1.2.2.A).

Russia's invasion of Ukraine is expected to further deepen poverty and worsen food insecurity in LICs (Husain 2022; Mitchell, Hughes, and Huckstep 2022). Food consumption in LICs accounts for over 45 percent of total household expenditure, and diets remain heavily based on staple foods, including wheat (OECD/FAO 2020, 2021). All LICs are food-deficit countries reliant on imported foods with imports of wheat from Russia and Ukraine accounting for about 14 of total caloric intake in a median LIC compared to just 3 percent in a median EMDE. Disruptions to wheat imports from Russia and Ukraine, along with surging global food prices, are therefore expected to exert a strong drag on LIC growth and stall progress in poverty reduction, particularly in those economies where large shares of the population are already experiencing food insecurity (Democratic Republic of Congo, Ethiopia, Madagascar, Mozambique, South Sudan).

BOX 1.2 Recent developments and outlook for low-income countries (*continued*)

FIGURE B1.2.2 LICs: Outlook and risks

Rapidly increasing prices of food and further disruptions of wheat imports could leave many millions in acute food insecurity and extreme poverty, depressing per capita incomes in many low-income countries (LICs). Elevated violence and insecurity could continue to stymie growth in fragile and conflict-affected countries. In many LICs, vaccination rates remain very low, heightening the risk of new and more severe COVID-19 outbreaks.

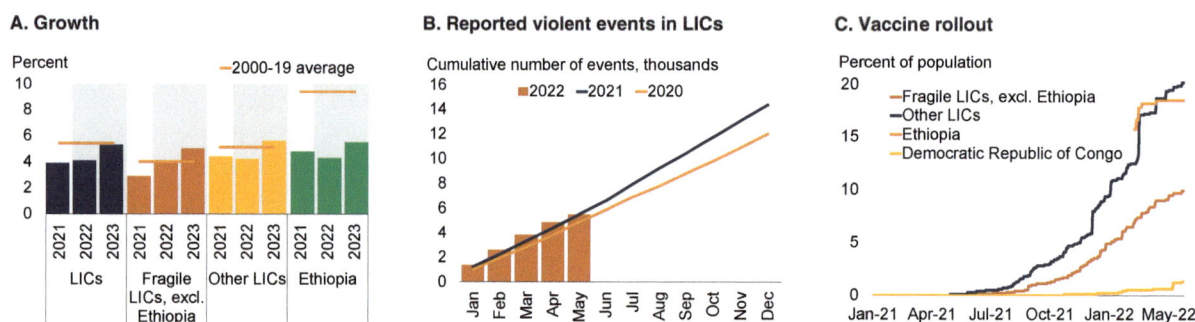

A. Growth

B. Reported violent events in LICs

C. Vaccine rollout

Sources: Armed Conflict Location & Event Data Project (ACLED), https://www.acleddata.com; Our World in Data (database); World Bank.
Note: Shaded area indicates forecasts. Fragile LICs = fragile and conflict-affected LICs; LICs = low-income countries.
A. Aggregate GDP growth rates calculated using constant GDP weights at average 2010-19 prices and market exchange rates. Sample comprises 22 LICs, which include 13 fragile LICs.
B. Violent events include battles, explosions, violence against civilians, riots, and protests, reported since the start of the year. Last observation May 20, 2022.
C. Share of population who are fully vaccinated. Last observation is May 31, 2022.

In some commodity exporters, the deleterious effects of higher food and fuel costs on real incomes are expected to be partly offset by gains from elevated prices of metals—particularly copper, aluminum, nickel, and gold. In Mozambique, higher prices of coal and natural gas are expected to support activity, though continued violence and insecurity weigh on the recovery. However, elevated oil prices are unlikely to boost growth substantially in LIC energy exporters, as aging oil fields and weak extractive investment limit prospects for increased oil production (Chad, South Sudan). In those commodity exporters where Russia has large stakes in extractive sectors (Guinea, Mozambique, Sudan), international sanctions due to the invasion of Ukraine are anticipated to weaken activity and investment in mining. The projected sharp growth slowdown in the European Union is also expected to slow growth in some LICs dependent on markets in high-income countries (Madagascar, Malawi).

Growth in fragile and conflict-affected LICs (excluding Ethiopia, the largest economy, accounting for 30 percent of total output in LICs) is projected to average 4.4 percent a year in 2022-23—0.6 percentage point below previous forecasts. In those countries, elevated levels of violence and insecurity are expected to lead to an even further deterioration of food security (Kuemmerle and Baumann 2021). As a result, real income per capita is projected to still fall short of pre-pandemic levels in almost 50 percent of fragile and conflict-affected LICs in 2023.

Agricultural production in a number of LICs is expected to remain subdued. A few countries have faced worsening drought conditions with delayed and below-average rainfall (Horn of Africa—Ethiopia, Somalia, Sudan, Uganda); others have experienced planting delays because of poor rainfall (Burundi, Madagascar, Malawi, Mozambique). In some LICs, higher prices of grains are expected to limit the ability of farmers, especially those dependent on subsistence agriculture, to purchase enough seeds for the new planting season and feed for livestock. The war in Ukraine has also markedly disrupted global fertilizer supply, with Russia the world's largest fertilizer exporter. Higher prices of fertilizers and fuels are expected to weigh heavily on farming output as well.

BOX 1.2 Recent developments and outlook for low-income countries (*continued*)

TABLE B1.2.1 Low-income country forecasts^a

(Real GDP growth at market prices in percent, unless indicated otherwise)

Percentage point differences from January 2022 projections

	2019	2020	2021e	2022f	2023f	2024f	2022f	2023f
Low-Income Country, GDP^b	4.8	1.9	3.9	4.1	5.3	5.7	-0.8	-0.6
GDP per capita (U.S. dollars)	1.9	-0.9	1.1	1.3	2.5	2.9	-0.8	-0.6
Afghanistan^c	3.9	-1.9	..	..	..	..	..	..
Burkina Faso	5.7	1.9	7.0	4.8	5.4	5.3	-0.8	0.1
Burundi	1.8	0.3	1.8	2.5	3.3	4.1	0.0	0.3
Central African Republic	3.1	0.9	0.9	3.2	3.4	4.0	-0.3	-1.1
Chad	3.2	-1.6	-1.2	2.8	3.5	3.9	1.0	0.6
Congo, Dem. Rep.	4.4	1.7	5.7	6.0	6.4	6.1	1.2	1.3
Eritrea	3.8	-0.6	2.9	4.7	3.6	3.7	0.0	0.0
Ethiopia^d	9.0	6.1	6.3	3.3	5.2	5.9	-1.0	-1.3
Gambia, The	6.2	-0.2	5.6	5.6	6.2	6.5	-0.4	-0.3
Guinea	5.6	4.6	3.1	4.3	5.9	5.8	-1.8	0.0
Guinea-Bissau	4.5	1.5	3.8	3.5	4.5	4.5	-0.5	-0.5
Liberia	-2.9	-3.0	4.0	4.4	4.8	5.2	-0.3	-0.2
Madagascar	4.4	-7.1	4.4	2.6	4.2	4.6	-2.8	-0.9
Malawi	5.4	0.8	2.8	2.1	4.3	4.2	-0.9	-0.1
Mali	4.8	-1.2	3.1	3.3	5.3	5.0	-1.9	0.3
Mozambique	2.3	-1.2	2.2	3.6	6.0	5.8	-1.5	-3.6
Niger	5.9	3.6	1.4	5.2	7.1	10.4	-1.0	-2.3
Rwanda	9.5	-3.4	10.9	6.8	7.2	7.4	-1.0	-0.6
Sierra Leone	5.3	-2.0	3.1	3.9	4.4	4.8	-2.1	0.1
South Sudan^d	3.2	9.5	-5.1	-0.8	2.5	4.0	-2.0	-1.0
Sudan	-2.2	-3.6	0.1	0.7	2.0	2.5	-2.8	-3.0
Syrian Arab Republic	3.7	1.3	-2.1	-2.6	..	..	..	..
Togo^e	5.5	1.8	5.1	5.0	5.8	6.4	-0.6	-0.4
Uganda^d	6.4	3.0	3.4	3.7	5.1	6.5	0.0	-0.4
Yemen, Rep.	1.4	-8.5	-2.1	0.8	2.5	..	..	..

Source: World Bank.

Note: e = estimate; f = forecast. World Bank forecasts are frequently updated based on new information and changing (global) circumstances. Consequently, projections presented here may differ from those contained in other Bank documents, even if basic assessments of countries' prospects do not significantly differ at any given moment in time.

a. The Democratic People's Republic of Korea and Somalia are not forecast on account of data limitations.

b. Aggregate growth rates are calculated using GDP weights at average 2010-19 prices and market exchange rates.

c. Forecast for Afghanistan (beyond 2020), the Syrian Arab Republic (beyond 2022), and the Republic of Yemen (beyond 2023) are excluded because of a high degree of uncertainty.

d. GDP growth rates are on a fiscal year basis. For example, the column labeled 2022 refers to FY2021/22.

e. For Togo, growth figures in 2019 are based on pre-2020 rebased GDP estimates.

Risks

Downside risks to the outlook predominate. With almost all LICs relying on imports of wheat, a prolonged disruption to global trade in cereals because of the Russia's invasion of Ukraine would significantly worsen affordability and availability of staple foods in the group. Moreover, further price increases of farming inputs—such as seeds, fuel, and fertilizers—could lead to stronger and more persistent food price pressures in LICs. Persistent inflation remains a major challenge for policy makers amid risks of stagflation in many LICs (World Bank 2022b).

Insecurity and violence continue to weigh on the outlook of many LICs, and more rapid increases in living costs risk further escalating social unrest (figure B1.2.2.B). Elevated levels of conflict could also dampen

BOX 1.2 Recent developments and outlook for low-income countries (*continued*)

growth and worsen food insecurity, especially in LICs where agriculture is already stressed by climate change (Anderson et al 2021). The scope for policy action to alleviate such problems is likely to be limited in most cases, especially in countries where public safety nets are predominantly donor-financed as donors reallocate resources to the ECA region (World Bank 2022b). Increased public spending on security, food support, and fertilizer subsidies, could further widen fiscal deficits, raising the risk of debt distress in many LICs.

Despite a recent uptick in vaccination rates, as of end-May only about 14 percent of LIC populations were fully vaccinated against COVID-19, reflecting a much slower vaccination rollout than in most other EMDEs. Vaccination rates remain particularly low in fragile and conflict-affected LICs (figure B1.2.2.C). Unvaccinated people remain at risk of severe illness, especially if new, more dangerous, variants of COVID-19 were to develop, which could lead to more severe and longer lasting interruptions to economic activity than with the Omicron wave.

With global financial conditions likely to tighten further, a sustained increase in risk aversion resulting from heightened geopolitical tensions could lead to further currency depreciations and sharp increases in borrowing costs in LICs. High levels of public debt and increased diversity of creditors could further stall progress in debt restructuring, while tighter sovereign-bank links could amplify financial distress if governments were to default on local currency debt. Interest rate and refinancing risks are particularly elevated for LICs that already spend high proportions of their tax revenues servicing external debt and rely on market-based borrowing (World Bank 2019). In the median LIC, the share of non-concessional debt in total external government debt has risen to over 70 percent from less than 60 percent in 2010, while about one quarter of all LIC external debt now has variable interest rates, compared to just 11 percent in 2010. Further increases in global interest rates, and thus LICs' borrowing costs, would limit other public spending, including food subsidies and investment in physical and human capital—to the detriment of LICs' pressing infrastructure and development needs.

supply bottlenecks. Global inflation is expected to peak around mid-year and then decline gradually thereafter as global growth slows, supply bottlenecks abate, and commodity supply increases and leads to lower prices (figure 1.10.C). Nonetheless, inflation is projected to remain above target in a majority of advanced economies and EMDEs well into 2023.

Despite new headwinds to growth, central banks across the world are expected to respond to inflationary pressures by withdrawing monetary accommodation over the forecast horizon. Pandemic-related fiscal support will continue to be withdrawn in advanced economies and EMDEs, albeit at a somewhat slower pace than previously anticipated in some economies as authorities introduce some targeted fiscal support measures to attenuate the effects from the war.

The war in Ukraine and its attendant impacts account for most of the 1.2 percentage points

downgrade to this year's global growth outlook. Almost one-third of this revision reflects the contraction envisaged in ECA owing to deep recessions in Russia and Ukraine. The combination of spillovers from the war, higher global inflation, and the associated faster withdrawal of monetary accommodation have also resulted in sizable downgrades to advanced economies and EMDEs outside of ECA. Sharp upward revisions to global energy prices, in particular, are weighing appreciably on activity in energy importers (Special Focus 2). As a result, downgrades among EMDEs are much more substantial among commodity importers, with growth forecasts for some energy exporters revised up because of improved terms of trade.

These baseline projections assume that the war persists in the near term but becomes increasingly contained to the eastern part of Ukraine. They also assume that sanctions due to the invasion are not lifted over the forecast horizon. Geopolitical and policy uncertainty are anticipated to remain above historical norms but to begin to gradually wane later this year as the intensity of the war and its repercussions abate. The outlook is also predicated on a pronounced but orderly tightening of global financing conditions and the continued withdrawal of pandemic-related macroeconomic policy support. Commodity prices are expected to remain high but moderate over the forecast horizon as supply disruptions ease (World Bank 2022a). The economic impacts of new COVID-19 outbreaks are expected to be markedly less severe than earlier outbreaks due to behavioral changes, alongside improved vaccine coverage and pandemic management (Bidani et al. 2022; McCahan 2022).

Risks to the outlook

The underlying assumptions for the baseline forecast are subject to significant uncertainty (figure 1.10.D). Russia's invasion of Ukraine and its implications are increasing the probability of negative tail risks, many of which are interlinked. Widening geopolitical turmoil could further destabilize global economic activity and, in the longer term, cause global trade, investment, and financial networks to fragment. The drag on activity from persistent supply disruptions and very high commodity prices may cause the global economy to become mired in stagflation, with low growth and high inflation. Rising price pressures could require substantially more monetary tightening than currently expected. Food shortages could weigh heavily on the most vulnerable and spark social unrest. Although the economic impact of new outbreaks of COVID-19 has faded over the course of the pandemic, the appearance of new, more virulent variants could lead to the re-introduction of disruptive control measures. If several of these downside risks were to materialize simultaneously, model-based quantifications suggest that global growth could fall more sharply in 2022 and nearly halve in 2023—declining to 2.1 percent and 1.5 percent, respectively.

Intensifying geopolitical tensions

Russia's invasion of Ukraine has led to a global weakening of confidence and a rise of policy uncertainty (figure 1.11.A). The situation could

FIGURE 1.11 Intensifying geopolitical tensions

Sustained geopolitical turmoil could weaken confidence and heighten policy uncertainty. The refugee crisis resulting from the war in Ukraine could worsen, with the sudden arrival of millions of newcomers putting pressure on public finances and the delivery of basic services in host countries.

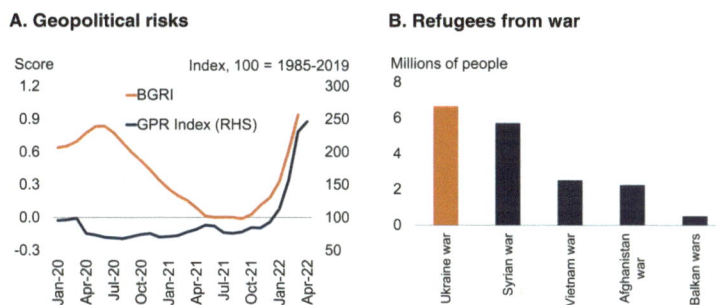

Sources: Barutciski (1994); BlackRock Investment Institute; Caldara and Iacoviello (2021); Matteo Iacoviello (data set); United Nations High Commissioner for Refugees; World Bank.
A. Figure shows the three-month moving average for the Geopolitical Risk (GPR) Index and the global BlackRock Geopolitical Risk Indicator (BGRI). The GPR, constructed by Caldara and Iacoviello (2021), is based on a count of newspaper articles that discuss geopolitical tensions. The BGRI tracks the relative frequency of brokerage reports and financial news stories associated with specific geopolitical risks.
B. Figure shows the number of registered refugees after each war.

worsen in a variety of ways, including through the spread of hostilities over a larger geographical area. It could also take the form of widespread state-sponsored cyberattacks on public infrastructure or financial systems, which could disrupt telecommunications, power grids, water supply, oil and gas pipelines, transportation networks, and critical manufacturing sectors. Such developments could have substantial destabilizing effects on the global economy, significantly heighten uncertainty and further erode confidence, and trigger additional sanctions or major retaliatory responses.

The existing refugee crisis could worsen. Global refugee levels were already historically high in recent years (figure 1.11.B; UNHCR 2021). The invasion of Ukraine—a country with more than twice the population of the Syrian Arab Republic (44 million versus 18 million)—has already caused nearly 7 million more to seek safety abroad. The sudden arrival of a large number of newcomers in host countries will put pressure on public finances and the delivery of basic services.

Global trade and financial networks could fragment if the war and its dislocating effects persist—especially if continued hostilities prompt

FIGURE 1.12 Stagflation

Rising inflation and slowing growth raise concerns that the global economy is entering a period of stagflation reminiscent of the 1970s. The surge in energy and food prices over the past two years has been the largest and second largest, respectively, since the early 1970s. It has been accompanied by a steep slowdown in global growth that was even more pronounced than the one following the 1975 recession.

A. Energy and food prices

B. Slowdown in growth after global recessions

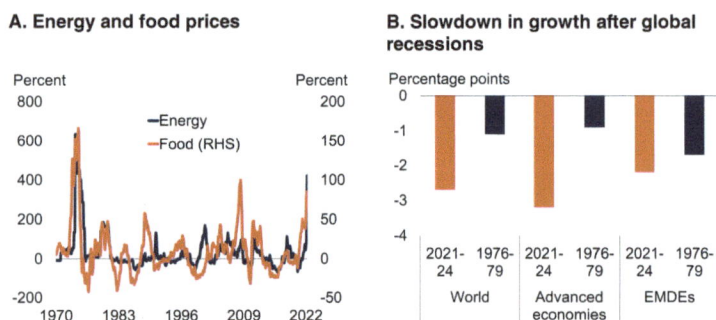

Source: World Bank.
Note: EMDEs = emerging market and developing economies.
A. Percent change in monthly price indices over a 24-month period. This facilitates a comparison of the April 2020 trough with the most recent data (April 2022). Due to data limitations, prior to 1979, the energy price change is proxied using the oil price change.
B. Figure shows changes in global growth (in percentage points) between 2021-24 and 1976-79; in both cases covering the rebound following a global recession. Aggregates are calculated using real U.S. dollar GDP weights at average 2010-19 prices and market exchange rates. Data for 2022-24 are forecasts.

the implementation of large-scale trade embargoes. The demonstrated impact of sanctions on the Russian economy may prompt some other countries to self-isolate and protect themselves from similar measures in the future. This could involve raising barriers to free trade and developing parallel payment systems independent of the U.S. dollar. The pace of global economic integration has slowed substantially in recent years, and an outright reversal could result in less specialization, fewer economies of scale, less competition, and the slower spread of innovations. This could slow output and income growth and add to inflation pressures.

Stagflation

The current multidecade high levels of inflation, combined with sharply slowing growth, raise concerns that the global economy is entering a period of stagflation reminiscent of the 1970s (Special Focus 1). In the 1970s, large supply shocks amid accommodative monetary and fiscal policies resulted in prolonged stagflation. The policy tightening in the early 1980s to contain high inflation played a major role in triggering a

global recession in 1982 and set off a string of EMDE debt crises.

The current juncture resembles the 1970s in several key aspects. First, supply disruptions driven by the pandemic and the recent supply shock dealt to global energy prices by the war in Ukraine resemble the oil shocks in 1973 and 1979-80. In fact, the increase in energy prices over the past two years has been the largest since the 1973 oil crisis (figure 1.12.A). Second, global growth is decelerating sharply, with the current slowdown even more pronounced than the one following the 1975 recession (figure 1.12.B). Third, then and now, monetary policy was highly accommodative in the run-up to these shocks, with interest rates negative in real (inflation-adjusted) terms for an extended period. Fourth, with EMDE debt at multidecade highs now, a rise in global borrowing costs may trigger financial crises, as it did in the early 1980s.[3]

The stagflation experience of the 1970s is a reminder that there is a considerable risk that inflation will remain high or continue to rise. The supply bottlenecks and rising commodity prices that have contributed to elevated inflation could persist in the near term as a result of renewed pandemic-related lockdowns or continued commodity market disruptions. In the longer term, inflation may remain elevated as many of the factors that have contributed to low inflation in recent decades are slowing or in outright retreat. The growth of global value chains and the global labor force has fallen, the productivity gains from the reallocation of resources away from agriculture have waned, and technological progress has slowed (Ha, Kose, and Ohnsorge 2022). In addition, the commitment among some policy makers to disciplined fiscal and monetary policy frameworks could soften.

---

[3] There are also important differences with the 1970s. Over the past three decades, many central banks have built considerable credibility in their commitment to price stability, which has helped anchor inflation expectations. Disinflation will also be supported by the planned fiscal consolidation underway in many economies. In addition, the 1970s were a time of considerable structural rigidities, including wage, price, and interest rate controls. Economies have become more flexible over time, reducing the likelihood of price-wage spirals that entrench inflation.

Alongside the possibility of elevated inflation, global activity could remain anemic. Growth is already slowing, including in the world's major economies. The United States is withdrawing policy accommodation, the euro area is suffering substantial spillovers from the invasion of Ukraine, and activity in China is being hindered by difficulties in the real estate sector and lockdowns to control COVID-19. Growth could remain feeble for a prolonged period, as many of its structural determinants have weakened. Demographics represent a growing headwind to potential growth. Labor productivity has slowed considerably since the global financial crisis, largely as a result of weakness in both investment and total factor productivity (Dieppe 2021). The pandemic has left deep scars in the form of lower investment, lower human capital, and a retreat from global supply chains, all of which are likely to dampen potential growth in the longer term (World Bank 2021a).

Financial stress across EMDEs

The current environment of elevated inflation and rising interest rates poses risks to the financial stability of many EMDEs. The increased cost of inputs, particularly energy, and of credit could trigger economic slowdowns, widen current account deficits, and generate significant financing gaps. Rising interest rates could result in fiscal pressures, widespread corporate defaults, and feeble global investment. These risks are particularly acute given that debt in many EMDEs has been on a decade-long upward trend capped by a broad-based surge during the pandemic, with increasingly tight interlinkages between the health of the government balance sheet and that of the banking system (Feyen and Zuccardi 2019; Kose et al. 2021). The most vulnerable EMDEs are those that could struggle to roll over debt in the face of significantly higher debt service obligations, or that hold large shares of debt that is denominated in foreign currencies, held by nonresidents, short-term, or subject to variable rates (figure 1.13.A).

Historically, financial crises in EMDEs have been more likely when the U.S. Federal Reserve pivots toward a more aggressive tightening stance, as it is currently doing to rein in inflation well above

FIGURE 1.13 Financial stress across emerging market and developing economies

Emerging market and developing economies with debt vulnerabilities—such as a high proportion of variable-rate debt—could face higher debt-servicing burdens or struggle to roll over debt in an environment in which aggressive monetary tightening, especially in the United States, may sharply raise borrowing costs. Inflation has risen to decade highs, which has kept real monetary policy rates negative despite recent nominal increases, suggesting that policy continues to be accommodative. The Phillips curve may have flattened, which suggests that central banks may need to significantly tighten monetary policy to rein in inflation.

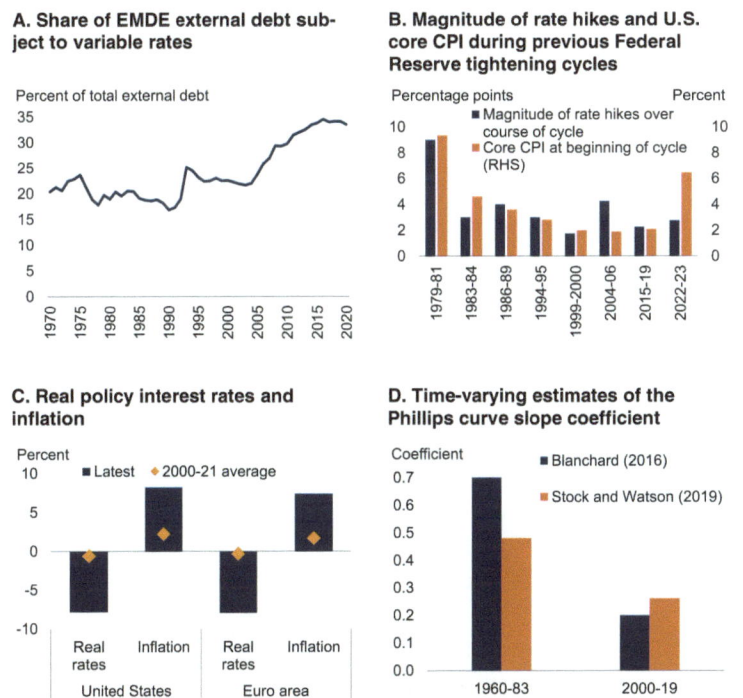

Sources: Eurostat (database); Federal Reserve Economic Data; Haver Analytics; World Bank.
Note: EMDEs = emerging market and developing economies.
A. Figure shows the EMDE average of variable rate external debt as a share of total external debt.
B. Blue bars show the extent of policy rate increases during previous tightening cycles. The value for 2023 is an estimate based on market expectations for the level of the Fed Funds rate in mid-2023. U.S. core CPI for 2023 shows latest data associated with tightening cycle.
C. "Real rates" are policy interest rates minus consumer price index inflation. "Latest" refers to the last available data, which are for April 2022.
D. Estimates from Blanchard (2016) and Stock and Watson (2019).

levels seen at the beginning of previous hiking cycles (figure 1.13.B). Some previous episodes of higher U.S. interest rates, such as the taper tantrum of 2013, have been followed by increased financial market volatility in EMDEs, including currency depreciation, rising bond spreads, portfolio outflows, equity price collapses, and liquidity shortages (Arteta et al. 2015; Hoek, Kamin, and Yoldas 2020). EMDE central banks may be forced to tighten monetary policy to stem capital outflows at the expense of domestic activity, as has occurred in the past.

More generally, central banks around the world may accelerate the pace of tightening if the current period of persistent and elevated inflation causes expectations to become de-anchored. Policy rates have been increasing at a far slower pace than prices, suggesting that policy continues to be accommodative (figure 1.13.C). In the near term, expectations of additional price increases could become baked into wage and price setting behavior, resulting in persistent above-target inflation (Blanchard 2022). The process of re-setting inflation expectations to match central bank targets through tighter monetary policy has been costly in the past (Cecchetti and Rich 2001; Ha, Kose, and Ohnsorge 2022). The evidence that the Phillips curve may have flattened in recent decades highlights the risk that central banks will have to engage in significantly tighter monetary policy to contain inflation (figure 1.13.D; Bank of Canada 2021; Blanchard 2016; Stock and Watson 2019).

Past banking crises have often been preceded by credit booms and relaxed macroprudential oversight, leading to high debt levels, currency and maturity mismatches, and concentrated credit risks (Claessens et al. 2014, Reinhart and Rogoff 2009). The health of bank balance sheets may be overstated because of the zero-risk weight given to sovereign securities. Strains may also emerge in market segments that are more opaque. For example, in many economies the nonbank financial sector has a high level of inter-connectedness with other parts of the financial system, and can potentially spread vulnerability through a high degree of leverage and liquidity mismatches (Pearce 2022). Tightening credit conditions or the unwinding of debt forbearance measures introduced during the pandemic could trigger disruptive financial sector dynamics (World Bank 2022c).

Widespread food shortages

Agricultural prices have been increasing significantly as a result of weaker grain production from Ukraine alongside higher costs for critical agricultural inputs such as fuel, chemicals, and fertilizers. Food shortages will result in millions of people being pushed into food insecurity and extreme poverty, particularly poor urban households in LICs that spend large shares of their income on food (Laborde, Lakatos, and Martin 2019). This will likely have adverse long-term consequences, as malnutrition causes persistent damage to human capital and insufficient access to agricultural inputs can lock an economy in a state of widespread, low productivity subsistence farming (McGovern et al. 2017; McArthur and McCord 2017). Further increases in the prices of food and agricultural inputs would magnify these risks.

Droughts, floods, wildfires, and other extreme events made more likely by climate change could further stress food systems. Events leading to sudden food production losses have become more frequent in recent decades, and they have had more severe impacts in areas where climate change has already slowed the growth of agricultural productivity and where the global poor are more concentrated (CSEP 2022; IPCC 2022). Food accounts for about half of consumption baskets and 20 percent of goods imports in LICs, on average; accordingly, even modest disruption to food supplies or increases in food prices can worsen food crises and contribute to severe inflationary pressures. LICs and EMDEs that import significant quantities of agricultural products from Russia and Ukraine are particularly vulnerable to disruption to the production and transportation of key commodities.

Food production is also at risk of being poorly distributed. Smaller producers such as subsistence farmers may lack the resources (or access to financial markets) required to purchase costly inputs. Low domestic yields combined with weak fiscal positions and the high cost of shipping may put adequate food stocks beyond the reach of poorer countries.

Food shortages have significant negative consequences in both the near and long term. In the near term, food shortages can contribute to rising social unrest (Barrett 2013; Hendrix and Brinkman 2013). Rising food prices can also cause fiscal balances to deteriorate, particularly in the presence of subsidies, which can either crowd out other spending or increase debt-related risks. In the long term, malnutrition has substantial human and economic costs that can persist for decades (Micha 2021).

Growth under alternative downside scenarios

A global macroeconomic projection model was used to further assess the impact of some key downside risks on the global economy.[4] These risks include widespread financial stress caused by faster U.S. monetary tightening, an intensification of geopolitical tensions in Europe, and recurring COVID-19 outbreaks in China.[5]

In the first scenario, the Federal Reserve would unexpectedly accelerate the pace of monetary policy tightening in response to resilient domestic demand, surging wage inflation, and rising inflation expectations. Policy rates would rise to 4 percent by the first quarter of 2023—about 1.5 percentage points higher than currently expected, and enough to bring real rates into positive territory—and stay at about that level for several quarters. A rapid tightening of global financial conditions would ensue, triggering widespread financial stress across EMDEs. Several major EMDEs would experience large scale capital outflows and soaring bond spreads, ultimately forcing authorities to accelerate fiscal consolidation efforts (World Bank 2021b). On net, EMDEs would experience much larger headwinds to activity than advanced economies, with EMDE growth reduced by 0.5 and 0.9 percentage point in 2022 and 2023, respectively, relative to baseline forecasts.

In the second scenario, Russia would respond to escalating EU sanctions by announcing an immediate ban on all energy exports to EU member countries starting in the third quarter.

Further, sanctions by the United States and the EU targeting shipping companies or third parties purchasing Russian oil could reduce the potential for trade diversion of Russian exports to other countries. The sudden implementation of the ban, combined with additional sanctions in response to Russia's invasion of Ukraine, would severely disrupt global energy supply routes. The resulting disruption to energy exports would be largest for natural gas, then oil, and lastly, coal. The price of these commodities would spike in 2022Q3 and remain elevated over the remainder of the scenario horizon, reflecting both precautionary buying and lower global supplies (figure 1.14.A). Meanwhile, uncertainty about geopolitical developments would also spike, contributing to a decline in consumer confidence across Europe (World Bank 2022d). In this scenario, growth would slow sharply in advanced economies—particularly in the euro area—while EMDEs would face notable headwinds from higher energy prices and weaker foreign demand.

In the third scenario, China would experience COVID-19 resurgences of steadily decreasing severity through the second half of 2022 and into 2023. Containing the spread of COVID-19 would require strict but short-lived lockdowns across several major cities. Pandemic control measures would sharply reduce private consumption and have adverse effects on domestic investment and regional trade networks (Guénette and Yamazaki 2021; World Bank 2022e, 2022g).[6] After each short-lived resurgence, activity would bounce back in the subsequent quarter as restrictions are lifted. Overall, pandemic resurgences and associated restrictions would lower growth relative to baseline in China by 0.5 percentage point in 2022 and 0.3 percentage point in 2023. Broader spillovers to EMDEs and advanced economies would be generally contained, owing to the short-lived nature of the shock.

There is a distinct possibility that all three scenarios materialize simultaneously. Each scenario layer would add headwinds to growth (of

---

[4] Similar scenario analysis at the regional level is presented in recent World Bank publications such as the Spring 2022 regional updates for Europe and Central Asia (World Bank 2022d), East Asia and Pacific (World Bank 2022e), and South Asia (World Bank 2022f).

[5] Each scenario is prepared using the Oxford Economics Global Economic Model, a global semi-structural macro projection model which includes 81 individual country blocks, most of which are available at a quarterly frequency, with behavioral equations governing domestic economic activity, monetary and fiscal policy, global trade, and commodity prices (Oxford Economics 2019).

[6] As described in the 2022 Spring EAP Economic Update, the magnitude of the zero-COVID shock would be scaled to one fifth of initial pandemic shock experienced in 2020H1 (World Bank 2022e).

FIGURE 1.14 Growth under alternative downside scenarios

A ban by the Russian Federation on energy exports to the European Union, coupled with sanctions in response to Russia's invasion of Ukraine targeting shipping companies or third parties purchasing Russian oil, could significantly disrupt global energy markets and send prices soaring. The Federal Reserve could significantly accelerate its pace of policy tightening if wage pressures increase or if inflation expectations continue to rise. Renewed COVID-19 outbreaks in China could lead to additional lockdowns. The simultaneous materialization of these downside risks could result in substantially weaker growth.

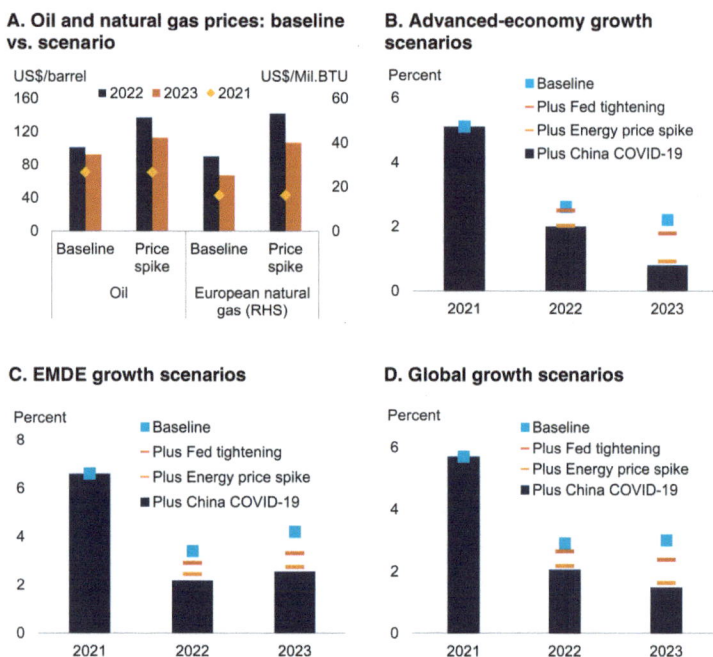

A. Oil and natural gas prices: baseline vs. scenario

B. Advanced-economy growth scenarios

C. EMDE growth scenarios

D. Global growth scenarios

Sources: Oxford Economics; World Bank.
Note: EMDEs = emerging market and developing economies.
A. Baseline scenario as described in the April 2022 *Commodities Market Outlook*. Alternative scenario paths are staff assumptions. Oil price is Brent oil benchmark in U.S. dollars per barrel.
B.-D. These scenarios are produced using the Oxford Economics Global Economic Model (OEM). The OEM is a global semi-structural macro projection model which includes 81 individual country blocks, most of which are available at a quarterly frequency, with behavioral equations governing domestic economic activity, monetary and fiscal policy, global trade, and energy prices (Oxford Economics 2019). The simulations assume that agents have adaptive expectations, monetary policy is endogenous, and fiscal policy is largely exogenous. Scenarios are linearly additive.

varying magnitudes) to advanced economies and EMDEs. Advanced economies—in particular the euro area—would be hard hit by soaring energy prices in addition to headwinds from faster Federal Reserve tightening and the pandemic-induced slowdown in China. Altogether, the three scenarios would see advanced-economy growth slow below 1 percent in 2023, compared to 2.2 percent in the baseline forecast (figure 1.14.B). Meanwhile, EMDEs would experience outsized impacts from the China COVID-19 shock in 2022 and acute financial stress amid faster Federal

Reserve tightening in 2023. The layered shocks would reduce EMDE growth by 1.2 and 1.6 percentage points in 2022 and 2023, respectively, all but eliminating the projected rebound from the effects of the war in Ukraine (figure 1.14.C). The combined scenarios would entail a sharp global downturn with the global economy only narrowly avoiding an annual recession next year.[7] Global growth would slow abruptly from 5.7 percent in 2021 to 2.1 percent in 2022 and 1.5 percent in 2023—0.8 and 1.5 percentage points slower than the baseline forecast in 2022 and 2023, respectively (figure 1.14.D).

Policy challenges

Urgent global efforts are needed to address the humanitarian crises from Russia's invasion of Ukraine and conflict elsewhere, alleviate the rise in worldwide food insecurity, and bolster COVID-19 vaccination efforts. Surging commodity prices and tightening financial conditions can be addressed in part with safeguards to central bank independence and targeted relief for vulnerable households. Policy makers in EMDEs will have to confront the rise in food insecurity and the growing risk of fragmentation in trade networks. Over the longer term, policies that improve education and raise labor participation rates will help reverse economic damage from the pandemic, war, and conflict.

Key global challenges

The global community needs to urgently step up efforts to limit the humanitarian cost of Russia's invasion of Ukraine and armed conflicts in other parts of the world, such as through the coordinated delivery of emergency food, medical, and financial aid to war-torn areas. A concerted effort will also be required to equitably share the burden of housing and possibly relocating refugees displaced by war in Ukraine and conflict elsewhere (OECD 2022). Once the geopolitical situation has stabilized, coordinated efforts will be required to support and finance the reconstruction of war-ravaged areas. One way to improve the economic effectiveness of reconstruction efforts is to offer

---

[7] As in Kose, Sugawara and Terrones (2020), a global recession is defined as an annual contraction in global real per capita output.

grants rather than loans when appropriate, while closely aligning international support with the affected nation's interests (Becker et al. 2022).

International assistance will be needed to cushion the blow from surging oil and food prices, particularly in poorer nations facing acute food insecurity risks (G7 2022). The impact of the war alone could tip millions back into food insecurity over the next two years (FAO 2022). Globally coordinated efforts can also help boost the supply of commodities. For energy commodities, this could entail drawing on strategic stockpiles, accelerating transitions to low-carbon energy sources, and introducing measures to reduce energy consumption—for example, by improving the energy efficiency of buildings and the fuel efficiency of motor vehicles (Special Focus 2; IEA 2022). For metals, major producers can work to expand production, taking full advantage of the metal-intensive nature of the green transition (Kabundi and Vasishtha 2022).

It will also be key for commodity-exporting economies, particularly food exporters, to safeguard the global commodity trade system by eschewing protectionist policies (such as export restrictions or bans) that could further magnify the rise and volatility in prices (Laborde, Lakatos, and Martin 2019). This is a serious challenge as several countries introduced food export restrictions since the invasion of Ukraine, affecting about 17 percent of globally traded calories (Glauber, Laborde, and Mamun 2022). Policy makers can also consider temporarily waiving biofuel mandates to help ease price pressures in key agricultural commodity markets.

The global community also needs to maintain efforts to end the COVID-19 pandemic, particularly in the poorest countries. Sustained collective action is required to bolster global pandemic preparedness and rapidly expand vaccination campaigns. Expanding vaccination coverage is a global priority—especially in LICs, where only about 14 percent of people have been fully vaccinated owing to a combination of insufficient supply, logistical challenges, and vaccine hesitancy. Much of the existing production capacity of vaccines continues to be allocated

to vaccinations and boosters in higher-income countries.

Globally coordinated debt relief efforts, including the G20 Common Framework for debt treatments, are critical to help EMDEs where debt sustainability has sharply deteriorated amid weak growth, surging commodity prices, and tighter financing conditions. Debt dynamics are especially unfavorable among LICs, about half of which were either experiencing or at high risk of experiencing debt distress prior to the invasion of Ukraine (World Bank 2022g). The same is true for about one-third of EMDE small states. In the past, delays in resolving unsustainable debt have had severe economic consequences for affected countries (Nagle 2022). Accordingly, debt relief needs to be rapid, comprehensive, and sizable to minimize risks to growth prospects. International financial institutions can help by easing near-term debt service pressures.

The global community also needs to foster a smooth transition toward low-carbon energy sources. To this end, countries can work collectively to reduce dependency on fossil fuels by aggressively expanding investments in electricity access and green energy, as well as increasing energy efficiency (OECD 2022). Governments need to work toward achieving consensus on priority reforms at the national level that can help achieve long-term climate and development objectives, while reducing global policy uncertainty. Key national policies can include creating climate-smart regulatory frameworks, introducing carbon pricing policy instruments, and strengthening land use regulations. Finally, policy makers need to renew support for a rules-based international economic order, guarding against the threat of fragmentation across trade, investment, and financial networks.

Challenges in advanced economies

Surging commodity prices have deepened the challenges facing monetary authorities, as they confront rising and above-target inflation at a time of slowing activity. Monetary policy normalization is also complicated by uncertainty about the effects of reducing the size of sizable central bank balance sheets.

FIGURE 1.15 Policy challenges in advanced economies

Central banks confronting rising inflationary pressures need to monitor the emergence of possible feedback loops between wages and core inflation. Fiscal support needs to ensure that possible increases in military spending amid heightened geopolitical risks do not crowd out social spending and public infrastructure investment.

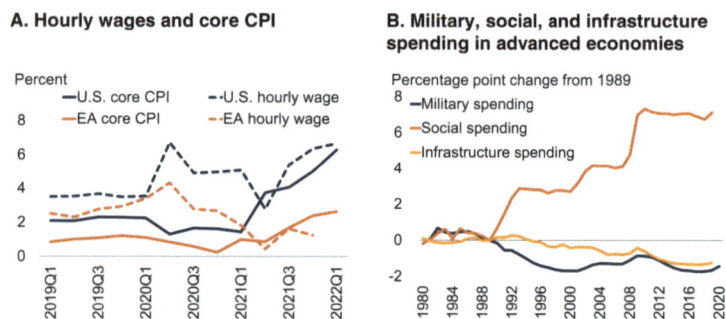

A. Hourly wages and core CPI

B. Military, social, and infrastructure spending in advanced economies

Sources: Haver Analytics; International Monetary Fund; Organisation for Economic Co-operation and Development; World Bank.
Note: EA = euro area.
A. Last observation for CPI and U.S. nominal hourly wages is 2022Q1. Last observation for EA nominal hourly wages is 2021Q4.
B. Figure shows the percentage point deviation from 1989 on military, social, and infrastructure spending as a share of GDP. Blue line shows GDP-weighted average for the euro area, Japan, the United Kingdom, and the United States. Red and orange lines show GDP-weighted average for France, Germany, Italy, Japan, Spain, the United Kingdom, and the United States. Last observation is 2020 for military spending and 2019 for social and infrastructure spending.

Central banks will need to carefully calibrate the timing and size of their policy actions, paying close attention to incoming data and the emergence of possible feedback loops between wages and core inflation (figure 1.15.A). A delay in the removal of monetary policy accommodation in an environment of above-target inflation and limited slack would risk de-anchoring inflation expectations. Clear and consistent communication with markets continues to be crucial, as does effective macroprudential regulation to maintain the resilience of financial institutions (García and Doehr 2022).

Russia's invasion of Ukraine has also further complicated fiscal policy, as accommodating the arrival of a large number of refugees will likely strain public finances in the near term in some countries. In addition, new fiscal support may be needed just as fiscal balances begin to improve. In the near term, fiscal policy can focus on mitigating the pernicious effects of high energy and food prices on the lower-income segments of the population, given the larger share of energy and food in their consumption basket. To that end, efforts that directly target vulnerable groups, such

as stronger social safety nets, may better support green objectives—unlike indirect measures (for example, energy subsidies) which often introduce economic distortions (World Bank 2013).

In the medium term, fiscal authorities need to promote resource reallocation to de-carbonize economic activity, including through carbon taxes when appropriate. These could help raise revenues to sustain investment in climate infrastructures and strengthen energy security in the face of rising energy prices (Islam 2022; Shang 2021). In addition, fiscal authorities need to ensure that social spending and productivity-enhancing expenditures, such as highly needed infrastructure, are not crowded out by possible increases in military spending in response to heightened geopolitical risk (figure 1.15.B). This is all the more important given that military expenditures have very low fiscal multipliers (van Gemert, Lieb, and Treibich 2022).

Widespread labor shortages in a number of advanced economies have slowed the recovery and put significant upward pressure on wages. This reflects a combination of declining labor supply and mismatches between available jobs and worker preferences. Active labor market policies that facilitate the reallocation of displaced workers and the recruitment of skilled and unskilled workers can foster increased labor force participation, helping to promote an equitable and sustained recovery (OECD 2021a).

Challenges in emerging market and developing economies

Concerns over high inflation and the rising risk of a de-anchoring of inflation expectations are expected to lead to further monetary policy tightening in many EMDEs. Having already experienced a marked erosion of fiscal space during the pandemic, commodity-importing EMDEs will face a further deterioration in fiscal positions due to the rise in borrowing costs. In contrast, some commodity exporters are likely to experience revenue windfalls. Russia's invasion of Ukraine threatens to raise food insecurity in many EMDEs and fragment broader trade and investment networks. Accordingly, it is critical that policy makers put in place measures to confront volatile food prices and provide targeted relief to vulnerable households, while also safeguarding trade networks and lowering trade costs. Over the longer term, policy makers can prioritize policies to reverse the damage inflicted by the back-to-back global shocks of the past two years, including policies that improve learning and enhance labor force participation.

EMDE monetary and financial policy challenges

Central banks in EMDEs face the challenge of tackling high inflation at the expense of economic activity when their cyclical recovery from the pandemic is fragile and incomplete. This is more daunting in countries with less well anchored inflation expectations and less established monetary policy credibility. ·

The war and the resulting surge in global commodity prices are compounding inflationary pressures, which are expected to trigger an acceleration in the pace of monetary tightening in many EMDEs (figure 1.16.A). Even if energy and food prices had no effect on core inflation, global inflation would rise markedly since energy alone accounts for about 10 percent of the consumption basket in the median EMDE. Past experience suggests that a 40 percent increase in oil prices—still below the increase projected for 2022—can increase EMDE inflation by about 4 percentage points within two years (figure 1.16.B; Ha et. al. 2019).

Although central banks face an inherent trade-off between supporting growth and containing inflation, the terms of this trade-off can be improved in various ways. Communicating monetary policy decisions clearly within credible monetary policy frameworks, and safeguarding central bank independence, can more strongly anchor inflation expectations, reducing the degree of policy tightening needed to achieve the desired effects on inflation and activity. Clear communication can help shape the expectations of financial markets, households, and firms so that inflation dynamics do not translate into destabilizing increases in wages and production costs (Coibion, Gorodnichenko, and Weber 2019).

FIGURE 1.16 Monetary policy challenges in emerging market and developing economies

The war and the resulting surge in global commodity prices are exacerbating inflationary pressures, which are expected to trigger additional monetary tightening in many emerging market and developing economies (EMDEs). Historical estimates suggest that an oil price shock that raises oil prices by 40 percent—still below the projected increase for 2022—can raise inflation in EMDEs by about 4 percentage points over two years.

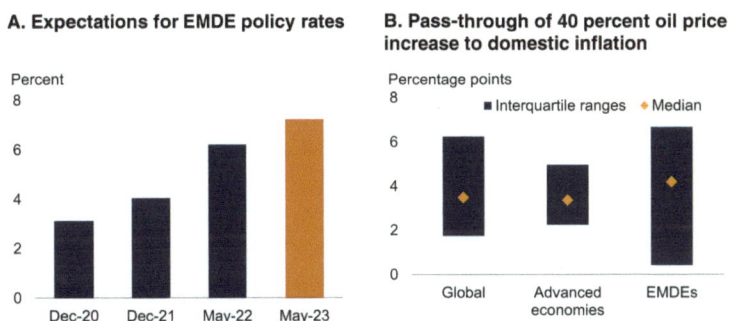

A. Expectations for EMDE policy rates

B. Pass-through of 40 percent oil price increase to domestic inflation

Sources: Consensus Economics; Ha, Kose, and Ohnsorge (2019); World Bank.
Note: EMDEs = emerging market and developing economies.
A. Consensus forecasts for one-year-ahead three-month treasury bill yields (or policy rates) for 18 EMDEs. Red bar based on May 2022 surveys.
B. Figure shows cumulative impulse responses after two years of domestic inflation to a positive 40 percent oil price shock. Orange diamonds indicate median and blue bars the 25th -75th percentiles of country-specific impulse responses. The results are based on the country-specific FAVAR models discussed in Ha, Kose, and Ohnsorge (2019), estimated for 29 advanced economies and 26 EMDEs for 1970-2017.

Rising global interest rates may cause financial stress in highly indebted corporate sectors, particularly if domestic activity remains weak. Refinancing debt would become more challenging in an environment where policy tightening in advanced economies and risk aversion lead to further increases in borrowing costs, capital flight, and currency depreciation. Countries can reduce these risks through the rapid and transparent treatment of nonperforming loans, insolvency reforms to allow for the orderly reduction of unsustainable debts, and innovations in risk management and lending models to ensure continued access to credit for households and businesses (Kose et al. 2021; World Bank 2020a).

More fundamentally, countries can reduce their vulnerability to volatile capital flows and exchange rate fluctuations by strengthening macroprudential regulation—including capital and liquidity buffers, building foreign exchange reserves, and increasing debt transparency. Banks' capital and liquidity buffers must be able to absorb shocks. Credit quality and nonperforming loans

FIGURE 1.17 Fiscal policy challenges in emerging market and developing economies

Tightening global financial conditions and higher borrowing costs are likely to exacerbate the burden of servicing record-high levels of debt, which could cause fiscal stress and increase fiscal adjustment needs. Many emerging market and developing economies are tightening fiscal policy to restore fiscal sustainability, but fossil fuel subsidies will make this more challenging.

A. Fiscal adjustment needs, stressed conditions

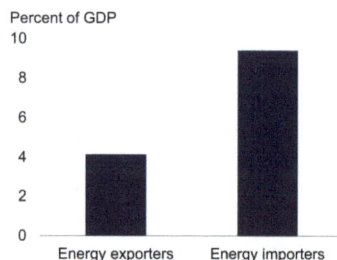

B. Cumulative change in cyclically adjusted primary balances

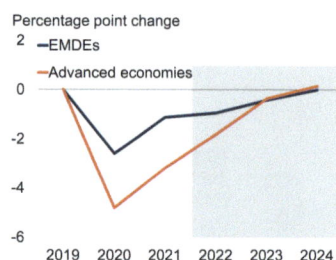

C. Share of EMDEs with tightening fiscal stances

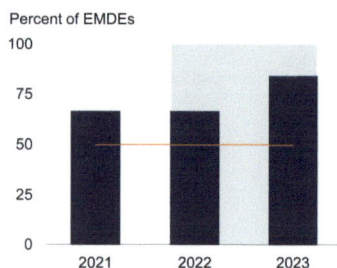

D. Fossil fuel subsidies in EMDEs, 2019-20 average

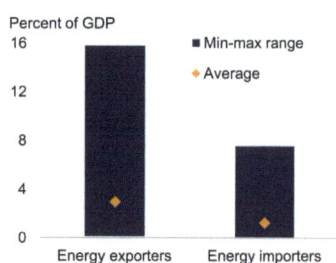

Sources: IMF (2022b); International Energy Agency; Kose et al. (2017); World Bank.
Note: EMDEs = emerging market and developing economies. Shaded areas indicate forecasts. Unless otherwise indicated, aggregates are calculated using real U.S. dollar GDP weights at average 2010-19 prices and market exchange rates.
A. Fiscal adjustment is the size of fiscal consolidation needed to return debt to a sustainable path, measured using the fiscal sustainability gap as in Kose et al. (2017). Stressed conditions are defined as nominal growth minus one country-specific standard deviation, or interest rates plus one standard deviation. Data as of 2021. Sample includes 77 EMDEs (17 energy exporters and 60 energy importers), excluding China, Russia, and Ukraine.
B. Figure shows the weighted cumulative change in cyclically adjusted primary balances (CAPB), as measured in IMF (2022b). Sample includes 34 advanced economies and 44 EMDEs, excluding China, Russia, and Ukraine.
C. Fiscal tightening defined as a decline in the fiscal impulse, with the impulse measured as the negative change in the CAPB from the previous year. Sample is limited to 45 EMDEs because of data availability.
D. Data are simple averages for 2019 and 2020. Sample includes 37 EMDEs (23 energy exporters and 14 energy importers).

need to be reported transparently, taking into account possible distortions from forbearance measures implemented during the pandemic, so that prompt corrective action is possible. Capital flow management measures may also help countries contend with large and volatile flows, but are best deployed sparingly—for example, to forestall immediate economic disruptions or to

prevent the build-up of financial vulnerabilities (IMF 2022a).

Crypto asset markets have grown rapidly since the pandemic—in some EMDEs, the volume of crypto asset transactions now rivals those of domestic equities (IMF 2021). Sound regulatory frameworks for crypto assets (and decentralized financial systems more generally) will be required to ensure macro-financial stability.

EMDE fiscal policy challenges

Tightening global financial conditions and higher borrowing costs present mounting challenges for EMDE fiscal policy makers. A further increase in borrowing costs and slowdown in growth could place some EMDEs in fiscal stress amid record-high debt levels and trigger sizable fiscal adjustment (figure 1.17.A). Compared to previous crises, EMDEs entered 2022 in more precarious fiscal positions, with incomplete economic recoveries and much narrower fiscal space following the pandemic. EMDEs have few available tools to support their economies, with fiscal policy buffers depleted and external financing costs rising. Placing debt on a more sustainable path will be a daunting challenge, especially in commodity importers given still-weak revenues from the pandemic and higher commodity prices. Even before the invasion of Ukraine, 60 percent of LICs were in or near debt distress. More broadly, EMDEs will have to carefully balance the need to ensure fiscal sustainability with that of mitigating the war's adverse effects, especially on the poor.

For the EMDEs most exposed to spillovers from the war, targeted fiscal relief may be warranted to shield vulnerable households from higher commodity prices, prevent further spikes in poverty and food insecurity, and manage any influx of refugees. The impact of targeted fiscal support can be improved by measures that strengthen public service delivery, such as expanding data and administrative capacity (Grosh et al. 2022). Given limited fiscal space, some relief for vulnerable populations may need to come at the expense of other categories of spending. Fiscal policy is expected to continue to tighten in most countries over the next few years, as EMDEs finish unwinding remaining pandemic support (figures 1.17.B and 1.17.C). Nonetheless, government debt in 2024 is anticipated to remain above 2019 levels in over two-thirds of EMDEs.

Food and energy subsidies are placing considerable strain on the budgets of households, public utilities, and some governments (figure 1.17.D). To mitigate the impact of sharp increases in commodity prices on households, numerous EMDEs have cut fuel taxes, increased subsidies, and imposed price controls on food and energy products. These measures are, in general, costly and ineffective at delivering benefits to low-income households, and can be challenging to dismantle.

Fiscal positions among many energy exporters will be improved by higher revenues related to rising commodity prices. This windfall may be best used to prepare for markedly higher borrowing costs, to bolster fiscal buffers, or to invest in improving human capital, accelerating business climate reforms, and strengthening governance. Prudent management of resource rents involves avoiding inefficient and distortive energy subsidies, and instead increasing export diversification, strengthening long-term growth prospects, and building resilience to external shocks. In commodity importers, measures that increase expenditure efficiency, such as strengthening expenditure review processes, can help ensure that limited fiscal space is used effectively. Across all EMDEs, leveraging private-sector involvement will be key given the necessary spending on longer-term investments and the limited degree of fiscal space.

More durable improvements in fiscal sustainability among EMDEs will be facilitated by efforts to increase domestic revenue mobilization and boost productivity. Broadening the tax base can improve government finances with limited impact on economic growth. Improvements in sovereign debt management would help preserve the ability of governments to support an equitable recovery.

EMDE structural policy challenges

EMDEs face various longer-term challenges, many of which have been aggravated by the pandemic and the invasion of Ukraine. These shocks have reversed progress made toward the achievement of the Sustainable Development Goals. Building resilience to food price volatility is critical, as the war has worsened food insecurity across many EMDEs. To counter the risk of costs being pushed up by trade and financial fragmentation, policy makers can put in place measures to enhance trade resilience and promote diversification. Moreover, reversing the scarring inflicted by COVID-19 on growth prospects will take substantial policy efforts, including investments in education and the enhancement of labor force participation through active labor market policies, especially for women.

Confronting food insecurity

Food insecurity, already pervasive in many EMDEs, is rising as the war in Ukraine pushes up global food prices and heightens the risk of severe food shortages (figure 1.18.A; WFP 2022). In 2020, more than 700 million people—nearly one in 10 people in the world—experienced severe food insecurity, while an estimated 2.3 billion lacked regular access to sufficient food (FAO et al. 2021). Improving access to safe and nutritious food, and maintaining food security in times of crisis, are critical for health and human development. Children who are properly nourished during the first 1,000 days of their lives are 33 percent more likely to escape poverty as adults (UNICEF 2019). Yet, currently, more than 150 million children under the age of five across the world have experienced chronic malnutrition, 90 percent of which are located in EMDEs and almost 40 percent in Sub-Saharan Africa (WHO, UNICEF, and World Bank 2021b). Addressing food loss and waste can improve food and nutrition security, while also helping to meet climate goals.

To the extent possible, policy makers in EMDEs should refrain from responding to rising prices of food and fertilizers by adding to the already-high number of price controls, which are often paired with subsidies (figure 1.18.B). Price controls can generate significant distortions, and their adverse consequences for growth, poverty reduction, and government policies can increase over time

FIGURE 1.18 Structural policy challenges in emerging market and developing economies

Food insecurity remains pervasive in many emerging market and developing economies (EMDEs) and is being exacerbated by the war. Policy makers can deploy targeted enhancements to safety nets rather than introducing distortionary price controls on food and energy, which are already widespread in EMDEs. Policies aimed at mitigating the expected slowdown in potential growth include reducing learning poverty, addressing investment needs, and increasing labor force participation, especially female participation, in part through education and labor market reforms.

A. People in acute food insecurity

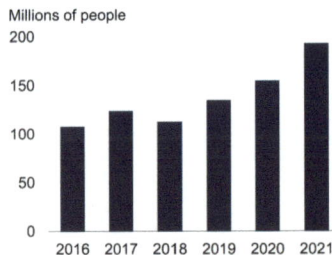

B. Economies with price controls

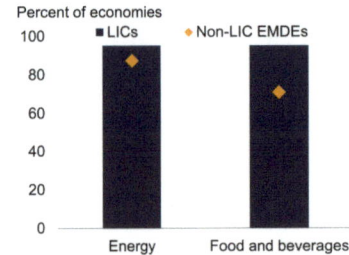

C. Learning poverty in 2019, by region

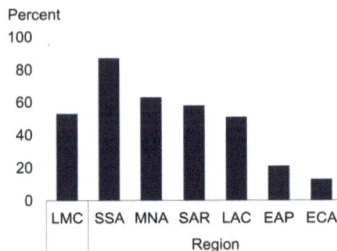

D. Learning poverty in EMDEs

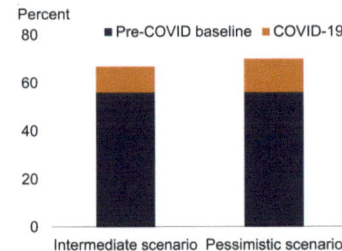

E. Labor force participation

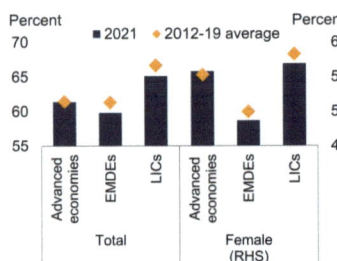

F. Impact of key structural reforms on potential growth in EMDEs

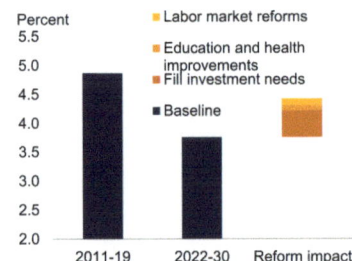

Sources: Azevedo et al. (2021); Barro and Lee (2010); FSIN and GNAFC (2022); Global Learning Assessment (database); Guénette (2020); Haver Analytics; ILO (database); International Monetary Fund; Organisation for Economic Co-operation and Development; PWT (database); UN Population Prospects; World Bank; World Trade Organization.
Note: EMDEs = emerging market and developing economies; LICs = Low-income countries; LMC = low- and middle-income countries; EAP = East Asia and Pacific, ECA = Europe and Central Asia, LAC = Latin America and the Caribbean, MNA = Middle East and North Africa, SAR = South Asia, SSA = Sub-Saharan Africa.
A. Data from the Food Security Information Network's *Global Report on Food Crises* 2022.
B. Listed price control policies are retrieved from WTO *Trade Policy Review* publications. Sample includes 21 low-income countries and 56 other EMDEs.
C.D. Learning poverty defined as the inability to read and understand a simple text by age 10.
C. Figure shows percent of children who are learning-poor in LMCs, by region.
D. Figure shows increase in learning poverty for LMCs in scenarios in Azevedo et al. (2021).
E. Figure shows labor participation rate for people older than 14 years old.
F. Period averages of annual GDP-weighted averages. Potential growth estimates are based on production function approach. Impact of structural reforms is computed as difference between 2020-30 potential growth under the baseline forecast and counterfactual reform scenarios. The latter assume a repeat of individual EMDEs best 10-year improvements in labor market participation, education and health, and investment over the period 1998-2020.

(Guenette 2020). Widespread subsidies negatively affect fiscal balances, limiting the ability to fund growth-enhancing investments. In addition, price controls often prove difficult to roll back after the crisis that led to their implementation has abated. In exceptional circumstances, a combination of price controls and subsidies may be warranted to cushion the short-term impact of dislocating commodity price developments in the absence of social protection programs. Nonetheless, price controls should be used as a last resort, and should include automatic sunset clauses. Trade restrictions should also be avoided and, where possible, pared back.

Instead of price controls and subsidies, EMDEs can improve social safety nets, encourage diversification of food sources, and promote efficiency in food production and trade. This can include investments aimed at promoting farming systems that use climate-smart techniques and produce a more diverse mix of foods. Improving supply chains to increase farmers' access to new markets, reduce postharvest food losses, and better link production to consumption is key. Reforms to leverage digital tools to improve the efficiency and integration of domestic food markets and reduce barriers to food trade can also be promoted (World Bank 2022b). When predictable and well-targeted, investment in social safety nets can also support households in new economic activities, boosting income levels in the longer-term and enabling access to healthy diets. Such comprehensive reforms can be both pro-poor and pro-growth.

Preventing fragmentation of trade and investment networks

Openness to trade and foreign direct investment is closely associated with positive technological spillovers, lower trade costs, and stronger long-term growth (World Bank 2020b). The war in Ukraine has heightened the risk of fragmentation in networks of trade, investment, and digital connectivity; EMDEs are particularly vulnerable to such fragmentation as they face high trade costs. Even before the invasion, trade costs in EMDEs were well in excess of 100 percent of the value of traded goods—substantially more than in advanced economies.[8] This was the result of many factors, including inadequate transportation infrastructure, a lack of logistics services, lengthy border processes, regulatory procedures, and elevated tariff barriers (World Bank 2021b).

Well-functioning and diversified GVCs are a source of resilience far more than they are a source of vulnerability (Bas Fernandes and Paunov 2022; Brenton, Ferrantino, and Maliszewska 2022; Constantinescu et al. 2022). Although participation in GVCs may increase exporters' vulnerability to foreign shocks, as experienced during the COVID-19 pandemic, it reduces their exposure to domestic shocks (Borin, Mancini, and Taglioni 2021; Espitia et al. 2021). In addition, the reshoring of production can lead to sustained welfare losses (OECD 2021b). Policy makers in EMDEs need to refrain from putting in place protectionist policies such as export restrictions that could magnify the recent increase in commodity prices.

Instead, they should favor multilateral measures that promote the resilience of GVCs, reduce the cost of trading, and facilitate capital flows. These include policies that encourage firms to diversify trade partners and inputs, especially in key strategic sectors, and measures that streamline border procedures and ease impediments to trade flows. Enhancing investment promotion capacity and expanding preferential trade agreements should also be pursued. Policy makers should also favor policies to deepen integration into GVCs, including by modernizing trade information and digital systems, strengthening contract enforcement and addressing market distortions, facilitating trade finance, and fostering competitiveness (Abreha et al. 2021).

Promoting education

Investing in education benefits society by driving long-term growth, spurring innovation, strengthening institutions, and fostering social cohesion. At the individual level, education promotes

employment, boosts earnings, and reduces poverty. Indeed, it is estimated that every extra year of schooling boosts hourly earnings by 9 percent (Psacharopoulos and Patrinos 2018).

Education systems across many EMDEs are experiencing the worst crisis of the last century (Saavedra 2021). With the spread of COVID-19, more than 180 countries, including the vast majority of EMDEs, mandated some form of school closures (Azevedo et al. 2020). Globally, about 131 million children missed three-quarters of their in-person learning from March 2020 to September 2021 (Mizunoya et al. 2021). Among them, 59 percent—or nearly 77 million—missed almost all in-person instruction time, with severe consequences for learning inequality. Given long school closures and the varying effectiveness of remote learning, learning poverty in low-and middle-income countries has risen sharply—the share of children under 10 who are unable to read and understand a simple text, which already exceeded 50 percent before the pandemic, is expected to surpass 70 percent (figures 1.18.C and 1.18.D; Azevedo et al. 2021). Unless governments act to recover these learning losses, they may continue to accumulate in coming years, potentially reaching about $17 trillion in global lifetime earnings in present value terms for the cohort of students affected by closures (Azevedo et al. 2021).

Past health emergencies suggest that the impact on education is likely to be most severe in countries with already low learning outcomes, high dropout rates, and low resilience to shocks. The harmful impact of the pandemic on households' ability to support children's education is also likely to be compounded by the fact that two-thirds of low-and lower-middle-income countries have cut their public education budgets since the onset of the pandemic (Al-Samarrai et al. 2021).

Against this sobering backdrop, it is critical for EMDEs to promote policies to enhance education and learning. These include learning recovery programs that prevent further learning losses once children return to school, as well as early-warning systems that monitor absenteeism or nonreturn of students (UNICEF 2022). Remote and hybrid

---

[8] Trade costs cover the full range of costs associated with trading and are expressed in excess of the costs that the same goods face when traded domestically, as defined in the ESCAP-World Bank (database).

education, which became a necessity during the pandemic, has the potential to transform the future of learning if systems are strengthened and technology is better leveraged (World Bank 2018). Enhancing digitalization and fostering connectivity are some of the steps that can increase the efficiency of education spending. Enhancing learning equality should also be promoted, including by channeling resources to disadvantaged pupils, such as those displaced by war and conflict. Finally, flexible programs aimed at lifelong learning and reskilling the unemployed are also needed.

Raising labor force participation

The pandemic resulted in widespread job losses in EMDEs, especially among vulnerable groups such as women and youth, leading to higher unemployment and lower participation rates (figure 1.18.E). In previous recoveries, the improvement in employment lagged behind activity, often resulting in long unemployment spells (Brown and Koettl 2012).

Promoting labor force participation is key to offsetting the labor market losses brought about by the pandemic and fostering long-run labor productivity. To that end, active labor market policies can increase labor demand and the efficiency of labor market matching. These include wage subsidies and job retention policies, measures that enhance job search assistance and on-the-job training, and pension reforms. A comprehensive policy package, including sustained investment, education policies and active labor market reforms, could enhance EMDEs labor force participation and help mitigate the slowdown in potential output expected over the next decade (figure 1.18.F; World Bank 2022g). Policy makers can also enhance participation through reforms that promote job market flexibility and improve the wider business environment, including those that spur competition and reduce red tape.

Boosting female labor participation can significantly increase household incomes among EMDEs (Pimkina and de la Flor 2020). This can be achieved by job training programs specifically aimed at women, including vocational training (Bandiera et al. 2020). Financial inclusion and access to savings and credit products, including noncollateralized credit, also need to be promoted to improve women's access to education and to enable them to set up new businesses, thus enhancing their participation in the labor force.

TABLE 1.2 Emerging market and developing economies[1]

Commodity exporters[2]		Commodity importers[3]	
Algeria*	Kyrgyz Republic	Afghanistan	Romania
Angola*	Lao PDR	Albania	Samoa
Argentina	Liberia	Antigua and Barbuda	Serbia
Armenia	Libya*	Bahamas, The	Sri Lanka
Azerbaijan*	Madagascar	Bangladesh	St. Kitts and Nevis
Bahrain*	Malawi	Barbados	St. Lucia
Belize	Mali	Belarus	St. Vincent and the Grenadines
Benin	Mauritania	Bosnia and Herzegovina	Thailand
Bhutan	Mongolia	Bulgaria	Tonga
Bolivia*	Mozambique	Cambodia	Tunisia
Botswana	Myanmar*	China	Turkey
Brazil	Namibia	Croatia	Tuvalu
Burkina Faso	Nicaragua	Djibouti	Vanuatu
Burundi	Niger	Dominica	Vietnam
Cabo Verde	Nigeria*	Dominican Republic	
Cameroon*	Oman*	Egypt, Arab Rep.	
Central African Republic	Papua New Guinea	El Salvador	
Chad*	Paraguay	Eswatini	
Chile	Peru	Georgia	
Colombia*	Qatar*	Grenada	
Comoros	Russian Federation*	Haiti	
Congo, Dem. Rep.	Rwanda	Hungary	
Congo, Rep.*	São Tomé and Príncipe	India	
Costa Rica	Saudi Arabia*	Jamaica	
Côte d'Ivoire	Senegal	Jordan	
Ecuador*	Seychelles	Kiribati	
Equatorial Guinea*	Sierra Leone	Lebanon	
Eritrea	Solomon Islands	Lesotho	
Ethiopia	South Africa	Malaysia	
Fiji	South Sudan*	Maldives	
Gabon*	Sudan	Marshall Islands	
Gambia, The	Suriname	Mauritius	
Ghana*	Tajikistan	Mexico	
Guatemala	Tanzania	Micronesia, Fed. Sts.	
Guinea	Timor-Leste*	Moldova	
Guinea-Bissau	Togo	Montenegro	
Guyana*	Uganda	Morocco	
Honduras	Ukraine	Nauru	
Indonesia*	United Arab Emirates*	Nepal	
Iran, Islamic Rep.*	Uruguay	North Macedonia	
Iraq*	Uzbekistan	Pakistan	
Kazakhstan*	West Bank and Gaza	Palau	
Kenya	Zambia	Panama	
Kosovo	Zimbabwe	Philippines	
Kuwait*		Poland	

* Energy exporters.

1. Emerging market and developing economies (EMDEs) include all those that are not classified as advanced economies and for which a forecast is published for this report. Dependent territories are excluded. Advanced economies include Australia; Austria; Belgium; Canada; Cyprus; the Czech Republic; Denmark; Estonia; Finland; France; Germany; Greece; Hong Kong SAR, China; Iceland; Ireland; Israel; Italy; Japan; the Republic of Korea; Latvia; Lithuania; Luxembourg; Malta; the Netherlands; New Zealand; Norway; Portugal; Singapore; the Slovak Republic; Slovenia; Spain; Sweden; Switzerland; the United Kingdom; and the United States.

2. An economy is defined as commodity exporter when, on average in 2017-19, either (1) total commodities exports accounted for 30 percent or more of total exports or (2) exports of any single commodity accounted for 20 percent or more of total exports. Economies for which these thresholds were met as a result of re-exports were excluded. When data were not available, judgment was used. This taxonomy results in the classification of some well-diversified economies as importers, even if they are exporters of certain commodities (for example, Mexico).

3. Commodity importers are EMDEs not classified as commodity exporters.

References

Abreha, K. G., W. Kassa, E. K. K. Lartey, T. A. Mengistae, S. Owusu, and A. G. Zeufack. 2021. *Industrialization in Sub-Saharan Africa: Seizing Opportunities in Global Value Chains.* Washington, DC: World Bank.

Al-Samarrai, S., P. Cerdan-Infantes, A. Bigarinova, J. Bodmer, M. J. A. Vital, M. Antoninis, B. F. Barakat, and Y. Murakami. 2021. "Education Finance Watch 2021." World Bank, Washington, DC.

Anderson, W., C. Taylor, S. McDermid, E. Ilboudo-Nébié, R. Seager, W. Schlenker, F. Cottier, Alex de Sherbinin, D. Mendeloff, and K. Markey. 2021. "Violent Conflict Exacerbated Drought-Related Food Insecurity Between 2009 and 2019 in Sub-Saharan Africa." *Nature Food* 2: 603–15.

Arteta, C., M. A. Kose, F. Ohnsorge, and M. Stocker. 2015. "The Coming U.S. Interest Rate Tightening Cycle: Smooth Sailing or Stormy Waters?" Policy Research Note, World Bank, Washington, DC.

Azevedo, J. P., A. Hasan, D. Goldemberg, S.A. Iqbal, and K. Geven. 2020. "Simulating the Potential Impacts of the COVID-19 School Closures on Schooling and Learning Outcomes: A Set of Global Estimates." Policy Research Working Paper 9284, World Bank, Washington, DC.

Azevedo, J. P., F. H. Rogers, S. E. Ahlgren, M. H. Cloutier, B. Chakroun, C.Gwang-Chol, S. Mizunoya et al. 2021. "The State of the Global Education Crisis: A Path to Recovery." World Bank, Washington, DC.

Bandiera, O., N. Buehren, R. Burgess, M. Goldstein, S. Gulesci, I. Rasul, and M. Sulaiman. 2020. "Women's Empowerment in Action: Evidence from a Randomized Control Trial in Africa." *American Economic Journal: Applied Economics* 12 (1): 210–59.

Bank of Canada. 2021. "Monetary Policy Framework Renewal (December 2021)." Bank of Canada, Ottawa.

Barrett, C. 2013. *Food Security and Sociopolitical Stability.* Oxford, U.K.: Oxford University Press.

Barro, R. and J. Lee. 2010. "A New Data Set of Educational Attainment in the World, 1950-2010." *Journal of Development Economics* 104 (September): 184–198.

Barutciski, M. 1994. "EU States and the Refugee Crisis in the Former the Yugoslavia." *Refuge: Canada's Journal on Refugees* 14 (3): 32–36.

Bas, M., A. M. Fernandes, and C. Paunov. 2022. "How Resilient Was Trade to COVID-19?" Policy Research Working Paper 9975, World Bank, Washington, DC.

Becker, T., B. Eichengreen, Y. Gorodnichenko, S. Guriev, S. Johnson, T. Mylovanov, K. Rogoff, and B. Weder di Mauro. 2022. "A Blueprint for the Reconstruction of Ukraine." CEPR Rapid Response Economics, Center for Economic Policy Research, London.

Benigno, G., J. Di Giovanni, J. Groen, and A. Noble. 2022. "Global Supply Chain Pressure Index: March 2022 Update." *Liberty Street Economics* (blog). March 3. https://libertystreeteconomics.newyorkfed.org/2022/03/global-supply-chain-pressure-index-march-2022-update/.

Bidani, B., R. Menon, S. N. Nguyen, R. Vakis, and Z. Afif. 2022. "Vaccine Hesitancy: 10 Lessons from Chatbotting about COVID-19 in 17 Countries." *Investing in Health* (blog). March 17. https://blogs.worldbank.org/health/vaccine-hesitancy-10-lessons-chatbotting-about-covid-19-17-countries.

BIS (database). Bank for International Settlements. Accessed on March 20, 2022. https://www.bis.org/statistics/.

BlackRock Investment Institute (Database). 2022. "Geopolitical Risk Dashboard | The BlackRock Geopolitical Risk Indicator (BGRI)." Accessed on March 24, 2022. https://www.blackrock.com/corporate/insights/blackrock-investment-institute/interactive-charts/geopolitical-risk-dashboard#risk-indicator.

Blanchard, O. 2016. "The US Phillips Curve: Back to the 60s?" Policy Brief 16-1, Peterson Institute for International Economics, Washington, DC.

Blanchard, O. 2022. "Why I Worry about Inflation, Interest Rates, and Unemployment." *PIIE Series* (blog). March 14. https://www.piie.com/blogs/realtime-economic-issues-watch/why-i-worry-about-inflation-interest-rates-and-unemployment.

Borin, A., M. Mancini, and D. Taglioni. 2021. "Measuring Exposure to Risk in Global Value Chains." Policy Research Working Paper 9785, World Bank, Washington, DC.

Brenton, P., M. J. Ferrantino, and M. Maliszewska. 2022. *Reshaping Global Value Chains in Light of COVID-19: Implications for Trade and Poverty Reduction in Developing Countries.* Washington, DC: World Bank.

Brown, A. J. G., and J. Koettl. 2012. "Active Labor Market Programs: Employment Gain or Fiscal Drain?" IZA Discussion Papers 6880, Institute for the Study of Labor (IZA), Bonn.

Caldara, D., and M. Iacoviello. 2021. "Measuring Geopolitical Risk." Working paper, Board of Governors of the Federal Reserve, Washington, DC.

Cecchetti, S. G., and R. W. Rich. 2001. "Structural Estimates of the U.S. Sacrifice Ratio." *Journal of Business and Economic Statistics* 19 (4): 416–27.

Chavez, D. 2022. "COVID-19 Trade Policy Database: Food and Medical Products." Brief, World Bank, Washington, DC.

Claessens, S., M. A. Kose, L. Laeven, and F. Valencia. 2014. *Financial Crises: Causes, Consequences, and Policy Responses.* Washington, DC: International Monetary Fund.

Coibion, O., Y. Gorodnichenko, and M. Weber. 2019. "Monetary Policy Communications and Their Effects on Household Inflation Expectations." NBER Working Paper 25482, National Bureau of Economic Research, Cambridge, MA.

Comtrade (database). United Nations. Accessed on March 15, 2022. https://comtrade.un.org.

Constantinescu, C., A. M. Fernandes, A. Grover, S. Poupakis, and S. Reyes. 2022. "Globally Engaged Firms in the COVID-19 Crisis." Policy Research Working Paper 9991, World Bank, Washington, DC.

CSEP (Centre for Social and Economic Progress). 2022. "Climate Change Policy for Developing Countries." CSEP Working Paper 23, New Delhi, India.

de Hoyos, R. E., and D. Medvedev. 2011. "Poverty Effects of Higher Food Prices: A Global Perspective." *Review of Development Economics* 15 (3): 387–402.

Dieppe, A., ed. 2021. *Global Productivity: Trends, Drivers, and Policies.* Washington, DC: World Bank.

ESCAP-World Bank Trade Cost (Database). UNESCAP-World Bank 2021. Accessed on May 23, 2022. https://www.unescap.org/resources/escap-world-bank-trade-cost-database#.

Espitia, A., A. Mattoo, N. Rocha, M. Ruta, and D. Winkler. 2021. "Pandemic Trade: Covid-19, Remote Work and Global Value Chains." Policy Research Working Paper 9508, World Bank, Washington, DC.

Eurostat (database). European Commission. Accessed on March 20, 2022. https://ec.europa.eu/eurostat/data/database.

FAO (Food and Agriculture Organization). 2021. *Food Outlook - Biannual Report on Global Food Markets.* Rome: Food and Agriculture Organization of the United Nations.

FAO (Food and Agriculture Organization). 2022. "The Importance of Ukraine and the Russian Federation for Global Agricultural Markets and the Risks Associated with the Current Conflict," Food and Agriculture Food and Agriculture Organization of the United Nations, Rome.

FAO (Food and Agriculture Organization), IFAD (International Fund for Agricultural Development), UNICEF (United Nations Children's Fund), WFP (World Food Programme), and WHO (World Health Organization). 2021. *The State of Food Security and Nutrition in the World 2021: Transforming Food Systems for Food Security, Improved Nutrition and Affordable Healthy Diets for All.* Rome: Food and Agriculture Organization of the United Nations.

Feyen, E., and I. Zuccardi. 2019. "The Sovereign-Bank Nexus in EMDEs: What Is It, Is It Rising, and What Are the Policy Implications?" Policy Research Working Paper 8950, World Bank, Washington, DC.

FSIN (Food Security Information Network) and GNAFC (Global Network Against Food Crises). 2021. *Global Report on Food Crises.* Food Security Information Network, Rome.

FSIN (Food Security Information Network) and GNAFC (Global Network Against Food Crises). 2022. *Global Report on Food Crises.* Food Security Information Network, Rome.

G7 (Group of Seven). 2022. "G7 Finance Ministers and Central Bank Governors' Statement on Russia's War of Aggression against Ukraine." Statement, Department of Finance, Government of Canada, Washington, DC.

García, E. M., and R. Doehr. 2022. "Interest Rate Expectations Shape the Federal Reserve's Path of Lift-Off." VoxEU.org, CEPR Policy Portal, March 6. https://voxeu.org/article/interest-rate-expectations-shape-federal-reserve-s-path-lift.

Glauber, J., D. Laborde, and A. Mamun. 2022. "Countries Implementing Food Export Restrictions." *IFPRI Blog* (blog). April 13. https://data wrapper.dwcdn.net/OHipi/3/.

Grosh, M., P. Leite, M. Wai-Poi, and E. Tesliuc. 2022. *Revisiting Targeting in Social Assistance: A New Look at Old Dilemmas*. Washington, DC: World Bank.

Guenette, J. D. 2020. "Price Controls: Good Intentions, Bad Outcomes." Policy Research Working Paper 9212, World Bank, Washington, DC.

Guenette, J. D., and T. Yamazaki. 2021. "Projecting the Economic Consequences of the COVID-19 Pandemic." Policy Research Working Paper 9589, World Bank, Washington, DC.

Ha, J., M. A. Kose, and F. Ohnsorge, eds. 2019. *Inflation in Emerging and Developing Economies: Evolution, Drivers and Policies*. Washington, DC: World Bank.

Ha, J., M. A. Kose, and F. Ohnsorge. 2022. "From Low to High Inflation: Implications for Emerging Market and Developing Economies," Centre for Economic Policy Research, London.

Ha, J., M. A. Kose, F. Ohnsorge, and H. Yilmazkuday, eds. 2019. "Sources of Inflation: Global and Domestic Drivers." In *Inflation in Emerging and Developing Economies: Evolution, Drivers, and Policies*, 143–206. Washington, DC: World Bank.

Hendrix, C., and H.-J. Brinkman. 2013. "Food Insecurity and Conflict Dynamics: Causal Linkages and Complex Feedbacks." *Stability: International Journal of Security and Development* 2 (2): 1-18.

Hoek, J., S. Kamin, and E. Yoldas. 2020. "When Is Bad News Good News? U.S. Monetary Policy, Macroeconomic News, and Financial Conditions in Emerging Markets." International Finance Discussion Papers 1269, Board of Governors of the Federal Reserve System, Washington, DC.

Husain, A. 2022. "Projected Increase in Acute Food Insecurity due to War in Ukraine." World Food Programme, New York.

IEA (International Energy Agency). 2022. "Oil Market Report—March 2022." International Energy Agency, Paris.

ILO (database). International Labour Organization. Accessed on March 15, 2022. https://ilostat.ilo.org/.

IMF (International Monetary Fund). 2021. *Global Financial Stability Report*. October. Washington, DC: International Monetary Fund.

IMF (International Monetary Fund). 2022a. "Review of The Institutional View on The Liberalization and Management of Capital Flows." IMF Policy Paper, International Monetary Fund, Washington, DC.

IMF (International Monetary Fund). 2022b. *Fiscal Monitor: Fiscal Policy from Pandemic to War*. Washington, DC: International Monetary Fund.

IPCC (Intergovernmental Panel on Climate Change). 2022. *Climate Change 2022: Impact, Adaptation and Vulnerability*. Geneva: Intergovernmental Panel on Climate Change.

Islam, R. 2022. "What a Carbon Tax Can Do and Why It Cannot Do It All." *Sustainable Energy for All* (blog). January 19. https://blogs.worldbank.org/energy/what-carbon-tax-can-do-and-why-it-cannot-do-it-all.

Ivanic, M., and W. Martin. 2014. "Short- and Long-Run Impacts of Food Price Changes on Poverty." Policy Research Working Paper 7011, World Bank, Washington, DC.

Ivanic, M., W. Martin, and H. Zaman. 2011. "Estimating the Short-Run Poverty Impacts of the 2010–11 Surge in Food Prices." Policy Research Working Paper 5633, World Bank, Washington, DC.

Kabundi, A., and G. Vasishtha. 2022. "Commodity Price Cycles: Drivers and Policies." In *Global Economic Prospects*. January. Washington, DC: World Bank.

Kose, M. A., S. Kurlat, F. Ohnsorge, and N. Sugawara. 2017. "A Cross-Country Database of Fiscal Space." Policy Research Working Paper 8157, World Bank, Washington, DC.

Kose, M. A., P. Nagle, F. Ohnsorge, and N. Sugawara. 2021. *Global Waves of Debt: Causes and Consequences*. Washington, DC: World Bank.

Kose, M. A., F. Ohnsorge, C. M. Reinhart, and K. S. Rogoff. 2021. "The Aftermath of Debt Surges." NBER Working Paper 29266, National Bureau of Economic Research, Cambridge, MA.

Kose, M. A., N. Sugawara, and M. E. Terrones. 2020. "Global Recessions." Policy Research Working Paper 9172, World Bank, Washington, DC.

Kuemmerle, T., and M. Baumann. 2021. "Shocks to Food Systems in Times of Conflict." *Nature Food* 2: 922-23.

Laborde, D., C. Lakatos, and W. Martin. 2019. "Poverty Impact of Food Price Shocks and Policies." In *Inflation in Emerging and Developing Economies—Evolution, Drivers, and Policies*, edited by J. Ha, M. A. Kose, and F. Ohnsorge, 371-401. Washington, DC: World Bank Group.

Mani, M., S. Bandyopadhyay, S. Chonabayashi, A. Markandya, and T. Mosier. 2018. *South Asia's Hotspots: Impacts of Temperature and Precipitation Changes on Living Standards*. Washington, DC: World Bank.

Matteo Iacoviello (data set). "Measuring Geopolitical Risk." Accessed on May 25, 2022. https://www.matteoiacoviello.com/gpr.htm

McArthur, J. W., and G. C. McCord. 2017. "Fertilizing Growth: Agricultural Inputs and Their Effects in Economic Development." *Journal of Development Economics* 127 (July): 133–52.

McCahan, C. 2022. "Building Health System Resilience by Supporting More Local Production." *Investing in Health* (blog). March 22. https://blogs.worldbank.org/health/building-health-system-resilience-supporting-more-local-production.

McGovern, M. E., A. Krishna, V. M. Aguayo, and SV Subramanian. 2017. "A Review of the Evidence Linking Child Stunting to Economic Outcomes." *International Journal of Epidemiology* 46 (4): 1171–91.

Melecky, M. 2021. *Hidden Debt: Solutions to Avert the Next Financial Crisis in South Asia*. Washington, DC: World Bank.

Micha, R., ed. 2021. *Global Nutrition Report: The State of Global Nutrition*. Bristol, U.K.: Development Initiatives.

Mitchell, I., S. Hughes, and S. Huckstep. 2022. "Price Spike Caused by Ukraine War Will Push Over 40 Million into Poverty: How Should We Respond?" Blog Post, Center for Global Development, Washington, DC.

Mizunoya, S., G. Avanesian, S. Mishra, Y. Wang, and H. Yao. 2021. "Education Disrupted: The Second Year of the COVID-19 Pandemic and School Closures." United Nations Children's Fund, New York.

Nagle, P. 2022. "5 Lessons from Past Episodes of Debt Relief." *Let's Talk Development* (blog). January 31. https://blogs.worldbank.org/developmenttalk/5-lessons-past-episodes-debt-relief.

OECD (Organisation for Economic Co-operation and Development). 2021a. *OECD Employment Outlook 2021: Navigating the COVID-19 Crisis and Recovery*. Paris: OECD.

OECD (Organisation for Economic Co-operation and Development). 2021b. "Global Value Chains: Efficiency and Risks in the Context of COVID-19." OECD, Paris.

OECD (Organisation for Economic Co-operation and Development). 2022. *OECD Economic Outlook, Interim Report March 2022: Economic and Social Impacts and Policy Implications of the War in Ukraine*. Paris: OECD.

OECD (Organisation for Economic Co-operation and Development) and FAO (Food and Agriculture Organization of the United Nations). 2020. *OECD-FAO Agricultural Outlook 2020-2029*. Rome: FAO; Paris: OECD Publishing.

OECD (Organisation for Economic Co-operation and Development) and FAO (Food and Agriculture Organization of the United Nations). 2021. *OECD-FAO Agricultural Outlook 2021-2030*. Rome: FAO; Paris: OECD Publishing.

Ohnsorge, F. L., M. Stocker, M. Y. Some. 2016. "Quantifying Uncertainties in Global Growth Forecasts." Policy Research Working Paper 7770, World Bank, Washington, DC.

Our World in Data (database). "Coronavirus Pandemic (COVID-19)." Accessed on March 15, 2022. https://ourworldindata.org/coronavirus.

Oxford Economics. 2019. "Global Economic Model." July, Oxford Economics, Oxford, U.K.

Pearce, T. 2022. "Non-Bank Financial Institutions Pose Significant Systemic Risk." *OMFIF* (blog). Official Monetary and Financial Institutions Forum. February 17. https://www.omfif.org/2022/02/non-bank-financial-institutions-pose-significant-systemic-risk/.

Pimkina, S., and L. de La Flor. 2020. "Promoting Female Labor Force Participation." Jobs Working Paper 56, World Bank, Washington, DC.

Psacharopoulos, G., and H. A. Patrinos. 2018. "Returns to Investment in Education: A Decennial Review of the Global Literature." Policy Research Working Paper 8402, World Bank, Washington, DC.

PWT (database). "Penn World Table." Accessed on May 5, 2022. https://www.rug.nl/ggdc/productivity/pwt/.

Reinhart, C. M., and K. S. Rogoff. 2009. *This Time Is Different: Eight Centuries of Financial Folly. This Time Is Different.* Princeton, NJ: Princeton University Press.

Ritchie, H., E. Mathieu, L. Rodés-Guirao, C. Appel, C. Giattino, E. Ortiz-Ospina, J. Hasell, B. Macdonald, D. Beltekian, and M. Roser. 2022. "Coronavirus Pandemic (COVID-19)." Accessed March 29, 2022. Available at https://ourworldindata.org/coronavirus.

Ruta, M. 2022. "The Impact of the War in Ukraine on Global Trade and Investment." Equitable Growth, Finance & Institutions Insight, World Bank, Washington, DC.

Saavedra, J. 2021. "A Silent and Unequal Education Crisis. And the Seeds for Its Solution." *Education for Global Development* (blog). January 5. https://blogs.worldbank.org/education/silent-and-unequal-education-crisis-and-seeds-its-solution.

Shang, B. 2021. "The Poverty and Distributional Impacts of Carbon Pricing: Channels and Policy Implications." IMF Working Paper 172, International Monetary Fund, Washington, DC.

Stock, J. H., and M. W. Watson. 2019. "Slack and Cyclically Sensitive Inflation." NBER Working Paper 25987, National Bureau of Economic Research, Cambridge, MA.

UNHCR (United Nations High Commissioner for Refugees). 2021. "Global Trends—Forced Displacement in 2020." UNHCR Global Data Service, Copenhagen, Denmark.

UNICEF (United Nations Children's Fund). 2019. "Children, Food, and Nutrition: Growing Well in a Changing World." United Nations Children's Fund, UNICEF, New York.

UNICEF (United Nations Children's Fund). 2022. "Where Are We on Education Recovery," United Nations Children's Fund, New York.

UNWTO (World Tourism Organization). 2021. *Yearbook of Tourism Statistics, Data 2015 – 2019.* 2021 Edition. Madrid: World Tourism Organization.

van Gemert, T., L. Lieb, and T. Treibich. 2022. "Local Fiscal Multipliers of Different Government Spending Categories." *Empirical Economics.*

Wang, D., B. P. J. Andree, C. Andres-Fernando, and P. Girouard Spencer. 2020. "Stochastic Modeling of Food Insecurity." Policy Research Working Paper 9413, World Bank, Washington, DC.

WEO (database). "World Economic Outlook Databases." Accessed on April 25, 2022. https://www.imf.org/en/Publications/WEO/weo-database/2022/April.

WFP (World Food Programme). 2022. "Food Security Implications of the Ukraine Conflict." World Food Programme, Rome.

WHO (World Health Organization), UNICEF (United Nations Children's Fund), and World Bank. 2021. *Levels and Trends in Child Malnutrition: UNICEF / WHO / The World Bank Group Joint Child Malnutrition Estimates: Key Findings of the 2021 Edition.* Geneva: World Health Organization.

Winkler, D., L. Wuester, and D. Knight. 2022. "Russia's Global Value Chain Participation: Implications of Russia's Invasion of Ukraine for its Trade Partners and Key Value Chains." World Bank, Washington, DC.

World Bank. 2013. "From Universal Price Subsidies to Modern Social Assistance: The Political Economy of Reform." World Bank, Washington, DC.

World Bank. 2014. *Turn Down the Heat: Confronting the New Climate Normal.* Washington, DC: World Bank.

Word Bank. 2015. "Hoping for the Best, Preparing for the Worst: Risks around U.S. Rate Liftoff and Policy Options." In *Global Economic Prospects: The Global Economy in Transition,* 63-91. June. Washington, DC: World Bank.

World Bank. 2018. *World Development Report 2018: Learning to Realize Education's Promise.* Washington, DC: World Bank.

World Bank. 2019a. Commodity Markets Outlook Report: Food Price Shocks: Channels and Implications. World Bank, Washington, DC.

World Bank. 2019b. *Global Economic Prospects - Darkening Skies.* January. Washington, DC: World Bank.

World Bank. 2020a. *EFI—Finance: Insolvency and Corporate Restructuring.* Washington, DC: World Bank.

World Bank, 2020b. *World Development Report 2020: Trading for Development in the Age of Global Value Chains.* Washington, DC: World Bank.

World Bank. 2021a. *Global Economic Prospects.* January. Washington, DC: World Bank.

World Bank. 2021b. *Global Economic Prospects.* June. Washington, DC: World Bank.

World Bank. 2022a. *Commodity Markets Outlook: Causes and Consequences of Metal Price Shocks.* Washington, DC: World Bank.

World Bank. 2022b. *Africa's Pulse: Boosting Resilience: The Future of Social Protection in Africa.* April. Washington, DC: World Bank.

World Bank. 2022c. *World Development Report 2022: Finance for an Equitable Recovery.* Washington, DC: World Bank.

World Bank. 2022d. *Europe and Central Asia Economic Update, Spring 2022: War in the Region.* Washington, DC: World Bank.

World Bank. 2022e. *East Asia and the Pacific Economic Update: Braving the Storm.* April. World Bank, Washington, DC.

World Bank. 2022f. *Reshaping Norms: A New Way Forward.* Washington, DC: World Bank.

World Bank. 2022g. *Global Economic Prospects.* January. Washington, DC: World Bank.

GLOBAL STAGFLATION

Global inflation has risen sharply from its lows in mid-2020, on rebounding global demand, supply bottlenecks, and soaring food and energy prices, especially since the Russian Federation's invasion of Ukraine. Markets expect inflation to peak in mid-2022 and then decline, but to remain elevated even after these shocks subside and monetary policies are tightened further. Global growth has been moving in the opposite direction: it has declined sharply since the beginning of the year and, for the remainder of this decade, is expected to remain below the average of the 2010s. In light of these developments, the risk of stagflation—a combination of high inflation and sluggish growth—has risen. The recovery from the stagflation of the 1970s required steep increases in interest rates by major advanced-economy central banks to quell inflation, which triggered a global recession and a string of financial crises in emerging market and developing economies (EMDEs). If current stagflationary pressures intensify, EMDEs would likely face severe challenges again because of their less well-anchored inflation expectations, elevated financial vulnerabilities, and weakening growth fundamentals. This makes it urgent for EMDEs to shore up their fiscal and external buffers, strengthen their monetary policy frameworks, and implement reforms to reinvigorate growth.

Introduction

The global economy is in the midst of a sharp growth slowdown following the extraordinarily strong rebound last year. This slowdown coincides with a steep runup in global inflation to multi-decade highs. Looking ahead, growth over the next decade is expected to be considerably weaker than over the past two decades. Although global inflation is for now projected to return close to its 2019 average by 2024, there is a growing risk that it may remain elevated as global supply disruptions persist and some structural drivers that depressed inflation over the past three decades dissipate.

These developments raise concerns about stagflation—a period of both weak growth and elevated inflation similar to what happened during the 1970s. The experience of the 1970s is a reminder of the damage this could cause to the global economy and, especially, to emerging market and developing economies (EMDEs).[1] The stagflation of the 1970s ended with a global

recession and a series of financial crises in EMDEs.

There has been considerable debate about current stagflation risks. Some researchers have warned that the recent surge in inflation around the world could mark a permanent ratcheting up of price pressures after two decades of low and stable inflation.[2] Some have also noted parallels between the current episode and the stagflation of the 1970s, including similarly negative real interest rates in both periods and the possibility of a wage-price spiral set off by rapid wage growth (Blanchard 2022; Summers 2022).[3] However, others have pointed to material differences from the 1970s, especially in the conduct of monetary policy, which may help prevent another bout of stagflation: the inflation-fighting credentials accumulated since the 1980s and recent evidence of broadly stable long-term inflation expectations (DeLong 2022, Reifschneider and Wilcox 2022).[4]

Thus far, markets expect that inflation in the near future will decline, albeit remaining elevated, as

---

Note: This Special Focus was prepared by Jongrim Ha, M. Ayhan Kose, and Franziska Ohnsorge.

[1] While there is no precise definition of stagflation, the term has been used to refer to a combination of high inflation and low growth (or high unemployment). Some researchers have focused on output growth and considered stagflation as a "combination of low or negative output growth, and inflation that is high by historical standards" (Barsky and Killian 2002). Others have focused on unemployment, and defined stagflation as "combinations of either increasing or persistently high levels of unemployment and inflation," even defining an "economic misery index" as the sum of the unemployment rate and inflation (Bruno and Sachs 1979, Welsch 2007).

[2] For these arguments, see Borio et al (2022); Eo, Uzeda, and Wong (2022); Forbes, Gagnon, and Collins (2021); and Ha, Kose, and Ohnsorge (2022).

[3] Gagnon (2022) cautions that the relationship between unemployment and inflation (the Phillips curve) is highly nonlinear and, as a result, current expectations of declining inflation with limited increases in unemployment may prove too optimistic. Rogoff (2021) discusses the role of politically motivated spending in driving inflation by drawing parallels between mounting fiscal pressures in the 1970s and the current growth in public pension obligations.

[4] Wilcox (2022) cautions against interpreting the 1970s as a lesson that only forceful policy tightening can lower inflation; instead, he argues, the lesson is that an excessive policy tightening in response to supply shocks, to compensate for previous excessive loosening, will cause a recession.

global growth cools, monetary policy gets tighter, fiscal support is withdrawn, energy and food prices level off, and supply bottlenecks ease. Moreover, most commentators argue that monetary policy has the tools to return inflation to target rates over time. However, if inflation expectations de-anchor, as they did in the 1970s, as a result of persistently elevated inflation and repeated inflationary shocks, the interest rate increases required to bring inflation back to target will be greater than those currently anticipated by financial markets. This raises the specter of the steep increases in interest rates that brought inflation under control but also triggered a global recession in 1982 (Goodfriend 2007). That global recession also coincided with a string of financial crises and marked the beginning of a protracted period of weak growth in many EMDEs.

Against this background of highly uncertain global economic prospects and complex policy challenges, this Special Focus addresses three questions:

- How have inflation and growth evolved over time?

- How does the current period compare with the stagflation of the 1970s?

- What challenges do stagflationary risks now pose for EMDEs?

The Focus makes several contributions to the literature. First, it provides the first systematic comparison of the current juncture with the stagflationary period of the 1970s. The previous literature has mostly focused on a comparison of high inflation during that period with today's inflationary challenges and studied the role of monetary policy and commodity price shocks in driving inflation in the two periods. This study considers the stagflation of the 1970s and examines the role of fiscal policy and broader structural differences in explaining weak output growth and high inflation. Second, in contrast to much of the earlier work, which has focused on the United States, this study presents a global perspective by examining the evidence of stagflation, and the challenges posed by it, for a

broad set of countries.[5] The threat of stagflation is global since the current combination of high inflation and weak growth is highly synchronized across many countries. Third, this Focus explicitly links the EMDE debt buildup of the 1970s that culminated in the debt crises of the 1980s to the stagflation of that era and its eventual resolution in advanced economies. The 1970s witnessed the first global debt wave fueled by a prolonged period of accommodative monetary policies in major advanced economies. Since 2010, the global economy has been experiencing the largest, fastest, and most synchronized debt wave of the past five decades amid a protracted period of monetary policy accommodation. The study considers the lessons of the debt accumulation of the 1970s for the current debt wave.

Evolution of inflation

Inflation in the 1960s and 1970s. Global consumer price inflation rose steadily in the 1970s, starting from a range of 1.7-4.4 percent a year through the 1960s and early 1970s (figure SF1.1.A). In 1973, inflation surged to 10.3 percent, when the first oil price shock struck. Inflation then rose steeply through the remainder of the 1970s and stayed elevated until the global recession of 1982. As a result, global inflation during 1973-83 averaged 11.3 percent a year, more than three times as high as the average of 3.6 percent a year during 1962-72. The inflation pickup over the course of the 1970s was accompanied by a double-digit depreciation of the U.S. dollar (in nominal effective terms).

During this period, however, there were marked differences across countries. While inflation subsided sharply in Germany, Japan, and Switzerland around the global recession of 1975, it dipped only briefly in the United States, France,

---

[5] Bruno and Sachs (1985) emphasize the importance of commodity price shocks (sharp increases in the prices of oil and food) as the main driver of inflation in the 1970s. Blinder (1979) and Blinder and Kilian (2009) attribute the U.S. stagflation in the 1970s mostly to supply shocks. Barsky and Kilian (2002 and 2004) find a prominent role for the monetary policy response to supply shocks. DeLong (1997) also notes these factors but also political pressure on the U.S. Federal Reserve.

and Spain, and remained high in the Nordics and Canada. Synchronous policy tightening around the world, including in the United States, contributed to the global recession of 1982, with global inflation waning to 5.4 percent per year, on average, in the remainder of the 1980s.

Inflation between the 1970s and the pandemic. Prior to the pandemic, many studies focused on the remarkable decline in inflation over the past five decades. Global inflation fell from a peak of 16.9 percent in 1974 to 2.3 percent in 2019 (figure SF1.1.A). This trend decline was broad-based, covering both advanced economies and EMDEs. Between 1974 and 2019, inflation in advanced economies declined from 15.3 percent in 1974 to 1.3 percent in 2019, while in EMDEs, it declined from 17.5 percent to 2.6 percent. These declines were driven by a sharper focus by monetary authorities on price stability as the primary objective of monetary policy and also by rapid globalization and the liberalization of product, labor, and financial markets (Ha, Ivanova, et al. 2019). In fact, inflation declined so much over the 1990s and 2000s, the period sometimes dubbed "The Great Moderation," that deflation had become a major concern in some advanced economies by the early 2000s. In 2019, before the COVID-19 pandemic struck, inflation was below target ranges in almost all inflation-targeting advanced economies. In about half of inflation-targeting EMDEs, inflation remained within target ranges in every year of the period 2012-2019.

Inflation since the outbreak of the pandemic. Since early 2020, global inflation has been highly volatile (figure SF1.1.B). In the early stages of the pandemic, between January and April 2020, global inflation declined by about 1 percentage point amid a collapse in demand and plunging oil prices. In May 2020, however, global inflation started to pick up with a rebound in oil and food prices and a recovery of activity following the easing of the lockdowns that had been introduced during the first wave of the pandemic. The surge in commodity prices resulting from Russia's invasion of Ukraine and supply disruptions due to renewed pandemic outbreaks and movement restrictions in China have further pushed up food

FIGURE SF1.1 Inflation

From its peak in the mid-1970s, global inflation has declined sharply. However, inflation has surged in 2021-22 as a result of the rebound in global demand from the pandemic and soaring commodity prices, especially since Russia's invasion of Ukraine. While inflation rose most in EMDEs in Europe and Central Asia, rising food and energy prices have also sharply increased inflation in Sub-Saharan Africa. Short-term inflation expectations have risen, especially since the start of the war, but medium-term expectations have remained broadly stable.

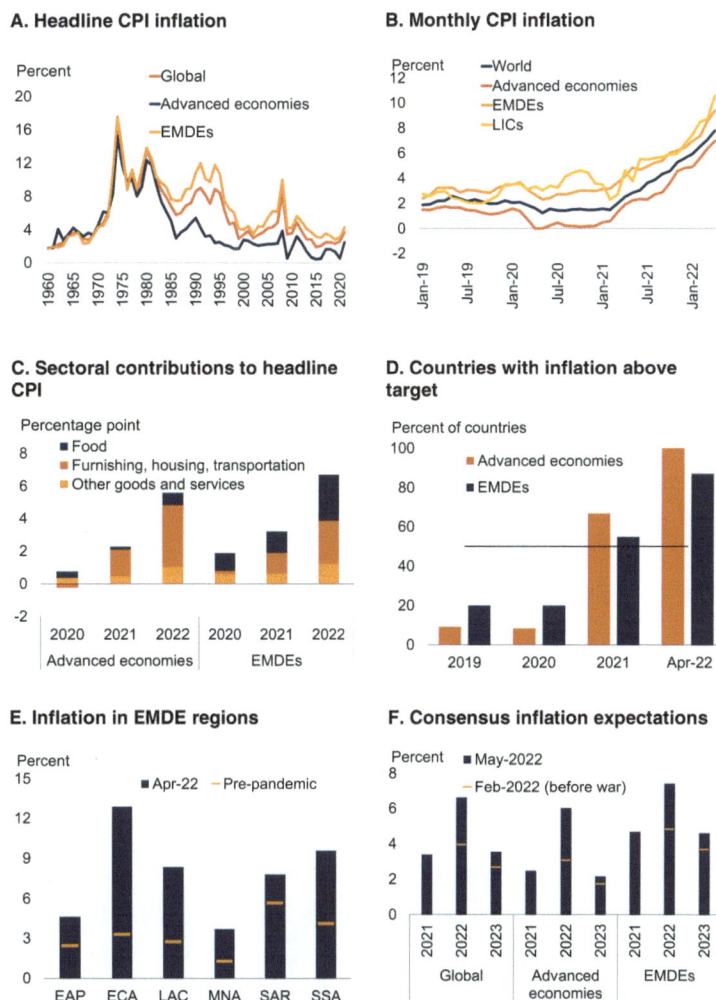

A. Headline CPI inflation

B. Monthly CPI inflation

C. Sectoral contributions to headline CPI

D. Countries with inflation above target

E. Inflation in EMDE regions

F. Consensus inflation expectations

Sources: Consensus Economics; Haver Analytics; International Monetary Fund; World Bank.
Note: CPI = consumer price index. EMDEs = emerging market and developing economies.
A. Based on a sample of 155 countries (30 advanced economies and 125 EMDEs). The values show year-on-year headline CPI inflation. Last observation is 2021.
B.E. Year-on-year inflation. Lines show group median inflation for 81 countries, of which 31 are advanced economies and 50 are EMDEs. Low-income country (LIC) inflation is based on 8 LICs. Last observation is April 2022.
C. Median headline CPI inflation (annual averages) in 12 sectors across 147 countries. Sectors are categorized following the International Financial Statistics. "Food" indicates food, beverages, tobacco, and narcotics sectors. "Furnishing" indicates furnishings, household equipment, and routine household maintenance sectors. "Housing" indicates housing, water, electricity, gas, and other fuels. "Other goods and services" include clothing, health, communication, recreation, education, restaurants, and miscellaneous sectors. 2022 is based on average inflation between January and April 2022.
D. Bars show the share of inflation-targeting economies (in percent) with average inflation during the course of the year (or month) above the target range.
E. EAP = East Asia and Pacific, ECA = Europe and Central Asia, LAC = Latin America and the Caribbean, SAR = South Asia, SSA = Sub-Saharan Africa. "Pre-pandemic" level is based on average inflation in 2019.
F. Figure shows forecasts from Consensus Economics for median headline CPI inflation for 2022-23 based on February 2022 and May 2022 surveys of 32 advanced economies and 50 EMDEs.

and energy prices, and inflation more broadly (figure SF1.1.C).

The most recent data, for April 2022, show inflation at multiyear highs: globally, at 7.8 percent, its highest level since 2008. Inflation in advanced economies is now at its highest level since 1982, up from near-zero during April-December 2020; inflation in EMDEs is at 9.4 percent, its highest level since 2008, up from a multidecade low in May 2020. As of April this year, inflation was above target in all advanced economies and almost 90 percent of inflation-targeting EMDEs (figure SF1.1.D). Among EMDE regions, the increase in inflation this year has been most pronounced in Europe and Central Asia (ECA) as a result of rebounding demand in advanced-economy Europe, disruptions driven by Russia's invasion of Ukraine, and the commodity price surge. In contrast, in East Asia and the Pacific (EAP), where recurring lockdowns have been implemented, inflation has also risen but has remained within most central banks' target ranges (figure SF1.1.E).

Drivers of recent inflation developments. To disentangle the quantitative importance of different forces driving global inflation, a factor-augmented VAR (FAVAR) model (annex SF1.1). The model is applied to three global variables—inflation, output growth, and oil price growth—all expressed as month-on-month growth rates.[6] The exercise is repeated for advanced economies and EMDEs separately, and for headline CPI inflation, core CPI inflation, and PPI inflation. The PPI tends to have larger tradables content than the headline CPI, whereas the core CPI tends to have smaller tradables content than the headline CPI (figure SF1.2.A; Ha, Kose, and Ohnsorge 2019b). The estimation results document how drivers of inflation have shifted since January 2020 and disturbances associated with demand, supply,

---

[6] Global inflation and output growth are proxied by the common global factors estimated using a dynamic factor model of cross-country inflation and industrial production growth, respectively (annex SF1.1). The dynamic factor model includes monthly data for 31 advanced economies and 52 EMDEs for January 2001 to March 2022. The global oil price is based on the average of Dubai, West Texas Intermediate, and Brent oil prices, as reported in the World Bank's Pink Sheet of commodity prices

and oil prices have affected different inflation measures. While demand shocks were the dominant force in pushing inflation down in the first half of 2020, oil price shocks and supply shocks have become more influential in pushing inflation up since early 2021, especially for core inflation and CPI in advanced economies.

- *January-May 2020.* Four-fifths of the decline in global inflation over this period reflected the collapse in global demand as both consumption and investment collapsed amid lockdowns and uncertainty about policies and growth prospects (figure SF1.2.B). Another one-fifth reflected the plunge in oil prices. For both advanced economies and EMDEs, disinflationary effects from collapsing demand and oil prices were partly offset by the inflationary effect of supply disruptions such as disruptions to firm operations and global shipping caused by pandemic restrictions to domestic economic activity and international travel (figures SF1.2.C and SF1.2.D).

- *May 2020-Mar 2022.* The collapses in demand and oil prices as well as supply disruptions began to unwind from May 2020 as consumers, firms, and investors began to adjust their behavior and operations. From May, as international trade and global manufacturing activity rebounded, easing supply bottlenecks began to lower inflation but sharp rebounds in demand and oil prices put upward pressure on inflation as consumption shifted from in-person to online transactions. Since mid-2021, when inflation accelerated and became more broad-based, the global growth rebound, rising oil prices and supply shocks—including shipping bottle-necks, non-oil commodity price pressures and, in some countries, wage pressures—have all contributed to rising inflation. Since Russia's inflation of Ukraine, oil price surges have further driven up inflation.

- *Alternative inflation measures.* The main drivers of inflation have been similar across different inflation measures. However, the measures differ in the relative roles of different types of shocks, reflecting their differing tradables contents. In particular, core inflation has been more susceptible to effects of supply shocks, with PPI inflation more susceptible to effects from oil price and global demand shocks (annex SF1.1).

Inflation prospects in the near term. The recent rise in inflation has led to a reassessment of near-term inflation prospects. Global inflation is expected to peak in about mid-2022 and to decline to about 3 percent in mid-2023 (chapter 1; figure SF1.1.F). This, however, would still be about 1 percentage point above its average in 2019. Russia's invasion of Ukraine has resulted in further increases in near-term inflation expectations because Russia and Ukraine are major exporters of many commodities (World Bank 2022a). The war-driven supply shortages and shipping disruptions have added to price increases in commodity markets, on top of the sharp price rises since mid-2020, and to global inflationary pressures.[7] Concerns about persistently above-target inflation have already prompted central banks in most advanced economies and many EMDEs to tighten monetary policy amid a sharp growth slowdown. Despite this tightening, as of May 2022, real policy rates (adjusted by actual inflation) remain deeply negative in the average advanced economy (-5.2 percent) and in the average EMDE (-3.2 percent).

Risks to inflation projections. There are material risks that inflation could rise higher or remain elevated for longer than currently projected. If supply disruptions persist or commodity prices continue to climb—in the event of a protracted war in Ukraine, for example, or recurring pandemic outbreaks and movement restrictions in China—inflation could remain above central banks' target ranges in many countries. If inflation remains elevated, the risk will also grow that expectations of higher inflation become baked

---

[7] Even if core inflation and inflation expectations remained unaffected by surging energy and food prices, global headline inflation would rise significantly, at least temporarily since energy and food together account for 40 percent of the consumption basket in a typical country. Model-based estimates suggest that an increase in oil prices alone of 50 percent (approximately the increase over the course of 2021) could be associated with a statistically significant increase in inflation of about 4.4 percentage points after two years (Ha, Kose, et al. 2019).

FIGURE SF1.2 Drivers of inflation in 2020-22

Between January and May 2020, demand factors played a major role in dampening global inflation. Since mid-2020, global supply and oil price shocks have also contributed significantly to rising inflation.

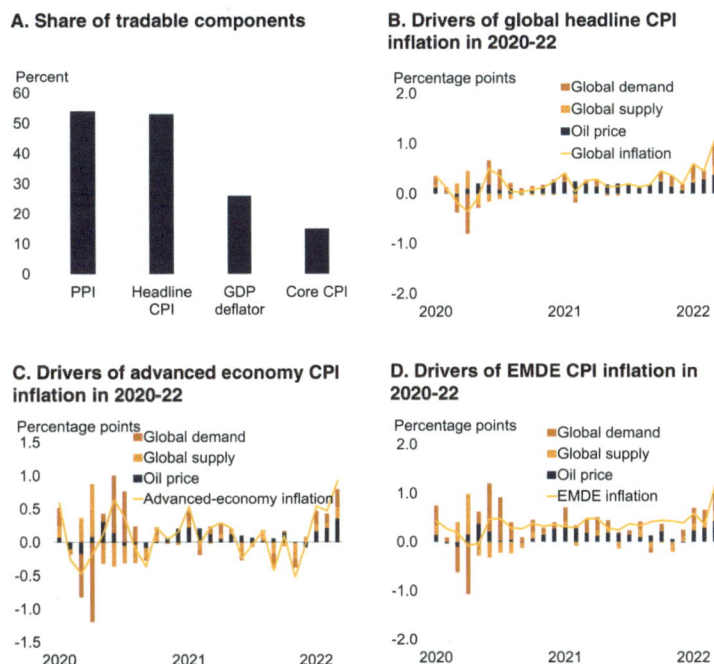

A. Share of tradable components

B. Drivers of global headline CPI inflation in 2020-22

C. Drivers of advanced economy CPI inflation in 2020-22

D. Drivers of EMDE CPI inflation in 2020-22

Sources: Ha, Kose, and Ohnsorge (2021a); U.S. Bureau of Labor Statistics; World Bank.
Note: CPI = consumer price index; EMDEs = emerging market and developing economies.
A. Share of tradable goods and services in different inflation measures in the United States. PPI =producer price index.
B.-D. Contributions to month-on-month inflation in headline CPI for 83 countries, of which 31 are advanced economies and 52 are EMDEs, based on FAVAR models over the period of 2001M1-2022M3. Unexplained residual is omitted from the graph.

into wage and price setting behavior. Financial market-based inflation expectations have already risen with Russia's invasion of Ukraine and the supply disruptions arising from pandemic outbreaks and control measures in major EMDEs, and there are concerns that a more significant unanchoring of inflation expectations could occur that would force major advanced-economy central banks to tighten policy by more than currently anticipated, slowing growth and even tipping some economies into recession. The implications of such a confluence of adverse shocks is explored in the global outlook and risks section of chapter 1.

Evolution of growth

Growth in the 1960s and 1970s. After two decades of robust global growth in the 1950s and

FIGURE SF1.3 Growth

The pre-pandemic decade was marked by slowing growth, especially in EMDEs. This partly reflected a decline in potential growth that cut across all EMDE regions. Prospects are for a further decline in potential growth over the 2020s. This has also been reflected in consensus forecasters' downgrades of long-term growth prospects.

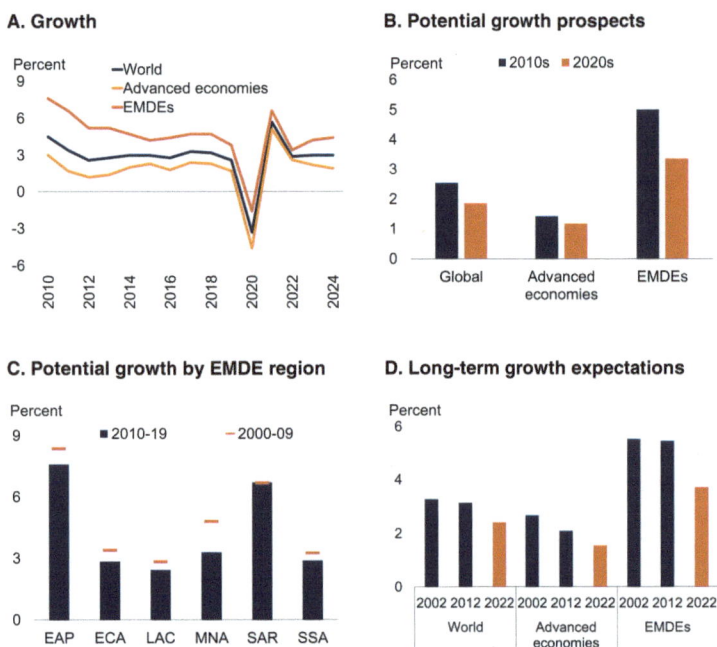

A. Growth

B. Potential growth prospects

C. Potential growth by EMDE region

D. Long-term growth expectations

Sources: Consensus Economics; Haver Analytics; World Bank.
Note: EMDEs = emerging market and developing economies.
A. 2022-24 growth rates are based on forecasts. GDP-weighted averages (at 2010-19 average prices and exchange rates).
B.C. GDP-weighted average (at 2010 prices and exchange rates) for 82 countries, including 52 EMDEs. Potential growth estimates based on a production function approach as described in Kilic Celik, Kose, and Ohnsorge (2020) and World Bank (2021b). 2020s forecasts in red bars assume that investment grows as expected by consensus forecasts, working-age population and life expectancy evolve as envisaged by the UN Population Projections, and secondary and tertiary school enrollment and completion rates decline by 2.5 percentage points.
C. EAP = East Asia and Pacific, ECA = Europe and Central Asia, LAC = Latin America and the Caribbean, SAR = South Asia, SSA = Sub-Saharan Africa.
D. Results from the latest Consensus Economics surveys in each year are presented. Sample includes 84 countries (33 advanced economies and 51 EMDEs). The horizontal axis shows the years when Consensus Economics forecasts are surveyed.

1960s, the 1970s were a period of sharply slowing global growth. The decade was marked by a global recession in 1975 and two recessions in the United States (1969-70, 1973-75) with a third U.S. recession (1980) ushering in the subsequent decade. Overall, global growth in the 1970s averaged 4.1 percent per year, well below the 5.5 and 5.1 percent, respectively, of the 1960s and 1950s. The global supply shocks that drove up inflation, like the two oil price shocks of the 1970s, also drove down growth.

Growth in the pre-pandemic decade. On the eve of the pandemic, in 2019, global growth reached a

decade low of 2.6 percent, about 1 percentage point below the 3.4 percent in 2011 (figure SF1.3.A). At 3 percent a year on average over the decade, growth in the 2010s was considerably below average growth of 3.4 percent per year in the preceding decade. The pre-pandemic decade was beset by crises and other adverse shocks that buffeted a wide range of countries and contributed to weaker output and trade growth (Kose and Ohnsorge 2020; World Bank 2021a). A rebound from the 2007-09 global financial crisis was followed by the euro area crisis in 2010-12; financial market jitters in 2013 (the "taper tantrum") highlighted financial stability risks in some major EMDEs; a steep commodity price slide during 2011-16 undercut the main drivers of growth in a wide swath of EMDEs; a policy-guided slowdown in China towards more sustainable growth rates eroded export demand for many EMDEs; a prolonged period of sluggish global trade and FDI flows dampened activity; and trade tensions between major economies starting in 2017 increased policy uncertainty and weakened confidence.

Growth prospects: Near-term. After its pandemic-related collapse in 2020, global growth rebounded to 5.7 percent in 2021, supported by unprecedented fiscal and monetary policy accommodation. It is now expected to slow to 2.9 percent in 2022 and 3.0 percent in 2023 because of the war in Ukraine, the fading of pent-up demand, and the withdrawal of policy support amid high inflation (chapter 1). Global growth is expected to remain at 3.0 percent in 2024 as output in advanced economies returns to its pre-pandemic trend. The recovery will lag in EMDEs, however, where output will remain about 5 percent below pre-pandemic trends even in 2024. These projections represent significant downgrades from forecasts six months ago. They are also subject to substantial uncertainty, with risks clearly tilted to the downside (see the risks section of chapter 1).

Growth prospects: Longer-term. Beyond the near-term, global growth is expected to slow further over the 2020s, reflecting a trend weakening of the fundamental drivers of growth (Dieppe 2021; Kose and Ohnsorge 2020; World

Bank 2021b; figures SF1.3.B SF1.3.C; annex SF1.2). Working age population shares in advanced economies began declining in the mid-1980s; in EMDEs, this process started in about 2010 and is set to continue over the next decade. The elevated uncertainty about the effects of both the pandemic and Russia's invasion of Ukraine on global trade and investment networks is expected to cause investment growth to remain weak (World Bank 2019). A global productivity growth slowdown since the early 2010s is expected to continue as the effects of earlier improvements to education and health outcomes as well as factor reallocation wane. As a result, global potential growth—the growth rate of the global economy at full capacity utilization, absent cyclical shocks—in the 2020s is expected to be 0.6 percentage points a year lower than in the 2010s (World Bank 2021b). Consensus forecasters have recognized the weakening of fundamental drivers of growth and have steadily downgraded their long-term (10 years ahead) growth forecasts since the early 2000s (figure SF1.3.D). This has been the case for both advanced economies and EMDEs: long-term growth forecasts for advanced economies have been downgraded by 0.6 percentage point between 2012 and 2022; for EMDEs, they have been downgraded by 1.8 percentage point.

Echoes of the stagflation of the 1970s?

The rapid emergence of above-target inflation around the world has raised concerns that an era of low inflation is coming to an end. Forces supporting the global expansion of output in recent decades—which included technological advances, the shift of labor out of agriculture in many EMDEs, globalization, and rapid population growth—were strongly disinflationary. As these fade, alongside recent supply shocks, inflationary pressures could build, echoing the experience of the 1970s, when large supply shocks, accommodative policies, and a fading of structural forces that promoted growth and disinflation triggered prolonged stagflation. A key difference that mitigates the risk of such a reoccurrence is that improved monetary policy frameworks in

advanced economies and many EMDEs have strengthened central bank credibility and helped anchored long-term inflation expectations.

Similarities to the 1970s

The current juncture resembles the early 1970s in three key respects: supply shocks and elevated global inflation in the near-term, preceded by a protracted period of highly accommodative monetary policy in major economies, together with recent marked fiscal expansion; prospects for weakening growth over the longer term, which echo the unforeseen slowdown in potential growth of the 1970s; and vulnerabilities in EMDEs to the monetary policy tightening by advanced economies that will be needed to rein in inflation.

Supply shocks after prolonged monetary policy accommodation. Supply disruptions driven by the pandemic and the recent supply shock dealt to global energy and food prices by Russia's invasion of Ukraine resemble the oil shocks in 1973 and 1979-80 (figure SF1.4.A). The 1970s witnessed the largest energy and food price shocks of the past fifty years. Price increases between April 2020 to March 2022 were the second largest for energy and third largest for food for any equivalent period since 1970 (figure SF1.4.B). Then and now, monetary policy generally was highly accommodative in the run-up to these shocks, with interest rates negative in real (inflation-adjusted) terms for several years (figures SF1.4.C and SF1.4.D). Global real interest rates averaged -0.5 percent over both the 1970-1980 and the 2010-2021 periods. The experience of the 1970s was that the delay in raising monetary policy rates ultimately made the required increase much greater (figure SF1.4.E). After several months of above-target inflation in major advanced economies, a steeper-than-anticipated policy tightening may now again be required to return inflation to target—and this might trigger a hard landing (Blanchard 2022; Summers 2022; Gagnon 2022). With EMDE debt at multidecade highs, the associated rise in global borrowing costs and exchange rate depreciations may trigger financial crises, as it did in the early 1980s.

Weaker growth. The global economy has been emerging from the pandemic-related global

FIGURE SF1.4 Developments in the 1970s and 2020s: Similarities

Recently, as in the 1970s, inflation has been rising amid surges in commodity prices and low interest rates. The recent rise in inflation has been accompanied by a steep slowdown in global growth, as in the 1970s.

A. Oil price

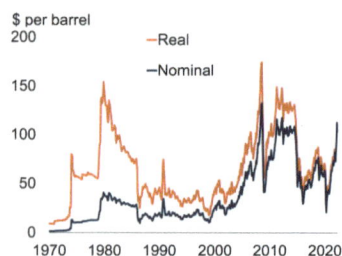

B. Change in food and energy prices

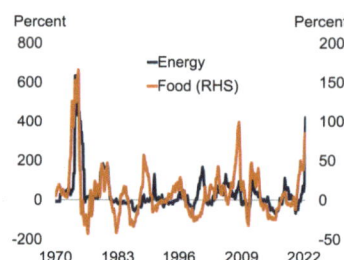

C. Interest rates

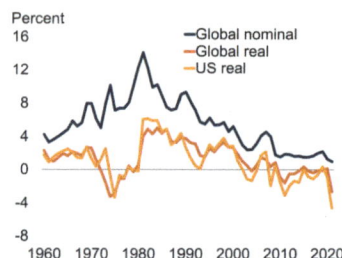

D. Real interest rates

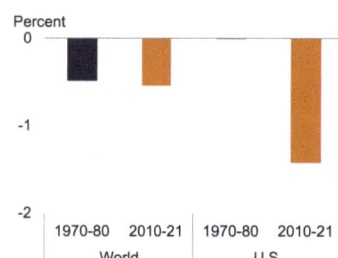

E. Magnitude of rate hikes and core CPI over previous U.S. Federal Reserve tightening cycles

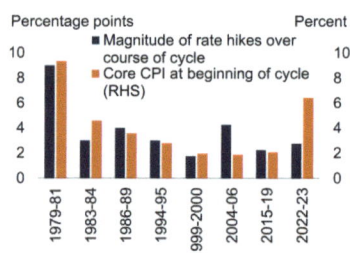

F. Slowdowns in growth after global recessions

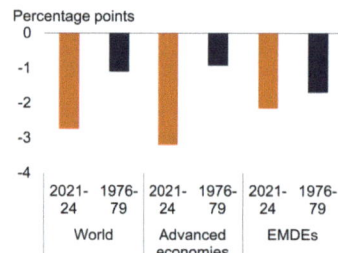

Sources: Federal Reserve Economic Data; Haver Analytics; World Bank.
Note: CPI = consumer price index.; EMDEs = emerging market and developing economies.
A. Nominal and real crude oil prices (averages of Dubai, Brent, and WTI prices). Real oil prices are deflated by U.S. CPI index (March 2022 = 100).
B. Percent change in monthly energy and food price indices over a 24-month period. Because of data limitations, prior to 1979, the energy price change is proxied using the oil price change.
C. D. Figure shows nominal and real (CPI-adjusted) short-term interest rates (Treasury bill rates or money market rates, with the maturity of three months or less). Global interest rates are weighted by GDP in U.S. dollars. Sample includes 113 countries, though the sample size varies by year.
E. Blue bars show the extent of policy rate increases during previous tightening cycles: 1979-81, 1983-84, 1986-89, 1994-95, 1999-2000, 2004-06, 2015-19. Value for 2023 is an estimate based on market expectations for the level of the Fed Funds rate in mid-2023. Core CPI for 2022-23 shows latest data associated with tightening cycle.
F. Figure shows changes in global growth (in percentage points) between 2021-24 and 1976-79; covers three years following a rebound from a global recession.

recession of 2020, just as it did during the stagflationary period after the global recession in 1975 (figure SF1.4.F).[8] While the inflation run-up since the 2020 global recession triggered by the COVID-19 pandemic has been less steep than that after the 1975 recession, the projected growth slowdown is considerably steeper. Between 2021 and 2024, global growth is projected to slow by 2.7 percentage points, more than twice as much as between 1976 and 1979. The slowdown is expected to be particularly pronounced for advanced economies, but it will also be significant for EMDEs. This slowdown mostly represents a return to potential growth after the post-recession rebound, which reflected the response to massive policy stimulus.

Over the 2020s as a whole, potential global growth is expected to slow 0.6 percentage point below the 2010s average. This structural weakening would resemble the prolonged growth slowdown during the stagflation of the 1970s. For comparison, annual average global growth slowed by 1.2 percentage point between the 1960s and 1970s and by another 1.1 percentage point during the 1980s (to 3 percent on average, Kose, Sugawara and Terrones 2021).[9] The current juncture also invites comparisons to the persistent overestimation of potential growth and underestimation of output gaps in the 1970s.[10]

[8] The global recession of 1975 followed the first major oil price shock the world economy had ever experienced (Kose and Terrones 2015). Oil prices shot up fourfold following the OPEC's oil embargo that began in October 1973. Although the embargo ended in March 1974, the supply shock associated with the sharp rise in oil prices quickly translated into a substantial increase in inflation and a deep contraction in output in a number of countries.

[9] This trend slowdown in global potential growth has also been reflected in a steady decline in the neutral real interest rate (Holston, Laubach, and Williams 2017). The gap between actual real interest rates and neutral real interest rates proxies the degree of monetary policy accommodation. Although real interest rates now are much more deeply negative (-3.4 percent in the 2020s) than in the 1970s (nil on average), the gap to the respective neutral rates (4.3 percent in the 1970s, 0.4 percent in the 2020s) is similar. Since the neutral interest rate is unobservable, its estimates are highly uncertain; depend on macroeconomic forces, policy regimes, and estimation approach; and have only a tenuous link to trend output growth (Brand, Bielecki, and Penalver 2018; Clark and Kozicki 2005; Hamilton et al. 2016; Summers and Rachel 2019).

[10] Some researchers discussed the roles of overoptimistic assessment of the output gap associated with the productivity slowdown of the late 1960s and early 1970s in driving inflation and monetary policy decisions (DeLong 1997, Orphanides 2003, and Blinder and Rudd 2013).

Significant EMDE vulnerabilities. In the 1970s and early 1980s, as now, high debt, elevated inflation and weak fiscal positions made EMDEs vulnerable to tightening financial conditions. The stagflation of the 1970s coincided with the first global wave of debt accumulation of the modern era (figures SF1.5.A and SF1.5.B; Kose et al. 2020).[11] Low global real interest rates and the rapid development of syndicated loan markets encouraged a surge in EMDE debt, especially in Latin America and many low-income countries (LICs), especially in Sub-Saharan Africa. In Latin America, total external debt rose by 12 percentage points of GDP over the course of the decade while, in LICs, it rose by 18 percentage points of GDP. Much of this debt was in foreign currency and short-term, as capital flowed from oil exporters to EMDEs with large fiscal and current account deficits (figure SF1.5.C). When major advanced-economy central banks—and especially the U.S. Federal Reserve—started to forcefully tighten monetary policy in the late 1970s to stem inflation, a series of debt crises erupted (figure SF1.5.D).

By comparison, the 2010s featured the fourth (and current) wave of global debt accumulation involving the largest, fastest, and most broad-based increase in government debt by EMDEs in the past 50 years. A number of LICs are already either in or near debt distress. The sheer magnitude and speed of the debt buildup heightens the associated risks. Additional vulnerabilities have arisen from increased exposure to nontraditional official creditors and to commercial debt (Kose et al. 2021). This, combined with the risk that inflation pressures will force steep monetary policy tightening among major advanced economies, raises the specter of a renewed series of financial crises in EMDEs, as in the 1980s.

Differences from the 1970s

There are some important cyclical and structural differences between the 1970s and the current situation.

FIGURE SF1.5 EMDE vulnerabilities

Previous waves of debt accumulation ended when real interest rates rose. In the 1970s, high debt, elevated inflation, and weak fiscal positions made EMDEs vulnerable to rising borrowing costs.

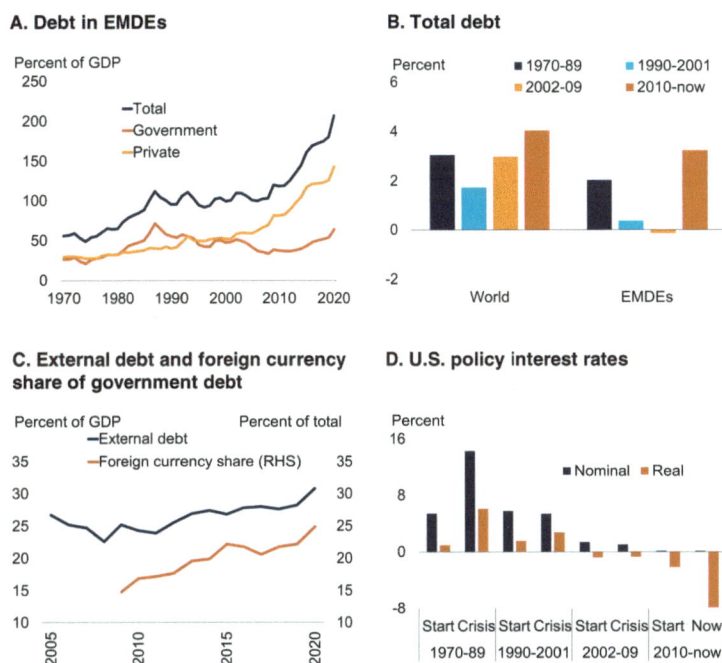

A. Debt in EMDEs

B. Total debt

C. External debt and foreign currency share of government debt

D. U.S. policy interest rates

Sources: Haver Analytics; International Monetary Fund; Kose et al. (2020); Kose, Sugawara, and Terrones (2021); World Bank.
Note: EMDEs = emerging market and developing economies.
A.B. GDP-weighted averages based on a sample of up to 153 EMDEs.
C. External debt (percent of GDP) is based on GDP-weighted average of up to 137 EMDEs. Foreign currency share of government debt is an average of up to 36 EMDEs.
D. Based on quarterly data. Start of a wave defined as the first three years of the wave. Crisis defined as the year before, and year of, widespread crises. First wave: 1970-72 and 1981-82; second wave: 1990-92 and 1996-97; third wave: 2002-04 and 2008-09; and fourth wave: 2010-12. The latest data (data for "now" in the fourth wave) are as of 2022Q1. Real interest rates are deflated by consumer price index.

Smaller shocks. At least thus far, the magnitude of commodity price jumps has been smaller than in the 1970s. In the wake of the two major oil crises, oil prices quadrupled (in U.S. dollar terms) in 1973-74 and doubled in 1979-80. As of May 2022, oil prices have roughly tripled from their lows of early 2020 and doubled since early 2021, but to a level that is still only about two-thirds of those in 1980. For now, global inflation in 2022 is still less broad-based than it was in the 1970s, and core inflation has remained relatively low in most countries, even if it has recently picked up.[12] This stands in contrast to 1979-80, when a steep global

---

[11] There have been four waves of broad-based debt buildup in EMDEs since 1970: 1970-89; 1990-2001; 2002-09; 2010 onwards.

[12] The Unites States is an exception among advanced economies in its much broader-based inflation pressures.

FIGURE SF1.6 Developments in the 1970s and 2020s: Cyclical differences

Inflation is still lower and less broad-based than in the 1970s. Wage growth and unemployment rates are mostly still below those in the 1970s.

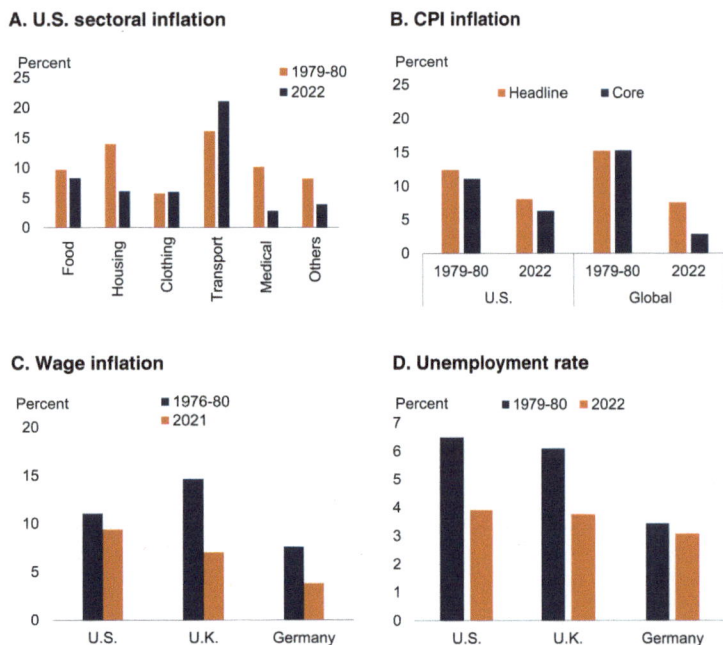

A. U.S. sectoral inflation

B. CPI inflation

C. Wage inflation

D. Unemployment rate

Sources: Haver Analytics; International Monetary Fund; OECD; World Bank.
Note: CPI: consumer price index.
A. Sectoral CPI inflation (monthly averages of year-on-year inflation) in the United States. 2022 is based on the averages of January to April 2022. "Others" includes communication, recreation, education, restaurants, and miscellaneous sectors.
B. Annual averages of headline and core CPI inflation in the United States and global (average across 66 countries). 2022 is based on the averages of January to April 2022.
C.D. Annual averages of wage growth (C) or unemployment rate (D). 2022 is based on the averages of January to April 2022.

inflation acceleration was broad-based across virtually all sectors (figures SF1.6.A and SF1.6.B). High inflation in some sectors is expected to return to low levels once supply disruptions ease and commodity prices stabilize (Ilzetzki 2022). However, the rate of unemployment is lower now than it was at the end of the 1970s implying potentially even larger wage and price pressures (figures SF1.6.C and SF1.6.D).

More credible monetary policy frameworks. Monetary policy frameworks have become increasingly focused on price stability over time. In the 1970s, central banks often faced competing objectives—aiming for both high output and employment, as well as for price stability. Monetary policy in the 1970s, in particular in the

United States, has been described as "go/stop" policy that oscillated between concerns about unemployment and inflation and, with the benefit of hindsight, ended up being accommodative (Blinder 1979; Goodfriend 2004). Many central banks in advanced economies, freed in 1971 from the constraints of the Bretton Woods system of fixed exchange rates, aimed to support economic activity with monetary expansion, without realizing that potential output growth had started to slow (DeLong 1997). Monetary policy was guided by a naïve view of the Phillips curve, which suggested tradeoffs between unemployment and inflation that could be exploited for policy purposes (Bernanke 2003).[13] Policy makers tended to attribute rising inflation to special factors, and underestimated the size of demand pressures and the persistence of inflation (Blinder 1979; Primiceri 2006).

The vast majority of EMDE central banks sought to maintain exchange rate pegs or tightly managed exchange rate regimes to anchor inflation during 1950-1980 (Ilzetzki, Reinhart, and Rogoff 2019). These central banks did not have operational independence but often dealt with challenges associated with high inflation, partly driven by chronic fiscal imbalances. In EMDEs, the financial sector was repressed as uncompetitive or government-owned banks kept nominal interest rates artificially low. International capital flows were also subject to controls (Frankel 2010).

In contrast, central banks in advanced economies and many EMDEs now have clear mandates for price stability, typically expressed as an explicit

---

[13] What became apparent over the 1970s was that the relationship between unemployment and inflation was unstable because changes in inflation expectations, so that a given level of unemployment could be accompanied by any number of inflation outcomes (Friedman 1968; Kuttner and Robinson 2010; Phelps 1968). As a result, central banks today estimate the Phillips curve using the concept of the non-accelerating inflation rate of unemployment, the NAIRU, and take into account inflation expectations (Tootell 1994; Coibion et al. 2018). They no longer consider themselves able to permanently change unemployment (that is, change the NAIRU) but instead focus on achieving inflation targets (Gordon 2011). In the United Kingdom, monetary policy was less reliant on the Phillips curve as a policy tool but generally skeptical of a major role for monetary policy as a driver of inflation (Nelson 2001, Nelson and Nikolov 2004).

inflation target (figure SF1.7.A). They have adopted transparent operating procedures, announcing and justifying their settings for the policy rate after regularly scheduled monetary policy decision meetings. Over the past three decades, many have established a credible track record of achieving their inflation targets (Bordo et al. 2007; Eichengreen 2022).

Better-anchored inflation expectations. As a result of improvements in policy frameworks and better anchored inflation expectations, inflation—in particular core inflation—has become much less sensitive to inflation surprises (figure SF1.7.B). The correlation of core inflation with import prices or producer prices, which are more sensitive to commodity price shocks, has declined significantly over time, despite continued high correlation between headline CPI inflation and PPI and import price inflation. This weakened correlation is also consistent with better-anchored inflation expectations (Ha, Kose, and Ohnsorge 2019). Similarly, the response of inflation expectations to inflation surprises, another indicator of the strength of the anchoring of inflation expectations, has fallen sharply over the past two decades, especially in advanced economies.

More flexible economies. The 1970s were a time of considerable structural economic rigidities, many of which have since been changed. In the average OECD country, collective bargaining covered four-fifths of employees; and the use of income and price policies as an instrument of inflation control (purportedly to help maintain low unemployment) was widespread among advanced economies, with price and wage controls were put in place in the United States in response to the oil price shock of 1973 (figure SF1.7.C).[14] In 1973, interest rate and credit controls were in place in all but three OECD countries and all EMDEs with available data had interest rate controls and all but one maintained credit controls (Abiad, Detragiache, and Tressel 2010).

FIGURE SF1.7 Developments in the 1970s and 2020s: Structural differences

Inflation expectations are better anchored than in the 1970s. Inflation targeting and lower energy intensity may help contain the transmission of surging global energy prices into core inflation. Wage-setting arrangements are less centralized now than in the 1970s.

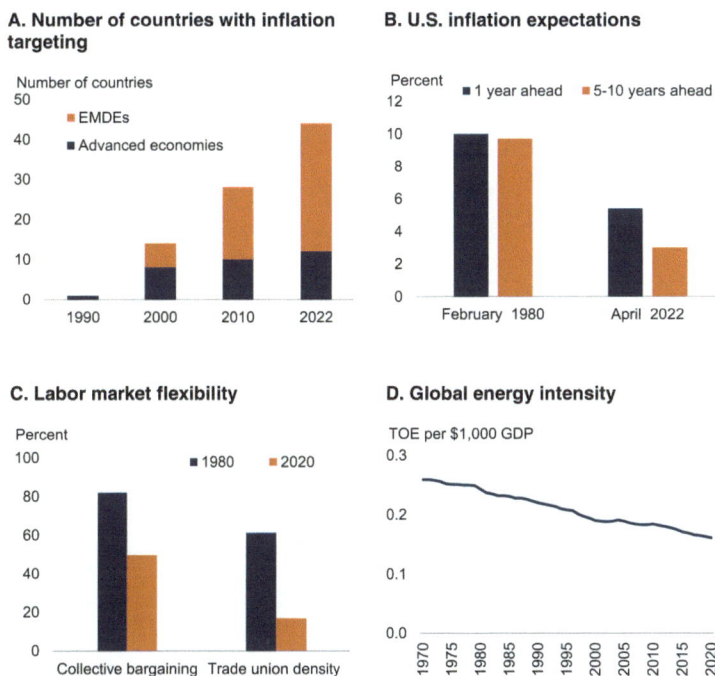

A. Number of countries with inflation targeting

B. U.S. inflation expectations

C. Labor market flexibility

D. Global energy intensity

Sources: BP Statistical Review; Haver Analytics; OECD; U.S. Energy Information Administration; World Bank.
Note: TOE=Tonnes of oil equivalent.
A. Based on the clarification of IMF *Annual Report on Exchange Arrangements and Exchange Restrictions* and country-specific sources.
B. U.S. consumer inflation expectations based on April 2022 University of Michigan survey.
C. Collective bargaining rates indicate percent of employees with bargaining powers. Trade union density rates indicate the number of union members as a percent of total employees. Aggregation is based on median across a balanced set of 25 economies.
D. Energy includes coal, natural gas, and oil. TOE stands for tonnes (metric tons) of oil equivalent. Aggregates calculated using GDP weights at average 2010-19 prices and market exchange rates.

The intervening decades have seen sweeping liberalizations of labor, product, and financial markets. By 2020, only half of employees in OECD countries were covered by collective bargaining; and by 2018, product market regulations had eased such that the OECD's product market regulation index has fallen to two-thirds its level two decades previously (Égert and Wanner 2016; OECD 2019). By 2005, interest rate and credit controls had been entirely eliminated in all but five OECD countries; interest rate controls had been removed in about three-quarters of EMDEs and credit controls in

---

[14] In the United States, in addition to rising energy and food prices, the relaxation of wage and price controls in 1973 also contributed to a jump in inflation in the early 1970s (Blinder 1982).

almost one-half (Abiad, Detragiache, and Tressel 2010; Calice, Diaz-Kalan, and Masetti 2020). Today's greater economic flexibility, with less centralized wage setting and less financial repression, allow a faster supply and demand response in sectors where prices are rising particularly rapidly and reduce the likelihood of price-wage spirals becoming entrenched.

In addition, the energy intensity of GDP has fallen considerably since the 1970s (figure SF1.7.D; World Bank 2022a; Igan et al. 2022). In advanced economies and EMDEs, energy efficiency has increased, with a steady decline in the amount of energy needed to generate a dollar of income. Oil-importing countries have taken numerous steps to reduce their vulnerability to energy shocks. Instead of oil, they have substituted other sources such as natural gas and renewables, including solar and wind.

Less fiscal accommodation. The 1960s and 1970s were marked by expansionary fiscal policy. In contrast, fiscal policy tightening is expected in coming years as governments withdraw the unprecedented fiscal support provided during the pandemic. In the two dozen advanced economies with available data, primary fiscal balances weakened by 1.5-6.5 percentage points of GDP and government spending rose by 5-25 percentage points of GDP over the course of the 1970s.[15] In contrast, today, fiscal policy is expected to tighten in advanced economies over the forecast horizon, as governments unwind fiscal support in 2020 that averaged 29 percent of GDP in advanced economies and 7 percent of GDP in EMDEs (World Bank 2022b). By 2023, two-thirds of advanced economies are expected to have unwound most of this stimulus and, by 2024, two-thirds of EMDEs are expected to have done so. This is likely to constitute a major brake on demand growth and help moderate price pressures.

End of stagflation of the 1970s and lessons for today

Policy tightening in the late 1970s and early 1980s to contain high inflation played a major role in triggering a global recession in 1982 and financial crises in EMDEs. This experience illustrates the risk of inflation remaining elevated amid weak growth, forcing a strong monetary policy response, and triggering a global recession and financial crises among the EMDEs. A key lesson from the 1970s is that central banks need to act in a pre-emptive manner to avoid a loss of confidence in their commitment to maintaining low inflation—specified today in their inflation targets—and to prevent a de-anchoring of inflation expectations. Fiscal policy also needs to do its part, not least since monetary policy will struggle to be credible if fiscal positions are unsustainable.

Aftermath of high inflation in the 1970s

Recessions in advanced economies. Eventually, in the late 1970s and early 1980s, monetary policy tightening—guided by prioritization of the aim of restoring price stability—reduced inflation in advanced economies to a median of 3 percent in 1986 from its peak of 15 percent in 1974, and established central bank credibility, although often at the cost of deep recessions with high unemployment.[16] In the United States, for example, short-term interest rates almost doubled between early 1979 and mid-1981, with the federal funds rate reaching a peak of 19.1 percent. In the wake of these interest rate increases, U.S. output contracted by more than 2 percent between early 1981 and mid-1982 and unemployment reached a peak of 10.8 percent in late 1982. The sharp increase in policy rates in the United States coincided with a synchronized decline in global activity and played a major role in triggering the 1982 global recession (figures SF1.8.A and SF1.8.B; Kose and Terrones 2015). In advanced-economy Europe, some central banks had prioritized inflation control early, and had

---

[15] Fiscal policy volatility was substantial in the United States during 1960-80. Great Society spending in the early 1960s was compounded by Vietnam war spending in the mid-1960s, only partially unwound with the 1968 tax surcharge to rein in inflation, followed by social spending in the run-up to the 1972 presidential election and a tax cut in 1975 to spur a recovery, and then followed by fiscal consolidation amid concerns about inflation (Blinder 2004).

[16] In addition to the United States, many advanced economies tightened monetary policy during this period, including Austria, Canada, Germany, and the United Kingdom.

responded earlier to rising inflation. As a result, in these countries, peak inflation was lower than in the United States, although the inflation declines were also accompanied by tighter monetary policy and recessions in the early 1980s.[17]

Financial crises in EMDEs. While inflation in advanced economies generally declined after the 1982 global recession, it remained high in EMDEs throughout the 1980s and was accompanied by financial crises (figure SF1.8.C). A number of Latin American countries and LICs were particularly vulnerable to rising borrowing costs because they had had accumulated large debts during the 1970s (mainly funded from the windfall reaped by the oil-exporting countries from high world oil prices). The sharp increase in global interest rates and the collapse of commodity prices in the early 1980s made servicing this debt very difficult (Arteta et al. 2015). Amid a contraction in global trade during the 1982 global recession, Mexico's default in August of that year marked the beginning of the Latin American debt crisis and the region's "lost decade." In LICs, especially in Sub-Saharan Africa, levels of debt were much lower in nominal terms than in Latin America, although they became very high relative to GDP over the same period. Many of these countries also experienced financial stress and faced sovereign debt crises in the 1980s.

Implications for the 2020s

In the near-term, inflation is likely to remain elevated as recent demand and supply shocks continue to affect wage and price setting. But there are reasons to expect that these pressures will prove temporary. Unlike the situation in the

---

[17] Central banks in Germany, Austria, and Switzerland, in particular, operated more transparent and discretionary monetary policies, based partly on their historical experiences of high inflation, compared with other advanced economies (Laubach and Posen 1997). The central banks in these countries kept money supply growth, their main monetary policy tool at the time, lower than in the United States and other major European countries. This resulted in lower inflation in these countries in the late 1970s—on average 2-5 percent in 1976-80—than in the United States (9 percent), the United Kingdom (14 percent), Italy (16 percent), and France (11 percent). Over the same period, output growth in these countries was about 3 percent, comparable to that in the United States and other major European countries.

FIGURE SF1.8 End of stagflation of the 1970s and vulnerabilities in EMDEs

Policy tightening in the late 1970s and early 1980s to contain high inflation contributed to a highly synchronized downturn in growth in many countries and a global recession in 1982. The global recession was followed by financial crises in EMDEs in the 1980s and 1990s. Because of high debt and sizable fiscal and current account deficits, there is a danger that financial stresses will again emerge in EMDEs.

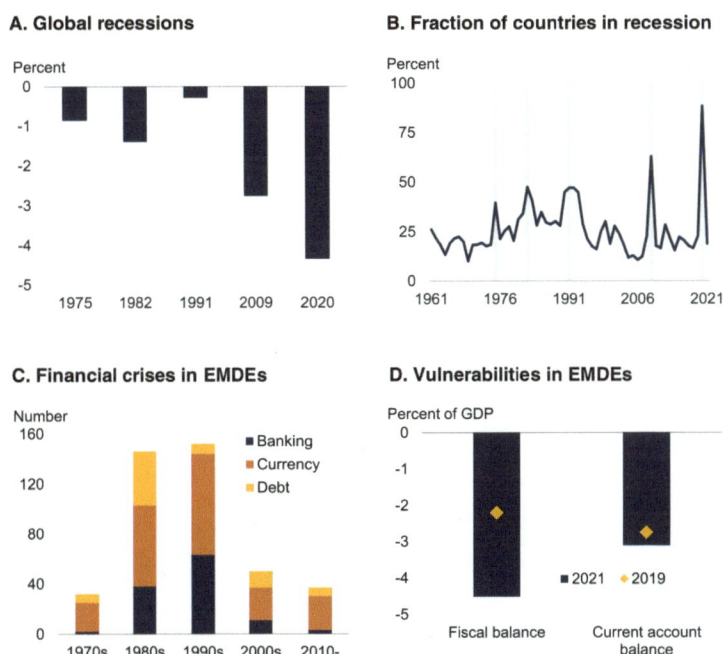

A. Global recessions

B. Fraction of countries in recession

C. Financial crises in EMDEs

D. Vulnerabilities in EMDEs

Sources: Kose, Sugawara, and Terrones (2020); Haver Analytics; International Monetary Fund; Laeven and Valencia (2020); World Bank.
Note:
A. Figure shows global per capita GDP growth in the years of global recessions since 1960.
B. Share of countries in recession, defined as a contraction in per capita GDP.
C. Total number of banking, currency, and sovereign debt crises in EMDEs over respective periods.
D. Medians based on a sample of up to 155 EMDEs.

1970s, central banks have well-established inflation targets, strengthened operational autonomy and, in many cases, substantial credibility built up over several decades. Inflation expectations are therefore more likely to remain well anchored, especially if central banks signal their resolve to contain price pressures (Armantier et al. 2022; Bordo and Orphanides 2013). As central banks tighten monetary policy and pandemic-related fiscal stimulus is unwound, demand pressures will moderate; as the supply disruptions caused by Russia's invasion of Ukraine are priced in, commodity prices will stabilize, albeit at high levels; and as global production lines and logistics adjust, supply bottlenecks will ease (Ilzetzki 2022; Reifenschneider and Wilcox 2022; World Bank 2022a).

However, the experience of the 1970s is a reminder that there is still a considerable risk that inflation remains high or continues to rise. First, there could be further supply shocks which could cause repeated inflation overshoots that may eventually de-anchor inflation expectations.

Second, central banks could fail to reach their inflation targets often or long enough that the public loses confidence in their commitment or ability to maintain price stability. While wage growth thus far has generally been moderate outside the United States, higher inflation expectations could eventually raise it and become entrenched in institutional arrangements such as automatic indexation and cost-of-living adjustments (Boissay et al. 2022).

Structural forces of disinflation

In addition to these short-term risks to inflation, the structural forces that have depressed inflation over recent decades may fade. Demographic changes, technological advances, globalization, and structural changes were instrumental in keeping inflation low over the past three decades (Ha, Kose, and Ohnsorge 2022). Should these forces recede, increases in short-term inflation may become more persistent, and thus threaten the anchoring of long-term inflation expectations (Gersbach 2021; Rogoff 2003, 2014).

While all these structural factors have been credited with contributing to the decline in inflation over the past three decades, the magnitudes of their effects remain poorly understood. These forces could also interact with cyclical shocks that could generate unpredictable swings in inflation.

Demographic changes. Rapid labor force growth, due to population growth and increased participation of women, helped dampen increases in wages and input costs (Goodhart and Pradhan 2020). There is possibility that the disinflationary benefits reaped from this process are now at an inflection

point as the share of the working-age population stabilizes even in EMDEs (World Bank 2018).

Technological advances. Automation, the increasing adaptability of computers, robotics, and artificial intelligence have improved production processes in many sectors. These factors have lowered demand for routine production and clerical workers and lowered wage and price pressures (Autor, Dorn, and Hanson 2015). In some advanced economies, disinflation has also been attributed to price transparency and competitive pressures introduced by the growing digitalization of services (Goolsbee and Klenow 2018; Dong, Fudurich, and Suchanek 2017). It is possible that the biggest gains from such technological advanced have now been exhausted and future progress will be slower.

Globalization. Over the past three decades, the entry of China and Eastern Europe into the global trading system has greatly reduced the prices of many manufactured goods. Over the past decade, however, the maturing of global value chains appears to have contributed to slowing trade growth (World Bank 2020b). New tariffs and import restrictions, rising protectionist sentiment and growing geopolitical risks may eventually slow or even reverse the pace of globalization and its disinflationary impact.

Sectoral shifts. In EMDEs, the large-scale shift of resources from agriculture to higher productivity employment in manufacturing offered productivity gains (Dieppe 2021). The momentum for such shifts has already slowed over the past decade and may slow further over the next decade. As this process slows, its disinflationary impacts may recede.

Policy frameworks. Over the past four decades, many advanced economies and EMDEs implemented macroeconomic stabilization programs and structural reforms, improved fiscal frameworks, and gave their central banks clear mandates to control inflation. Mounting public and private debt in EMDEs or populist sentiment could weaken commitment to disciplined fiscal and monetary policy frameworks (Ha and Kindberg-Hanlon 2021; Kose et al. 2019).

Challenges for EMDEs

In response to intensifying inflationary risks, major advanced-economy central banks have already begun to tighten policy. Buttressed by decades of building inflation-fighting credibility, well-calibrated interest rate changes and adjustments to long-term asset holdings should engineer a soft landing, in which a reduction in inflation is achieved without a recession. However, even in such a benign disinflationary scenario, EMDEs may face significant challenges.

Weaker anchoring of inflation expectations. The sensitivity of long-term inflation expectations to inflation surprises—the lack of anchoring of inflation expectations—is greater in EMDEs than in advanced economies although, in both country groups, it has declined over the past several decades (figures SF1.9.A and SF1.9.B).[18] In the median advanced economy, the sensitivity of inflation expectations to inflation surprises has declined to essentially zero and inflation expectations are pinned close to 2 percent. However, in EMDEs, inflation expectations have remained more sensitive to inflation surprises (figure SF1.9.C).

Since the beginning of the pandemic, there have been marked increases in inflation and medium-term inflation expectations in many EMDEs in Europe and Central Asia, Latin America and the Caribbean, and South Asia, while expectations remained stable or even declined in EMDEs in East Asia and Pacific and Middle East and North Africa (figure SF1.9.D). The risk remains that the energy and food price increases triggered by Russia's invasion of Ukraine, or the supply disruptions triggered by the renewed pandemic outbreaks and pandemic control measures in China, will lead to further increases in long-term inflation expectations among EMDEs.

FIGURE SF1.9 Long-term inflation expectations

Long-term inflation expectations have declined and become better anchored over the past three decades. However, in EMDEs, they remain sensitive to inflation surprises and have recently begun to rise in some EMDE regions.

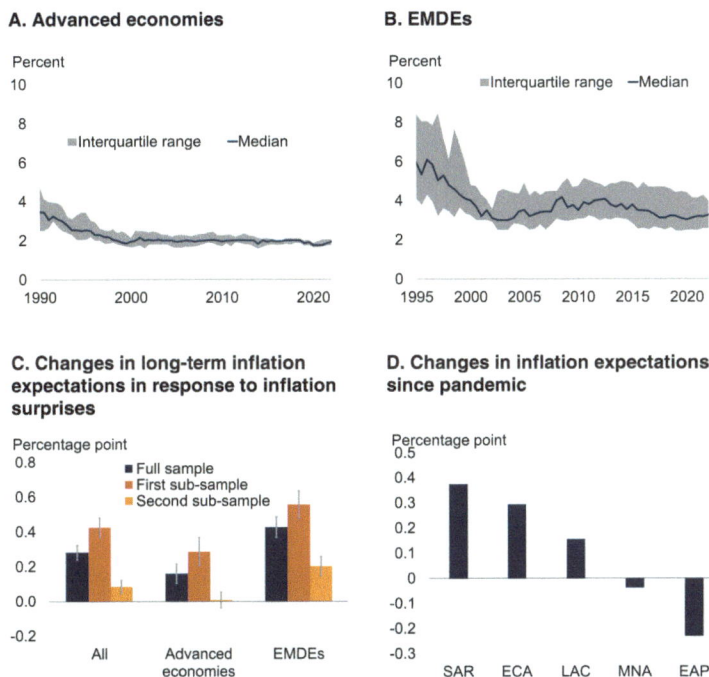

A. Advanced economies

B. EMDEs

C. Changes in long-term inflation expectations in response to inflation surprises

D. Changes in inflation expectations since pandemic

Sources: Consensus Economics; Kose et al. (2019); World Bank.
Note: EMDEs = emerging market and developing economies. Inflation expectations are five-year-ahead expectations of annual inflation.
A.B.D. Based on a sample of 24 advanced economies for 1990H1-2022H1 (A) and 20 EMDEs for 1995H1-2022H1 (B).
C. Inflation surprises are defined as the difference between realized inflation and short-term inflation expectations in the previous period (that is, six months prior). Sensitivity is estimated using a panel regression of the change in five-year-ahead inflation expectations on inflation shocks. Bars denote medians and vertical lines denote 90 percent confidence intervals of the regression coefficients. The regression is based on a sample of 24 advanced economies and 23 EMDEs. Full sample refers to 1990-2018, divided into first (1990-2004) and second (2005-2018) subsamples.
D. Bars show changes in the inflation expectations since the beginning of the COVID-19 pandemic, by five EMDE regions. EAP = East Asia and Pacific, ECA = Europe and Central Asia, LAC = Latin America and the Caribbean, MNA = Middle East and North Africa, SAR = South Asia.

Concerned about weak anchoring and rising inflation expectations, most inflation-targeting EMDEs began to tighten monetary policy much earlier than advanced economies, a few of them already in late 2020. To the extent that recent commodity price rises lead to broader price increases and work their way into core inflation, EMDE central banks will likely need to continue tightening policy to contain inflation expectations. This tightening of policy is taking place well before their economic recoveries from the pandemic are complete and will slow the return to full employment.

---

[18] Following Gürkaynak, Levin, and Swanson (2010) and Beechey, Johannsen, and Levin (2011), Kose et al. (2019) assess the anchoring of inflation expectations by measuring the sensitivity of five-year-ahead inflation expectations to inflation surprises—defined as the difference between realized inflation and inflation expectations in the previous period. They report that for a 1 percentage point positive inflation surprise, in a typical EMDE, inflation expectations were revised up by about 0.2 percentage point six months later.

Financial vulnerabilities. Should inflation turn out to be more persistent or higher than currently anticipated, advanced-economy central banks may tighten monetary policy faster, or over a longer period, than currently expected. In the past, unexpectedly rapid policy tightening has tended to put downward pressure on asset prices and led to capital outflows and currency depreciation pressures, with especially adverse consequences for EMDEs. Coupled with high debt and sizable fiscal and current account deficits of many EMDEs, there is a danger that financial stresses will emerge in these economies and further hold back their recoveries from the pandemic (figure SF1.8.D; Hoek, Kamin, and Yoldas 2020, 2021). These risks are particularly acute among those EMDEs with large current account deficits and a heavy reliance on foreign capital inflows, as well as EMDEs with high levels of short-term or foreign-currency denominated government or private debt.

Increasingly influential global inflation cycle. In the 1970s, global inflationary pressures also led to a significant increase in EMDE inflation, including in those economies that had experienced low and stable inflation in the late 1960s and early 1970s (Cline 1981). During the 1970s stagflation, about two-thirds of EMDEs experienced a synchronized increase in inflation. Since then, inflation has become even more globally synchronized. The contribution of global factors to domestic inflation variation has doubled over the recent two decades (based on the median contribution across a large group of 99 countries) and now accounts for 22 percent of inflation variation (Ha, Kose, and Ohnsorge 2019b). Partly reflecting the increased influence of the global inflation cycle, inflation rates rose in almost all EMDEs in 2021 (from the previous year), and three-quarters of them are experiencing even higher inflation this year. Central banks in about two-fifths of EMDEs—in particular those in inflation-targeting countries—raised policy rates in 2021. Many more EMDEs have started tightening monetary policy in 2022. For EMDE central banks wishing to bring down domestic inflation, persistently high global inflation could require them to tighten monetary policy more forcefully than otherwise.

Policy options for EMDEs

A protracted period of weak growth likely lies ahead for the 2020s as the fundamental drivers of growth continue to weaken. In addition, a prolonged period of high inflation may be in store, unless central banks act promptly and decisively to stem persistent price pressures. The implication is that EMDE policy makers are facing the first significant global monetary policy tightening cycle after more than a decade of highly accommodative external financial conditions and in the midst of a major energy and food price shock. Amid deteriorating growth prospects and until inflation is reined in again, they may need to adjust to more expensive borrowing terms.

EMDE commodity exporters and importers may face somewhat different policy challenges. Commodity importers may need to contain inflation pressures without unduly dampening growth while at the same time containing fiscal and external pressures resulting from high commodity prices. Commodity exporters may need to be more aggressive in containing inflationary pressures in the face of rapidly expanding resource sectors.

Low-income countries face additional challenges because of the impact of double-digit food price inflation on food insecurity and poverty (World Bank 2022b). Broader policy efforts aimed at protecting the poorest, strengthening fiscal and monetary policy frameworks, and improving debt management are required in these economies.

Notwithstanding differences in some of the specifics of these policy challenges, EMDE policies will require careful *calibration*, *credible* formulation, and clear *communication* (Ha, Kose, and Ohnsorge 2022; Orphanides and Williams 2013). This approach can go a long way in making these economies more resilient to sudden shifts in global financial markets.

Monetary policy. Calibrating policy levers to get ahead of inflation without stifling the recovery will be key. Many EMDEs already began tightening monetary policy in 2021, to contain increases in inflation. Communicating monetary policy decisions clearly, leveraging credible monetary frameworks, and safeguarding central bank independence will be critical for EMDEs to manage the cycle. To reinforce the anchor of low inflation expectations, policy makers need to communicate clearly not only with financial markets but also with households and firms so that inflationary pressures do not translate into destabilizing increases in wages and production costs (Coibion et al. 2022; D'Acunto and Weber 2022).

Financial policies. Policy makers need to rebuild foreign exchange reserve buffers and realign prudential policy to prepare for potential financial stress. Such policies could also help dampen demand pressures. During the pandemic, at least three-fourths of EMDEs implemented regulatory forbearance measures to prevent a credit crunch. Many governments supported lending to firms to address liquidity constraints through loan guarantees and payment moratoria (World Bank 2022c). In light of these earlier interventions and rising risks, banking system exposures to exchange rate risk and rollover risk need to be monitored carefully and, if necessary, contained through macro- and micro-prudential policies. Credit quality and nonperforming loans need to be reported transparently such that prompt corrective action can be taken. Banks' capital and liquidity buffers need to be sufficiently sound to be able to absorb shocks. If deployed appropriately, foreign currency reserves can help stem temporary exchange rate pressures.

Fiscal policy. The pace and magnitude of withdrawal of fiscal support must be finely calibrated and closely aligned with credible medium-term fiscal plans. Fiscal balances deteriorated sharply during the pandemic, and these deteriorations will not have fully returned to pre-pandemic levels by 2022. EMDE fiscal deficits are still 1.1 percentage points of GDP wider than in 2019 and government debt is 10 percentage points of GDP higher. In part to contain the fiscal deteriorations, EMDEs already tightened fiscal policy in 2021, unwinding about one-half of the 2020 fiscal impulse. Policy makers need to address

investor concerns about long-run debt sustainability by strengthening fiscal frameworks, enhancing debt transparency, upgrading debt management functions, and improving revenue collection and spending efficiency. Inflation expectations are unlikely to be well anchored if there are concerns about long-term fiscal sustainability because of fears that monetary policy is constrained, especially in cases where high interest rates imply unstable public debt dynamics.

Structural policies. Export restrictions and disrupted global food markets due to the war in Ukraine are expected to contribute to rising global food inflation. The use of trade policy interventions and price controls to insulate domestic markets from food price shocks could compound the volatility of international prices and lead to even higher domestic prices (Laborde, Lakatos, and Martin 2019). To help alleviate the consequences of food price volatility on the poor, EMDE policy makers need to strengthen social safety nets and enhance the resilience of food production and distribution systems, while refraining from price control measures. Price controls tend to distort markets, have adverse consequences for growth and poverty reduction, and often prove difficult to roll back after price pressures ease (Guenette 2020). If price controls or untargeted subsidies are unavoidable, their longer-term damage can be contained if they are introduced with automatic sunset clauses. Moreover, in the medium-term, policy measures that increase productivity and tackle supply chain disruptions can support higher growth and help reduce price pressures (Baqaee and Farhi 2022; Dieppe 2020).

These policy interventions are easier said than implemented, especially when fiscal space is limited and financial vulnerabilities are prominent. However, sticking to the basic principles of policy making—carefully *calibrating* and clearly *communicating* cyclical policies within *credible* policy frameworks—can pay large dividends in making EMDEs more resilient as they navigate stagflationary pressures.

ANNEX SF1.1 Methodology: Decomposing inflation

This annex briefly presents a novel factor-augmented vector autoregression (FAVAR) model. The empirical framework is based on recent studies that employ standard sign-restricted VAR models to explore the drivers of global inflation (Charnavoki and Dolado 2014; Ha, Kose, et al. 2019; Ha, Kose, and Ohnsorge 2021a), or more generally, the Philips-curve framework (Forbes 2019). However, it deviates from these approaches in three ways to accommodate the circumstances of the 2020 pandemic.

First, the model employs higher-frequency (monthly) data rather than quarterly or annual data, to minimize the concerns over the endogeneity among variables. The use of monthly data is particularly important when the pace of recessions and recoveries differs. That said, monthly data are available only for a smaller set of countries for services activity. Therefore, the exercise with monthly data relies on industrial production series, which rebounded faster than services from the global recession of 2020.

Second, on top of the standard sign restrictions, an additional set of narrative restrictions is imposed for the periods of large oil price fluctuations. The sign restrictions are not sufficient to identify the structural shocks, in particular in the presence of multiple large shocks. Third, the model allows for time-varying volatility in the global variables.

Model specification

The model consists of three global variables: global inflation, global output growth, and oil price growth. All variables are detrended such that, effectively global output proxies the output gap. Global output growth and global inflation are proxied by the global industrial production growth and global inflation factors estimated separately using the following dynamic factor models:

$$\pi_t^i = \beta_{global}^{\pi,i} f_t^{\pi,global} + e_t^{\pi,i}$$

$$Y_t^i = \beta_{global}^{Y,i} f_t^{Y,global} + e_t^{Y,i}$$

where Y_t^i and π_t^i are output growth and inflation in country i in month t, respectively, while $f_t^{\pi,global}$ and $f_t^{Y,global}$ are the global factors for inflation and output growth in month t, respectively. In its structural form, the FAVAR model is represented by:

$$B_o Z_t = \alpha + \sum_{i=1}^{L} B_i Z_{t-i} + \varepsilon_t$$

where ε_t is a vector of orthogonal structural innovations, and Z_t consists of global inflation, global output growth, and oil price growth. The vector ε_t consists of a shock to the global supply of goods and services ("global supply shock"), a shock to the global demand for goods and services ("global demand shock"), and a shock to oil prices ("oil price shock").

While the traditional VAR model assumes that the variance-covariance matrix of residuals are constant over time, this assumption could be problematic in this analysis, given the exceptionally large macroeconomic volatility induced by the COVID-19 pandemic (Lenza and Primiceri 2020; Primiceri and Tambalotti 2020). To resolve the issue, the model assumes stochastic volatility of structural shocks—the residuals are independently but not identically distributed across time. Their variance-covariance is allowed to be period-specific, hence rendering volatility stochastic and introducing heteroskedasticity (Carriero et al. 2019).

Identification of shocks

Sign restrictions. The Special Focus follows the methodology in Charnavoki and Dolado (2014) and Ha, Kose, et al. (2019) in using sign restrictions to identify the global shocks. Postulating that B^{-1} as a recursive structure such that the reduced form errors (u_t) can be decomposed according to $u_t = B^{-1}\varepsilon_t$, as follows:

$$\begin{bmatrix} u_t^{Y,global} \\ u_t^{OilPrice} \\ u_t^{\pi,global} \end{bmatrix} = \begin{bmatrix} + & - & + \\ + & + & + \\ + & + & - \end{bmatrix} \begin{bmatrix} \varepsilon_t^{GlobalDemand} \\ \varepsilon_t^{OilPrice} \\ \varepsilon_t^{GlobalSupply} \end{bmatrix}$$

- A positive *global demand shock* is assumed to increase global output growth, global inflation, and oil price growth.

- A positive *global non-oil supply shock* (hereafter "*global supply shock*") is assumed to raise global output and oil price growth but reduce global inflation.

- A positive *oil price shock* is defined as raising oil prices and global inflation but depressing global output growth.

Narrative restrictions. Since oil price shocks are the main drivers of variations in global inflation, the identification of oil price shocks deserves further robustness checks. In particular, similar to Antolín-Díaz and Rubio-Ramírez (2018), these identified oil price shocks (or historical decompositions of the shocks) can further be constrained to ensure that they agree with the established narrative account of historical episodes. The narrative sign restrictions are imposed by considering the subset of successful draws in Bayesian estimation that result in negative oil price shocks (or negative historical contributions to oil prices) during key historical episodes since 2000 identified in Baffes et al. (2015) and Wheeler et al. (2020):

- Structural oil price shocks are negative in January 2015 and March 2020.

- Historical contributions of oil price shocks to oil prices are negative in January 2015 and March 2020.

- Historical contributions of oil price shocks to oil prices are more sizeable (in absolute values) than other global shocks in January 2015.

Bayesian estimation

The model is estimated by using monthly data with four lags, as is standard in the literature. The Bayesian estimation first searches for 2,000 successful draws from 1,000 iterations with 1,000 burn-ins; the results reported are based on the median of these 1,000 successful draws, along with 16-84 percent confidence intervals. The estimation process is standard Gibbs sampling

FIGURE A.SF1.1 Drivers of inflation in 2020-22: Alternative inflation measures

The inflation increase has been relatively more muted, and the contribution of oil price movements smaller, in inflation measures with lower tradables content, such as core inflation.

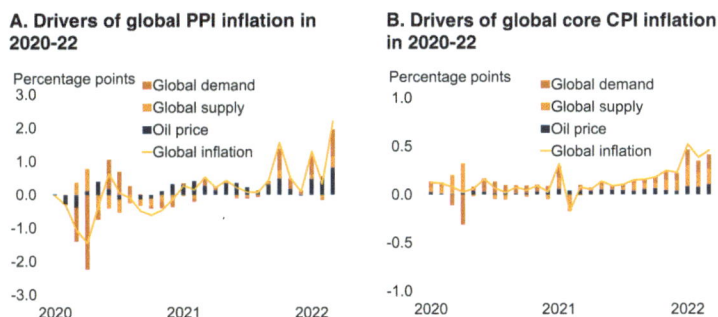

Source: Ha, Kose, and Ohnsorge (2021a).
Note: Contributions to month-on-month inflation in producer price index (PPI, A) and core CPI (B) for 83 countries, of which 31 are advanced economies and 52 are EMDEs, based on FAVAR models over the period of 2001M1 - 2022M3. Unexplained residual is omitted from the graph.

except that the volatility of residuals is endogenously determined.

To reflect a sudden change in the volatility in variables around global recessions and oil price shocks, stochastic volatility is assumed to have random inertia—this introduces an extension of the standard stochastic volatility model by turning it into an endogenous variable integrated to the Bayesian estimation process. In the model, the inertia of stochastic volatility is endogenously estimated, allowing for variable-specific inertia (Cogley and Sargent 2005).

Database

The sample for the monthly estimation includes data for up to 31 advanced economies and 52 EMDEs for 2001 M1-2022 M3. Global output growth is the global common factor of month-on-month, seasonally adjusted industrial production growth. Global inflation is defined as the global common factor of month-on-month headline CPI inflation, producer price (PPI) inflation, or core inflation (figure A.SF1.1). The estimation is repeated using core inflation and producer price index inflation, similarly defined. Oil price growth is the month-on-month growth rate of nominal oil prices (average of Dubai, West Texas Intermediate, and Brent).

ANNEX SF1.2 Methodology: Estimating potential growth

Potential growth is estimated using the production function approach employed by Kilic Celik, Kose, and Ohnsorge (2020) and World Bank (2018). It assumes that potential output can be captured by a Cobb-Douglas production function:

$$Y_t = A_t \, K_t^{\alpha-1} \, L_t^{\alpha}$$

where Y_t is potential output, A_t is potential total factor productivity (TFP), K_t is the potential capital stock, and L_t is potential employment.

TFP data are calculated as the Solow residual of output, employment (extended using data from Haver Analytics) and capital (extended using investment data from Haver Analytics and the perpetual inventory method). Labor and capital shares are the within-country averages of those reported in Penn World Tables. Two of the three components of potential output—potential TFP and potential employment—are proxied by the fitted values from panel regression estimates. The third component, the contribution of capital to potential growth, is assumed to be the same as the contribution of capital to actual growth.

This approach yields an unbalanced panel data set for 34 advanced economies and 63 EMDEs for 1988- 2030. Capital stock data from Penn World Table 9.1 are used until the latest available year in the data set (2017 for most countries in the sample). For 2017-19, investment data are compiled from national statistics offices and Haver Analytics, while the capital stock is estimated from investment data by the perpetual inventory method using historical average depreciation rates.[19]

Estimating potential total factor productivity

Potential TFP growth is defined as the fitted value of a panel fixed effects regression for 35 advanced

economies and 83 EMDEs for 1983-2017 of Hodrick Prescott-filtered trend of actual TFP growth (the Solow residual) on determinants of productivity. These include GDP per capita relative to advanced economies, education (secondary school completion rate), the working-age share of the population, and the five-year moving average real investment growth (as in Abiad, Leigh, and Mody 2007; Bijsterbosch and Kolasa 2010; Feyrer 2007).[20] To allow for nonlinearities in the productivity dividends from education, schooling is interacted with a dummy for schooling in the bottom two-thirds across the sample. A dummy for commodity exporters between the period 2003-07 captures the impact of credit boom in commodity exporters.

$$\Delta tfp_{i,t} = \beta_0 + \beta_1 GDP \ per \ capita_{i,t} + \beta_2 \ wap_{i,t} + \beta_3 education_{i,t} + \beta_4 \ education_{i,t} * \Delta edu + \beta_5 \Delta ceb_{i,t} + \beta_6 \Delta inv_{i,t} + \varepsilon_{i,t}$$

where Δtfp is the logarithmic first difference of trend TFP, *GDP per capita* is GDP per capita in percent of advanced economies per capita GDP, *wap* is the working-age share of the population, *education* is the percent share of the population who completed secondary school, Δinv is the five-year moving average real investment growth, Δedu is a dummy variable taking the value of 1 if the secondary completion rate is in the bottom two-thirds of the distribution, and Δceb is a dummy variable taking the value 1 if the country is a commodity exporter for the period 2003-07.

The data were compiled using UN Population Statistics (for population growth, the working-age share of the population), Barro and Lee (for secondary school completion), the World Development Indicators (for GDP per capita relative to the advanced economies, and life expectancy), and Haver Analytics (for investment). The results are broadly in line with the existing literature (World Bank 2018).

---

[19] Implicitly, this approach does not account for the possibility that inefficient investment is written off during downturns but depreciates only gradually. Hence, it may overstate the capital stock during downturns.

[20] The results are robust to using GDP per capita instead of GDP per capita in percent of advanced-economy GDP per capita. GDP per capita relative to a frontier (advanced economies) is used here to proxy the catch-up effect highlighted in the literature on frontier analysis (Growiec et al. 2015).

Estimating labor force participation rates

Potential employment is defined as the product of the working-age population and the fitted value of age- and gender-specific regressions of labor force participation rates ($lfpr_{a,g,t}$) on their structural determinants ($X_{a,g,t}$) and controlling for cohort effects, fixed effects, and the state of the business cycle, defined as the deviation of the logarithm of real GDP from the Hodrick-Prescott-filtered trend. The vector $X_{a,g,t}$ includes gender-specific education outcomes (secondary and tertiary completion and enrollment rates), age-specific fertility rates and life expectancy. The vector $C_{a,g,t}$ includes all the control variables.

$$lfpr_{a,g,t} = \alpha_{a,g} + \beta_{a,g} X_{a,g,t} + \delta_{a,g} X_{a,g,t} * \Delta emde + \gamma_{a,g} C_{a,g,t} + \varepsilon_{a,g,t}$$

Data on the working-age population come from the UN Population Statistics Database. Data for age- and gender-specific labor force participation rates are available from *Key Indicators of the Labor Market* (KILM) of the ILO *Population Statistics Database* for 1990-2019 for up to 36 advanced economies and 146 EMDEs.[21] Completion rates of secondary and tertiary education are from Barro and Lee (2013); age-specific fertility rate and life expectancy are from the UN's *World Population Projections database*; gender-specific secondary and tertiary school enrollment rates are from the *World Development Indicators*.[22] The results are broadly in line with findings in the existing literature (World Bank 2018).

---

[21] This is an unbalanced sample because some of the exogenous variables are not available for the full period for all countries. However, the regression results are robust to restricting the sample to the balanced panel with fully available data.

[22] UN data for life expectancy are for five-year periods so life expectancy for historical years is used from the *World Developing Indicators* database and then spliced with UN *World Population Statistics* and *Prospects* data for the projection years or if the data are not available in the *World Development Indicators* database.

References

Abiad, A., E. Detragiache, and T. Tressel. 2010. "A New Database of Financial Reforms." *IMF Staff Papers* 57 (2): 281-302.

Abiad, A., D. Leigh, and A. Mody 2007. "International Finance and Income Convergence: Europe is Different," IMF Working Papers 64, International Monetary Fund.

Antolín-Díaz, J., and F. Rubio-Ramírez. 2018. "Narrative Sign Restrictions for SVARs." *American Economic Review* 108 (10): 2802-29.

Armantier, O., L. Goldman, G. Kosar, G. Topa, W. van der Klaauw, and J. C. Williams. 2022. "What Are Consumers' Inflation Expectations Telling Us Today?" Federal Reserve Bank of New York Liberty Street Economics, New York.

Arteta, C., M. A. Kose, F. Ohnsorge, and M. Stocker. 2015. "The Coming U.S. Interest Rate Tightening Cycle: Smooth Sailing or Stormy Waters?" Policy Research Note 15/02, World Bank, Washington, DC.

Autor, D. H., D. Dorn and G. H. Hanson. 2015. "Untangling Trade and Technology: Evidence from Local Labour Markets." *The Economic Journal* 125 (584): 621-46.

Baffes, J., M. A. Kose, F. Ohnsorge, and M. Stocker. 2015. "The Great Plunge in Oil Prices—Causes, Consequences, and Policy Responses." Policy Research Note 1, World Bank, Washington, DC.

Baqaee, D., and E. Farhi. 2020. "Supply and Demand in Disaggregated Keynesian Economies with an Application to the Covid-19 Crisis." *American Economic Review* 112 (5): 1397–1436.

Barsky, R. B., and L. Kilian. 2002. "Do We Really Know that Oil Caused the Great Stagflation? A Monetary Alternative." *NBER Macroeconomics Annual* 16: 137-183.

Barsky, R. B. and L. Kilian. 2004. Oil and he Macroeconomy Since the 1970s," *Journal of Economic Perspectives* 18(4): 115-134.

Beechey, M. J., B. K. Johannsen, and A. T. Levin. 2011. "Are Long-Run Inflation Expectations Anchored More Firmly in the Euro Area Than in the United States?" *American Economic Journal: Macroeconomics* 3 (2): 104-29.

Bernanke, B. 2003. "'Constrained Discretion' and Monetary Policy." Speech before the Money

Marketeers of New York University, February 3, New York.

Bijsterbosch, M., and M. Kolasa. "FDI and Productivity Convergence in Central and Eastern Europe: An Industry-level Investigation." *Review of World Economics* 145 (4): 689-712.

Blanchard, O. 2022. "Why I Worry About Inflation, Interest Rates, and Unemployment." *Peterson Institute for International Economics* (blog). March 14. https://www.piie.com/blogs/realtime-economic-issues-watch/why-i-worry-about-inflation-interest-rates-and-unemployment.

Blinder, A. S. 1979. *Economic Policy and the Great Stagflation.* New York: Academic Press.

Blinder, A. S. 2004. "The case Against the Case Against Discretionary Fiscal Policy." Working Paper 100, Center for Economic Policy Studies, Princeton University.

Blinder, A. S., and L. Kilian. 2009. "Causes and Consequences of the Oil Shock of 2007–08. Comments and Discussion." *Brookings Papers on Economic Activity* (Spring): 262-283.

Blinder, A. S., and J. B. Rudd. 2013. "The Supply-shock Explanation of the Great Stagflation Revisited." In *The Great Inflation: The rebirth of modern central banking,* edited by M. D. Bordo and A. Orphanides, 119-175.

Boissay, F., F. de Fiore, D. Igan, A. Pierres-Tejada, and D. Rees. 2022. "Are Major Advanced Economies on the Verge of a Wage-Price Spiral?" Bulletin 53, Bank for International Settlements, Basel, Switzerland.

Bordo, M. D., C. Erceg, A. Levin, and R. Michaels. 2007. "Three Great American Disinflations." NBER Working Paper 12982, National Bureau of Economic Research, Cambridge, MA.

Bordo, M. D., and A. Orphanides, eds. 2013. *The Great Inflation: The Rebirth of Modern Central Banking.* Chicago: University of Chicago Press.

Borio, C., P. Disyatat., D. Xia, and E. Zakrajšek. 2021. "Inflation, Relative Prices and Monetary Policy: Flexibility Born Out of Success." *BIS Quarterly Review* September: 15–29.

Brand, C., M. Bielecki, and A. Penalver. 2018. "The Natural Rate of Interest: Estimates, Drivers, and Challenges to Monetary Policy." Occasional Paper 217, European Central Bank, Frankfurt.

Bruno, M., and J. Sachs. 1979. *Supply Versus Demand Approaches to the Problem of Stagflation.* Cambridge, MA: National Bureau of Economic Research.

Calice, P., F. Diaz Kalan, and O. Masetti. 2020. "Interest Rate Repression: A New Database." Policy Research Working Paper 9457, World Bank, Washington, DC.

Carriero, A., T. E. Clark, and M. Marcellino, 2019. "Large Vector Autoregressions with Stochastic Volatility and Non-conjugate Priors." Journal *of Econometrics* 212 (1): 137-154.

Charnavoki, V., and J. Dolado. 2014. "The Effects of Global Shocks on Small Commodity-Exporting Economies: Lessons from Canada." *American Economic Journal: Macroeconomics* 6 (2): 207-237.

Clark, T. E., and S. Kozicki. 2005. "Estimating Equilibrium Real Interest Rates in Real Time." The *North American Journal of Economics and Finance* 16 (3): 395-413.

Cline, W. R. 1981. *World Inflation and the Developing Countries.* Washington, DC: BrookingsInstitution.

Cogley, T. and T. J. Sargent. 2005. "Drift and Volatilities: Monetary Policies and Outcomes in the Post WWII U.S." *Review of Economic Dynamics* 8 (2): 262-302.

Coibion, O., Y. Gorodnichenko, and R. Kamdar. 2018. "The Formation of Expectations, Inflation, and the Phillips Curve." *Journal of Economic Literature* 56 (4): 1447-91.

Coibion, O., Y. Gorodnichenko, and M. Weber. 2022. "Monetary Policy Communications and their Effects on Household Inflation Expectations." *Journal of Political Economy* 130 (6): 1537- 1584.

D'Acunto, F., and M. Weber. 2022. "Rising Inflation Is Worrisome. But Not for the Reasons You Think." VoxEU.org, CEPR Policy Portal, January 4. https://voxeu.org/article/rising-inflation-worrisome-not-reasons-you-think.

DeLong, J. B. 1997. "America's Peacetime Inflation: The 1970s.*"* In *Reducing Inflation: Motivation and Strategy,* edited by C. D. Romer and D. H. Romer, 247-280. Chicago: University of Chicago Press.

DeLong, J. B. 2022. "No, the Fed Is Not (Far) Behind the Curve!" *Brad DeLong's Grasping Reality* (blog), March 16. https://braddelong.substack.com/p/no-the-fed-is-not-far-behind-the.

Dieppe, A., ed. 2021. *Global Productivity: Trends, Drivers, and Policies*. Washington, DC: WorldBank.

Dong, W., J. Fudurich, and L. Suchanek. 2017. "Digital Transformation in the Service Sector: Insights from Consultations with Firms in Wholesale, Retail and Logistics." Staff Analytical Note 2017-19, Bank of Canada, Ottawa.

Égert, B., and I. Wanner. 2016. "Regulations in Services Sectors and Their Impact on Downstream Industries: The OECD 2013 REGIMPACT Indicator." OECD Economics Department Working Paper 1303, Organisation for Economic Co-operation and Development, Paris.

Eo, Y., L. Uzeda., and B. Wong. 2022. "Understanding Trend Inflation through the Lens of the Goods and Services Sectors." Working Paper 28, Center for Applied Macroeconomic Analysis, Canberra.

Eichengreen, B. 2022. "America's Not-so-Great Inflation." *Project Syndicate* (blog), February 10. https://www.project-syndicate.org/commentary/why-current-us-inflation-is-nothing-like-the-1970s-by-barry-eichengreen-2022-02.

Feyrer, J. 2007. "Demographics and productivity." *Review of Economics and Statistics* 89 (1): 100-109.

Forbes, K. 2019. "Has Globalization Changed the Inflation Process?" BIS Working Paper 791, Bank for International Settlements, Basel.

Forbes, K., J. Gagnon, and C. G. Collins. 2021. "Pandemic Inflation and Nonlinear, Global Phillips Curves," Voxeu.org, CEPR Policy Portal, December 21, https://voxeu.org/article/pandemic-inflation-and-nonlinear-global-phillips-curves

Frankel, J. A. 2010. "Monetary Policy in Emerging Markets: A Survey." NBER Working Paper 16125, National Bureau of Economic Research, Cambridge, MA.

Friedman, M. 1968. "The Role of Monetary Policy," *American Economic Review* 58 (March): 1-17.

Gagnon, J. E. 2022. "Why US Inflation Surged in 2021 and What the Fed Should Doto Control It." Real Time Economic Issues (blog). March 11. https://www.piie.com/blogs/realtime-economic-issues-watch/why-us-inflation-surged-2021-and-what-fed-should-do-control-it.

Gersbach, H. 2021. "Another Disinflationary Force Vanishes: The Tightening of Bank Equity Capital Regulation." VoxEU.org, CEPR Policy Portal, February 18. https://voxeu.org/article/tightening-bank-equity-capital-regulation.

Goodfriend, M. 2004. "Inflation Targeting in the United States?" In *The Inflation-Targeting Debate,* edited by B. S. Bernanke and M. Woodford , 311-352. Chicago: University of Chicago Press.

Goodfriend, M. 2007. "How the World Achieved Consensus on Monetary Policy." *Journal of Economic Perspectives* 21 (4): 47-68.

Goodhart, G., and M. Pradhan. 2020. *The Great Demographic Reversal: Ageing Societies, Waning Inequality, and an Inflation Revival.* London: Palgrave Macmillan.

Goolsbee, A. D., and P. J. Klenow. 2018. "Internet Rising, Prices Falling: Measuring Inflation in a World of E-Commerce." *AEA Papers and Proceedings* 108: 488-92.

Gordon, R. J. 2011. "The History of the Phillips Curve: Consensus and Bifurcation." *Economica* 78 (309): 10-50.

Guenette, J. D. 2020. "Price Controls: Good Intentions, Bad Outcomes." Policy Research Working Paper 9212, World Bank, Washington, DC.

Gürkaynak, R. S., A. Levin, and E. Swanson. 2010. "Does Inflation Targeting AnchorLong- Run Inflation Expectations? Evidence from the US, UK, and Sweden." *Journal of the European Economic Association* 8 (6): 1208-42.

Ha, J., A. Ivanova, F. Ohnsorge, and F. D. Unsal. 2019. "Inflation: Concepts, Evolution, and Correlates." Policy Research Working Paper 8738, World Bank, Washington, DC.

Ha, J., and G. Kindberg-Hanlon. 2021. "Asset Purchases in Emerging Markets: Unconventional Policies, Unconventional Times." In *Global Economic Prospects*, 169-198. January. Washington, DC: World Bank.

Ha, J., M. A. Kose, and F. Ohnsorge, eds. 2019a. *Inflation in Emerging and Developing Economies: Evolution, Drivers, and Policies.* Washington, DC: World Bank.

Ha, J., M. A. Kose, and F. Ohnsorge. 2019b. "Global Inflation Synchronization." CEPR Discussion Paper 13600, Centre for Economic Policy Research, London.

Ha, J., M. A. Kose, F. Ohnsorge, and H. Yilmazkuday. 2019. "Sources of Inflation: Global and Domestic

Drivers." In *Inflation in Emerging and Developing Economies: Evolution, Drivers, and Policies,* edited by J. Ha, M. A. Kose, and F. Ohnsorge, 143-199. Washington, DC: World Bank.

Ha, J., M. A. Kose, and F. Ohnsorge. 2021a. "Inflation During the Pandemic: What Happened? What is Next?" CEPR Discussion Paper 16328, Centre for Economic Policy Research, London.

Ha, J., M. A. Kose, and F. Ohnsorge. 2021b. "One-Stop Source: A Global Database of Inflation." CEPR Discussion Paper 16327, Centre for Economic Policy Research, London.

Ha, J., M. A. Kose, and F. Ohnsorge. 2022. "From Low to High Inflation: Implications for Emerging Market and Developing Economies." CEPR Policy Insight 99, Centre for Economic Policy Research, London.

Hamilton, J. D., E. S. Harris, J. Hatzius, and K. D. West. 2016. "The Equilibrium Real Funds Rate: Past, Present, and Future." *IMF Economic Review* 64 (4): 660 -707.

Hoek, J., S. Kamin, and E. Yoldas. 2020. "When is Bad News Good News? U.S. Monetary Policy, Macroeconomic News, and Financial Conditions in Emerging Markets." International Finance Discussion Paper 1269, Board of Governors of the Federal Reserve System, Washington, DC.

Hoek, J., S. Kamin, and E. Yoldas. 2021. "Are Rising U.S. Interest Rates Destabilizing for Emerging Market Economies?" FEDS Notes, Board of Governors of the Federal Reserve System, Washington, DC.

Holston, K., T. Laubach, and J. C. Williams. 2017. "Measuring the Natural Rate of Interest: International Trends and Determinants." *Journal of International Economics* 108 (May): S59-S75.

Igan, D., E. Kohlscheen, G. Nodari and D. Rees. 2022. "Commodity Market Disruptions, Growth and Inflation?" Bulletin 54, Bank for International Settlements, Basel, Switzerland.

Ilzetzki, E. 2022. "Surging Inflation in the UK." VoxEU.org, CEPR Policy Portal, February 10. https://voxeu.org/article/surging-inflation-uk.

Ilzetzki, E., C. M. Reinhart, and K. S. Rogoff. 2019. "Exchange Arrangements Entering the 21st Century: Which Anchor Will Hold?" *Quarterly Journal of Economics* 134 (2): 599–646.

Kilic Celik, S., M. A. Kose, and F. Ohnsorge. 2020. "Subdued Potential Growth: Sources and Remedies." In *Growth in a Time of Change: Global and Country Perspectives on a New Agenda,* edited by H. W. Kim and Z. Qureshi, 25-74. Washington, DC: Brookings Institution Press.

Kose, M. A., H. Matsuoka, U. Panizza, and D. Vorisek. 2019. "Inflation Expectations: Review and Evidence." CEPR Discussion Paper 13601, Centre for Economic Policy Research, London.

Kose, M. A., P. Nagle, F. Ohnsorge, and N. Sugawara. 2020. *Global Waves of Debt: Causes and Consequences.* Washington, DC: World Bank.

Kose, M. A., P. Nagle, F. Ohnsorge, and N. Sugawara. 2021. "What has Been the Impact of COVID-19 on Debt? Turning a Wave into a Tsunami." Policy Research Working Paper 9871, World Bank, Washington, DC.

Kose, M. A., and F. Ohnsorge. 2020. *A Decade after the Global Recession: Lessons and Challenges for Emerging Market and Developing Economies.* Washington, DC: World Bank.

Kose, M. A., N. Sugawara, and M. E. Terrones. 2021. "What Happens During Global Recessions?" In *A Decade after the Global Recession: Lessons and Challenges for Emerging and Developing Economies*, edited by M. A. Kose and F. Ohnsorge, 57-116. Washington, DC: World Bank.

Kose, M. A., and M. E. Terrones. 2015. *Collapse and Revival: Understanding Global Recessions and Recoveries.* Washington, DC: International Monetary Fund.

Kuttner, K., and T. Robinson. 2010. "Understanding the Flattening Phillips Curve." *The North American Journal of Economics and Finance* 21 (2): 110-125.

Laborde, D., C. Lakatos, and W. J. Martin. 2019. "Poverty Impact of Food Price Shocks and Policies." Policy Research Working Paper 8724, World Bank, Washington, DC.

Laeven, L., and F. Valencia. 2020. "Systemic Banking Crises Database II." *IMF Economic Review*, 68(2): 307-361.

Laubach, T., and A. S. Posen. 1997. "Disciplined Discretion: The German and Swiss Monetary Targeting Frameworks in Operation." Research Paper 9707, Federal Reserve Bank of New York.

Lenza, M., and G. E. Primiceri. 2020. "How to Estimate a VAR after March 2020." NBER Working

Paper 27771, National Bureau of Economic Research, Cambridge, MA.

Nelson, E. 2001. "What Does the UK's Monetary Policy and Inflation Experience Tell Us About the Transmission Mechanism?" Discussion Paper 3047, Center for Economic Policy Research, London, UK.

Nelson, E., and K. Nikolov. 2004. "Monetary Policy and Stagflation in the UK." *Journal of Money, Credit and Banking* 36 (3): 293-318.

OECD (Organisation for Economic Co-operation and Development). 2019. *Indicators of Product Market Regulation.* Paris: OECD.

Orphanides, A. 2003. "The Quest for Prosperity Without Inflation." *Journal of Monetary Economics* 50 (3): 633-663.

Orphanides, A., and J. C. Williams. 2013. "Monetary Policy Mistakes and the Evolution of Inflation Expectations." In *The Great Inflation: The Rebirth of Modern Central Banking,* edited by M. D. Bordo and A. Orphanides. New York: Academic Press.

Phelps, E. 1968. "Money-Wage Dynamics and Labor Market Equilibrium," *Journal of Political Economy* 76 (August): 678-711.

Primiceri, G. E. 2006. "Why Inflation Rose and Fell: Policy-Makers Beliefs and U.S. Postwar Stabilization Policy." *Quarterly Journal of Economics* 121 (3): 867-901.

Primiceri, G. E., and A. Tambalotti. 2020. "Macroeconomic Forecasting in the Time of COVID19." Unpublished paper.

Reifenschneider, D., and D. Wilcox. 2022. "The Case for a Cautiously Optimistic Outlook for U.S. Inflation." Policy Brief 22-3, Peterson Institute for International Economics, Washington, DC.

Rogoff, K. S. 2003. "Globalization and Global Disinflation." *Federal Reserve Bank of Kansas City Economic Review* 88 (4): 45-78.

Rogoff, K. S. 2014. "The Exaggerated Death of Inflation." *Project Syndic*ate, September 2. https://www.project-syndicate.org/commentary/kenneth-rogoff-debunks-rumors-of-the-demise-of-threats-to-price-stability.

Rogoff, K. S. 2021. "Back to the Seventies?" *Project Syndicate,* August 31. https://www.project-syndicate.org/commentary/america-facing-1970s-style-stagflation-threat-by-kenneth-rogoff-2021-08.

Summers, L. H. 2022. "The Stock Market Liked the Fed's Plan to Raise Interest Rates. It's Wrong." *Washington Post,* March 17.

Summers, L. H., and L. Rachel. 2019. "On Falling Neutral Real Rates, Fiscal Policy and the Risk of Secular Stagnation." Brookings Papers on Economic Activity, BPEA Conference Drafts, March 7.

Tootell, G. M. 1994. "Restructuring, the NAIRU, and the Phillips Curve." New England Economic Review 1994: 31-45.

Welsch, H. 2007. "Macroeconomics and Life Satisfaction: Revisiting the "Misery Index." *Journal of Applied Economics* 10 (2): 237-51.

Wheeler, C. M., J. Baffes, A. Kabundi, G. Kindberg-Hanlon, P. S. Nagle, and F. Ohnsorge. 2020. "Adding Fuel to the Fire: Cheap Oil during the COVID-19 Pandemic." Policy Research Working Paper 9320, World Bank, Washington, DC.

Wilcox, D. 2022. "Wherein I Try to Calm Professor Blanchard's Nerves." *Uneasy Money* (blog), March 15. https://uneasymoney.com/tag/david-wilcox/.

World Bank. 2018. *Global Economic Prospects: The Turning of the Tide?* June. Washington, DC: World Bank.

World Bank. 2019. *Global Economic Prospects: Heightened Tensions, Subdued Investment.* June. Washington, DC: World Bank.

World Bank. 2020. *World Development Report: Trading for Development in an Age of Global Value Chains.* Washington, DC: World Bank.

World Bank. 2021a. *Global Economic Prospects.* June. Washington, DC: World Bank.

World Bank. 2021b. *Global Economic Prospects.* January. Washington, DC: World Bank.

World Bank. 2022a. *Commodity Markets Outlook: The Impact of the War in Ukraine on Commodity Markets.* April. Washington, DC: World Bank.

World Bank. 2022b. *Global Economic Prospects.* January. Washington, DC: World Bank.

World Bank. 2022c. *World Development Report: Finance for an Equitable Recovery.* Washington, DC: World Bank.

RUSSIA'S INVASION
OF UKRAINE

Implications for
Energy Markets and Activity

The Russian Federation's invasion of Ukraine has disrupted global energy markets and damaged the global economy. Compared to what took place in the 1970s, the shock has led to a surge in prices across a broader set of energy-related commodities. In energy-importing economies, higher prices will reduce real disposable incomes, raise production costs, tighten financial conditions, and constrain policy space. Some energy exporters may benefit from improved terms of trade and higher commodities production. However, on net, model-based estimates suggest that the war-driven surge in energy prices could reduce global output by 0.8 percent after two years. The experience of previous oil price shocks has shown that these shocks can provide an important catalyst for policies to encourage demand reduction, substitution to other fuels, and development of new sources of energy supply.

Introduction

Volatility in energy markets, driven by a strong demand recovery from the pandemic and numerous pandemic-related supply constraints, is being exacerbated by Russia's invasion of Ukraine. The invasion has led to significant disruptions to the trade and production of energy commodities as Russia is the world's largest exporter of natural gas and accounts for a significant share of global coal and crude oil exports (figure SF2.1.A). However, the ultimate impact of these disruptions will depend on their magnitude, the availability of inventories, the development of other supplies or a ramping up of production in other countries, and the extent to which demand can be reduced.

Already, the United States and the European Union (EU) have announced plans to ban or phase out fossil fuel imports from Russia, and Russia has cut off direct natural gas exports to Bulgaria, Finland, the Netherlands, and Poland (World Bank 2022a). The United States and other International Energy Agency members announced the release of 180 million and 60 million barrels of oil, respectively, from April to October 2022. And in any event, tighter financial conditions, reduced investment, and restricted access to technology are likely to have a longer-term impact on Russia's energy production.

Reflecting these developments, coal and oil prices have risen sharply, European natural gas prices have reached record highs, and the World Bank's energy price index increased by 34 percent between January and March 2022, on top of a 50

percent increase between January 2020 and December 2021 (figures SF2.1.B-D). Based on current projections, energy prices are expected to rise by 50 percent in 2022, reflecting an 81 percent increase in coal prices, a 74 percent rise in natural gas prices (average of the European, Japan, and U.S. benchmarks), and a 42 percent increase in the price of oil. Relative to January projections, the prices of energy commodities are now expected to be 46 percent higher on average in 2023.[1]

Supply disruptions of key energy commodities could severely affect a wide range of industries, including food, construction, petrochemicals, transport, and firm-level effects (Lafrogne-Joussier et al. 2022). Concerns about energy security have already prompted public policies aimed at bolstering national self-sufficiency and reducing energy prices for consumers; however, lessons from previous energy price shocks show that these policies are often costly and ineffective, compared with steps to encourage consumers to reduce demand, to substitute for other forms of energy, and to develop alternative energy sources.

The increase in energy prices is likely to weigh on global economic activity. Higher energy prices will reduce activity in energy-importing economies by lowering real incomes, raising production costs, tightening financial conditions, and constraining macroeconomic policy. Stronger activity in some energy-exporting emerging market and developing economies—supported by more favorable terms of trade, expanded production, and stronger investment—will only provide a partial offset to the drag on global growth.

Note: This Special Focus was prepared by Justin-Damien Guénette and Jeetendra Khadan with contributions from Peter Stephen Oliver Nagle, John Baffes, and Garima Vasishtha.

[1] On average over 2022-23, oil, natural gas, and coal prices are now expected to be 87 percent, 40 percent, and 69 percent higher than in January.

The Russian Federation is a major exporter of energy commodities. All coal and natural gas prices have reached historic highs in nominal terms. However, in real terms, only the European natural gas price has reached an all-time high, and it is substantially above its previous peak in 2008. Real coal prices are close to their 2008 peak, while real oil prices remain some distance below.

A. The Russian Federation's share of global energy exports

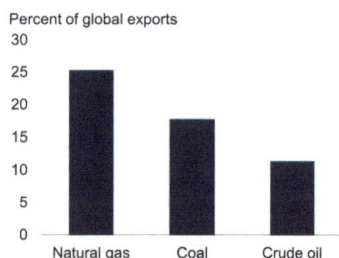

B. Commodity price changes in 2022

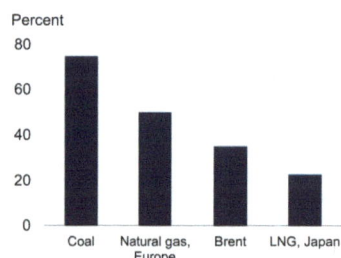

C. Coal and oil prices (real)

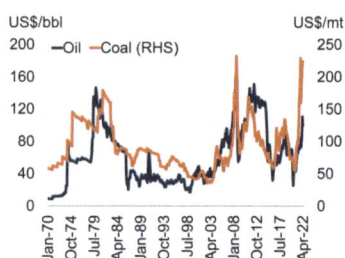

D. Natural gas prices (real)

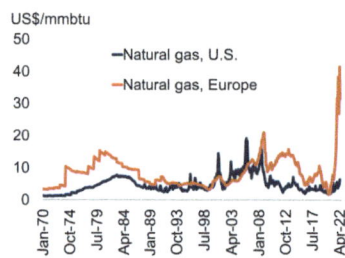

Sources: BP Statistical Review; Eurostat; Haver Analytics; Comtrade (database); World Bank.
A. Data for energy are trade volumes. Data are for 2020.
B. Three-month change in commodity prices through end-March 2022. LNG stands for liquefied natural gas.
C.-D. Monthly data from 1970 to April 2022. Prices deflated by the U.S. Consumer Price Index.

Against this background, this Special Focus addresses the following questions:

- How does the latest energy price shock compare with previous major shocks?

- What are the lessons from previous energy price shocks?

- What are the likely implications of the current energy price shock for global activity?

Comparison with previous energy shocks

The current energy shock differs from previous oil price spikes to the extent that the current episode has had a broader impact on energy commodities,

implying less opportunity for substitution toward cheaper fuels. At the same time, however, the energy intensity of GDP now is much lower than in the 1970s, so consumers may be less sensitive to relative price changes, at least in the short term. And in the current episode, policy responses have tended to focus on adjustments to fuel subsidies and taxes to mitigate the effects on consumer prices, rather than on measures to address underlying supply/demand imbalances.

Prices. Crude oil prices have increased by 350 percent (in nominal terms) from their pandemic low in April 2020 to April 2022, making it the largest increase for any equivalent two-year period since the 1970s.[2] Also, all energy prices rose sharply in 2022, in contrast to earlier episodes where oil prices rose much more sharply than those for coal and gas. In nominal terms, coal and gas prices have all reached historic highs. However, in real terms, only the European natural gas price has reached an all-time high (and it is substantially above its previous peak in 2008). Coal prices are close to their 2008 peak, while oil prices remain some way below. With all energy prices elevated, there is less opportunity to substitute for cheaper fuel in the current energy shock. In addition, the increase in prices of some energy commodities is also driving up prices of other commodities. For example, higher natural gas prices have already pushed fertilizer prices to their highest level since 2010.

Smaller energy intensity of GDP. The oil intensity of GDP has fallen considerably since the 1970s. Similarly, prior to the price shock, consumer spending on energy as a share of total spending is also lower, especially in advanced economies, which means that consumers may respond less to energy price changes, at least in the short term, than in the 1970s.

Different policy focus. Many countries have responded to the current shock by prioritizing energy subsidies and tax breaks with fewer policies

_____

[2] Another shock took place during the early 2000s in a more gradual fashion as a result of strong demand growth in emerging market and developing economies, especially in China and India (Baffes et al. 2018). At their peak, in July 2008, nominal oil prices exceeded $130/bbl (or $172/bbl in inflation-adjusted 2022 terms).

designed to tackle the underlying imbalance between supply and demand. However, several countries have announced plans to increase production of fossil fuels (coal and LNG), while others have announced faster increases in fuel efficiency requirements to reduce energy demand.

By comparison, policy responses to previous oil price shocks were focused on establishing institutions, such as the creation of the International Energy Agency in 1974, to safeguard oil supplies and promote common policy making. Key policy decisions included the requirement to create national oil reserves equal to 60 days of imports (later expanded to 90 days) and a ban on building new oil-powered electricity plants with a directive to switch to coal (enacted in 1977; Scott 1994). Measures were also implemented to address the underlying demand and supply imbalance (Ilkenberry 1988; Shibata 1982; U.S. Congress 1975). For example, the United States adopted policies to reduce demand and boost production after the steady increase in prices in the 2000s (EPA 2007). Demand-side measures included fiscal incentives to improve energy efficiency in vehicles and housing. Supply-side measures included a mandate to sharply increase the use of biofuels; establishing renewable fuel standards; providing energy-related tax incentives for fossil fuels, nuclear, and renewable energy sources; and providing loan guarantees for zero-carbon technologies. The EU and many EMDEs adopted similar policies.

Lessons from previous energy shocks

The experience of the past 50 years suggests that there are three channels through which market mechanisms respond to energy price shocks and associated policies: demand reduction, substitution, and supply responses (Baffes and Nagle 2022).

Demand reduction. Between 1979 and 1983, global oil demand fell by 11 percent, or 6 million barrels per day (mb/d). While the drop in oil demand was partly a result of the global recession in 1982, energy efficiency and policies to encourage a substitution from oil implemented by

oil-importing countries contributed to a permanent reduction in underlying demand. Changes in consumer preferences in response to higher prices also played a role in reducing demand, for example, the shift toward more fuel-efficient vehicles in the United States (Cole 1981). In the 2000s, there was less substitution to other fuels as a much smaller amount of crude oil was being used in electricity generation. After reaching its peak in 2005, oil consumption in advanced economies steadily declined and was 14 percent lower by 2014. The decline in oil consumption was largely due to a shift toward more fuel-efficient automobiles, including hybrid electrics (Hamilton 2009). Among EMDEs, oil demand also decelerated in the 2010s.

Substitution. In the five years after the 1979 oil price shock, the share of crude oil in the energy mix in advanced economies fell by more than 7 percentage points, owing to the prohibition of the construction of new oil-fired power stations and their gradual replacement with nuclear and coal-powered stations. Among EMDEs, the share of oil in the energy mix fell by 4 percentage points and was largely replaced by natural gas. In the years following the 2008 oil price increase, the share of natural gas and renewables in the energy mix rose, reflecting the U.S. shale boom for natural gas, as well as mandates and technological improvements for renewables. However, substituting other energy commodities for oil in its main current uses—transport and petrochemicals—has proved to be more difficult.

New sources of production. High oil prices in the 1970s induced investment in oil production by non-OPEC countries, particularly for reserves with a higher cost of production. These included Prudhoe Bay in Alaska, the North Sea offshore fields of the United Kingdom and Norway, the Cantarell offshore field of Mexico, and oil sands in Canada (figure SF2.2.A). High and stable prices in the 2000s also facilitated the development of alternative sources of crude oil. The most notable of these was the development of U.S. shale oil deposits, output from which rose from 0.6 mb/d in 2008 to 7.8 mb/d in 2019, resulting in a sustained expansion in total U.S. production (figure SF2.2.B).

The oil price increases in the 1970s led to increased oil production from non-OPEC countries, notably in the North Sea and Alaska in the 1970s-80s. Similarly, high and stable prices in the 2000s induced investment in the development of alternative sources of crude oil, the most notable being U.S. shale and Canadian tar sands in the 2000s.

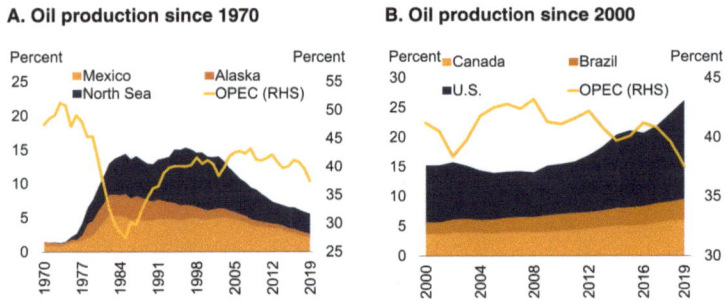

A. Oil production since 1970

B. Oil production since 2000

Sources: BP Statistical Review; International Energy Agency; World Bank.
Note: OPEC = Organization of the Petroleum Exporting Countries.

The lessons from previous energy shocks will be key to inform a long-term solution to the current price hike, especially one that could make achieving climate change goals less challenging. Measures to promote energy efficiency and changes in consumer preferences have proven to be instrumental in significantly reducing oil demand after the 1970s oil shocks. On the other hand, policies that encouraged the use of coal for electricity generation and price controls have led to environmental problems and market distortions, respectively (World Bank 2022a). These lessons would suggest that countries should focus their policies on promoting energy efficiency, investing in renewable energy sources, and pursuing policies to encourage consumers to shift toward low carbon technologies.

Implications for the global economy

Channels

Energy prices affect growth and inflation through various channels: direct effects on prices and activity for both importers and exporters; indirect effects via trade and other commodity markets; monetary and fiscal policy responses; and investment uncertainty. Through these channels, energy prices can also have immediate reper-

cussions—even absent discretionary policy responses—on fiscal and external balances.

Shifts in national incomes and activity. Developments in global oil and energy markets are accompanied by significant real income shifts from energy-importing countries, where the propensity to spend tends to be higher, to energy-exporting countries, which tend to have higher average saving rates. This generally results in weaker global demand over the medium term. Yet, the ultimate impact of higher energy prices on individual countries depends on a wide range of factors, including the share of oil and other energy inputs in their exports or imports, their reliance on the oil sector for tax revenues, their cyclical positions, and their amount of monetary and fiscal policy room to react. While the positive impact on exporters is immediate and, in some cases, accentuated by financial market easing, the negative impact on energy importers could be more diffuse and take some time to materialize.

Higher costs. For consumers, higher energy costs decrease real disposable income and reduce consumption. This effect is particularly prominent in commodity-importing low-income countries for which fuel constitutes a large fraction of consumption (World Bank 2022b). For firms, rising energy prices often imply a sizeable increase in input costs. For energy and oil-intensive sectors, including transportation, petrochemicals, and agriculture, this would worsen conditions for investment and employment. Agriculture, for instance, is 4–5 times more energy intensive than manufacturing (Baffes et al. 2015).

Procyclical policy responses. In energy exporters, rising energy prices can trigger procyclical increases in public spending (Arezki, Hamilton, and Kazimov 2011; Frankel, Végh, and Vuletin 2013; World Bank 2022b). This procyclicality is particularly acute in commodity exporting countries, where governments have tended to raise spending in response to an increase in government revenues during booms (Frankel 2017). Fiscal policy thus often accentuates the impact of the commodity price cycle on economic growth and increases the amplitude of cycles in economic activity (Mendes and Pennings 2020; Riera Crichton, Végh, and Vuletin 2015). In contrast, oil importing countries may see their fiscal positions deteriorate as domestic economic activity weakens and the cost of providing fuel subsidies rises.

Procyclical financial flows. The economic impact of rising energy prices can also be magnified by the financial channel. In energy exporters, higher energy prices can trigger increases in domestic credit creation and compression of country risk premia, leading to large capital inflows and currency appreciation (World Bank 2022b). A surge in capital inflows can be particularly problematic if not properly invested, as evidenced by the Latin American debt crises of the 1980s (Eberhardt and Presbitero 2021; Kose et al. 2021; Reinhart, Reinhart, and Trebesch 2016). In contrast, energy importers may experience a tightening of domestic financial conditions, including as a result of lenders pulling back in the face of weaker credit quality. This may be further exacerbated if monetary policy is tightened to resist inflation pressures (Baffes et al. 2015).

Uncertainty. Abrupt changes in energy prices, by increasing uncertainty, can also have an outsized adverse impact on investment and durable goods consumption. For instance, uncertainty generated by sharp movements in oil prices can hinder the consumption of durable goods (Kilian 2014). Rising uncertainty of future oil prices can also lead to more precautionary demand of crude oil, with second-order impacts on activity (Anzuini, Patrizio and Pisani 2014).

Impact on global activity

Impact of higher oil prices

Global economy. Oil price movements driven by supply shocks in oil markets are often associated with significant changes in global output and income shifts between oil exporters and importers (Cashin, Mohaddes, and Raissi 2014; Kilian 2009; Peersman and Van Robays 2012). Recent studies using large-scale macroeconomic models indicate that a supply-driven increase in oil prices averaging about 40 percent over two years—the size of the upward revision to World Bank projections—would lower global activity by about 0.2-0.6 percent after two years (figure SF2.3.A;

Andrle et al. 2015; Blagrave et al. 2020; Dieppe et al. 2017).[3]

The results of these previous studies are confirmed here using simulations of a global semi-structural model, which suggest that global output would decline by a cumulative 0.3 percent in the second year of the shock (figure SF2.3.B).[4] The impact on the global economy could be even bigger as oil price increases generally appear to have larger output effects on oil importing economies than oil price decreases (Hoffman 2012; Jimenez-Rodriguez and Sanchez 2005). This asymmetry could be caused by uncertainty, frictions such as wage rigidities, and varying monetary policy responses to different types of movements in oil prices (Bachmeier and Keen 2018; Kilian and Lewis 2011; Rahman and Serletis 2011).

Oil importers. Activity in oil importers should deteriorate in response to higher oil prices since these reduce household and corporate real incomes. Past research suggests that a 40 percent increase in oil prices could lower growth in oil-importing economies by some 0.4–2.0 percentage points, depending on the share of oil imports in GDP (Rasmussen and Roitman 2011; World Bank 2013). Broadly in line with these estimates from the literature, simulations of the global model suggest that this shock would lower output growth in oil-importing advanced economies and EMDEs by 0.25 percentage point in the first year.

Oil exporters. In addition to an expansion of the oil sector, rising oil prices can have a number of indirect effects on oil-exporting economies. In many, government finances rely heavily on taxing

---

[3] The literature offers a range of estimates of the impact of a sustained, supply-driven oil price increase (Baffes et al. 2015; IMF 2014; OECD 2014). More recent studies report smaller estimates primarily because of the recent expansion of oil production in the United States which has reduced the economy's overall sensitivity to oil prices (Gervais 2019).

[4] These simulations are conducted using the Oxford Economics Global Economic Model (OEM). The OEM is a global semi-structural macro projection model which includes 81 individual country blocks, most of which are available at a quarterly frequency, with behavioral equations governing domestic economic activity, monetary and fiscal policy, global trade, and energy prices (Oxford Economics 2019). The simulations assume that agents have adaptive expectations, monetary policy is endogenous, and fiscal policy is largely exogenous.

FIGURE SF2.3 Implications for global economic activity

The World Bank has significantly increased its projections for oil and natural gas prices over the near term. According to a large-scale global macroeconomic model, the upward revision to oil prices included in baseline forecasts, if driven by supply shocks, would lower global output by about 0.3 percent after two years. The much larger upward revision to baseline natural gas price forecasts over 2022 and 2023 would be expected to lower global output by a similar magnitude. Combined, supply-driven upward revisions to the prices of oil, natural gas, and coal could lower global output by a cumulative 0.8 percent in 2023.

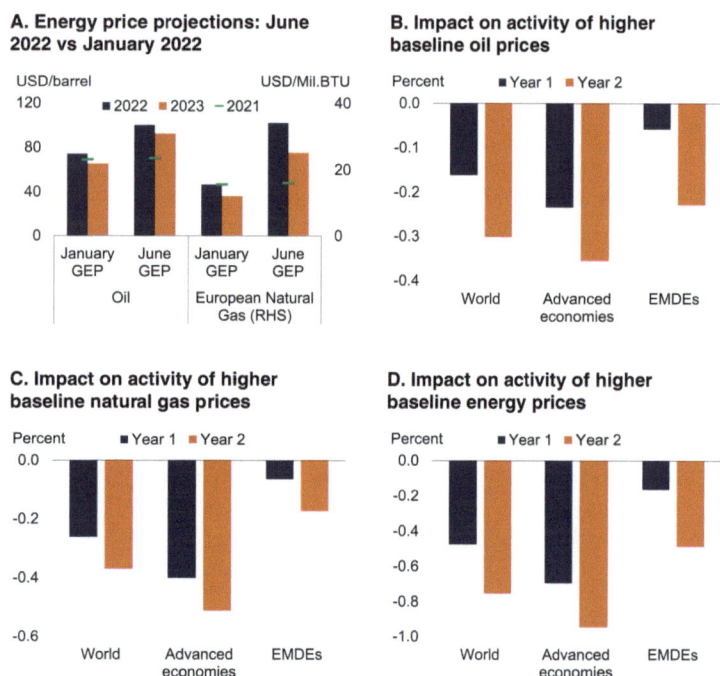

A. Energy price projections: June 2022 vs January 2022

B. Impact on activity of higher baseline oil prices

C. Impact on activity of higher baseline natural gas prices

D. Impact on activity of higher baseline energy prices

Sources: Oxford Economics; JP Morgan; World Bank.
Note: BTU = British Thermal Unit; EMDEs = emerging market and developing economies; Mil. = million; USD = U.S. dollar.
A. GEP refers to the *Global Economic Prospects* report. Oil price is the simple average of Brent, Dubai, and West Texas Intermediate prices.
B.D. These scenarios are produced using the Oxford Economics Global Economic Model.
B. Simulation is for supply-driven increases in Brent oil prices averaging 40 percent above baseline for two years.
C. Simulation is for supply-driven increases in natural gas prices averaging 70 percent above baseline for two years.
D. Chart combines the impacts on global output of the supply-driven increases in Brent oil prices, natural gas prices, and coal prices. Coal price shock is a supply driven increase in coal prices averaging 87 percent above baseline for two years.

the oil sector, so that higher oil prices tend to boost revenues and may trigger a fiscal expansion. In addition, an increase in oil prices generally improves their current account and precipitates currency appreciation. Previous research suggests that output in oil-exporting countries could increase by about 0.6–4.8 percent in the year following a 40 percent rise in the annual average oil price (Feldkircher and Korhonen 2012; World Bank 2013). A similar shock in the global model would raise the aggregate output of oil-exporting

EMDEs by about 1 percent over the same time horizon.

Impact of higher natural gas prices

In addition to the drag from elevated oil prices, several countries are likely to face significant headwinds from sharply higher natural gas prices, and to a lesser extent, higher coal prices. Simulations of the global model indicate that a supply-driven 70 percent increase in natural gas prices—equivalent to the average upward revision to World Bank forecasts over 2022-23—would lower global output by 0.4 percent after two years (figure SF2.3.C).[5] The impact of the gas supply shock would be greatest for continental Europe owing to its outsized dependence on Russian supplies (Bachmann et al. 2022). The larger incidence on global output of the natural gas price shock compared to that of oil is a function of the size of the shock—the projected revision to natural gas prices is nearly double that for oil.

Impact of combined energy price shocks

On net, model simulations suggest that the upward revisions to energy prices, including to oil, natural gas and coal, could reduce global growth by 0.5 percentage point in 2022 and a further 0.3 percentage point in 2023, lowering global output by a cumulative 0.8 percent by 2023 (figure SF2.3.D).[6] The estimated impact on global growth for the first year is in line with the results of a similar exercise conducted by the OECD (OECD 2022). Advanced economies would experience a cumulative reduction in output of 0.9 percent by 2023 compared to a 0.6 percent output reduction in oil-importing EMDEs. The outsized impact on advanced economies would reflect a particularly

---

[5] The impact of the natural gas price shock, which is not well explored in the literature, is nonetheless broadly in line with model-based estimates for a gas-importing advanced economy (Millard 2011).

[6] OEM simulations suggest that an 87 percent rise in global coal prices—equivalent to the average upward revision to World Bank forecasts over 2022-23—would only reduce global activity by about 0.1 percent cumulatively after two years. This negligible impact may reflect the peripheral role of coal in the current version of the model. Historically, adverse coal supply shocks are estimated to have caused marked but short-lived declines in output (van de Ven and Fouquet 2017).

large drag in Europe from surging natural gas prices as a result of Russia's invasion of Ukraine (Federle et al, 2022; Guénette, Kenworthy and Wheeler 2022). This is broadly in line with other model-based studies (Ferrara, Mogliani and Sahuc 2022; Mahlstein et al. 2022).[7] The adverse impact on EMDEs would be blunted by the positive impact on EMDE oil exporters, who would see their level of output rise by a net 0.5 percent in 2023.[8]

These model-based estimates could, however, underestimate the combined drag of higher oil, natural gas, and coal prices on global growth. For instance, the model may underestimate the drag on global activity caused by a near doubling of global coal prices. It could also fail to appreciate how elevated prices for all hydrocarbon energy sources could limit the ability of countries to substitute for lower-cost energy sources in the near term.

Lastly, an even more severe scenario for energy prices could be envisioned, such as a Russian embargo on energy exports to the EU and the imposition by the EU and the U.S. of sanctions targeting shipping companies or third parties purchasing Russian oil, possibilities that are explored in the risk section of chapter 1. This scenario would include further unanticipated shocks to energy markets and a material deterioration of confidence in the euro area, resulting in an additional drag on global growth of 0.4 percentage point in 2022 and 0.8 percentage point in 2023. Thus, when combined, energy supply-related shocks in the baseline and in the energy price spike scenario could reduce global output growth by 0.9 percentage point in 2022

and 1.1 percentage points in 2023, resulting in a 2 percent reduction in global output by 2023.

Policy implications

Policy responses to previous energy shocks have shown that some polices can be highly effective and beneficial (such as increasing energy efficiency and renewable energy mandates), while others can lead to market distortions and environmental problems (such as price controls and the promotion of coal use for electricity generation in the 1970s). Given these lessons, policy makers today can prioritize policies that encourage greater energy efficiency and accelerate the transition towards low-carbon energy sources. To cushion the adverse effects of households, temporary targeted support to vulnerable groups can be prioritized over energy subsidies, which in the current context, could delay the transition to a zero-carbon economy (World Bank 2022a).

References

Andrle, M., P. Blagrave, P. Espaillat, M. K. Honjo, M. B. Hunt, M. Kortelainen, R. Lalonde, et al. 2015. "The Flexible System of Global Models – FSGM." IMF Working Paper 15/64, International Monetary Fund, Washington, DC.

Anzuini, A., P. Pagano, and M. Pisani. 2014. "Macroeconomic Effects of Precautionary Demand for Oil." *Journal of Applied Econometrics* 30 (6): 968-86.

Arezki, R., K. Hamilton, and K. Kazimov. 2011. "Resource Windfalls, Macroeconomic Stability and Growth: The Role of Political Institutions." IMF Working Paper 11/142, International Monetary Fund, Washington, DC.

Bachmann, R., D. Baqaee, C. Bayer, M. Kuhn, A. Löschel, B. Moll, A. Peichl, et al. 2022. "What If Germany Is Cut Off From Russian Energy?" VoxEU.org, CEPR Policy Portal, March 25. https://voxeu.org/article/what-if-germany-cut-russian-energy.

Bachmeier, L., and B. D. Keen. 2018. "Modeling the Asymmetric Effects of an Oil Price Shock." Kansas State University, New York.

Baffes, J., M. A. Kose, F. Ohnsorge, and M. Stocker. 2015. "The Great Plunge in Oil Prices: Causes,

---

[7] Several other studies have quantified the global growth impacts of scenarios related to a worsening of disruptions to Russia's energy exports. IMF (2022) finds that more severe disruptions to European imports of Russian energy, combined with global supply disruptions and adverse confidence shocks would lower global output by about 0.5 percent in 2022 and 1 percent in 2023—over and above downward revisions to the baseline outlook. Similarly, McFee (2022) presents an alternative baseline featuring a worsening of the war in Ukraine accompanied by sharply higher oil and natural gas prices. In this scenario, global output would be lower by 0.6 percent in 2022 and 1.1 percent in 2023.

[8] Growth in oil-exporting EMDEs would be 0.8 percentage point higher in 2022 and 0.3 percentage point lower in 2023 as a result of the upward revision to oil prices.

Consequences, and Policy Responses." Policy Research Note 15/01, World Bank, Washington, DC.

Baffes, J., A. Kabundi, P. Nagle, and F. Ohnsorge. 2018. "The Role of Major Emerging Markets in Global Commodity Demand." Policy Research Paper 8495, World Bank, Washington, DC.

Baffes, J., and P. Nagle. 2022. *Commodity Markets: Evolution, Challenges, and Policies.* Washington, DC: World Bank.

Blagrave, P., C. Godbout, J.D. Guénette, R. Lalonde, and N. Perevalov. 2020. "Impact: The Bank of Canada's International Model for Projecting Activity." Technical report, Canadian Economic Analysis Department, Bank of Canada, Ottawa.

Cashin, P., K. Mohaddes, and M. Raissi. 2014. "The Differential Effects of Oil Demand and Supply Shocks on the Global Economy." *Energy Economics* 44 (July): 113-134.

Cole, R. 1981. "The Japanese Automotive Industry. Model and Challenge for the Future?" Center for Japanese Studies, University of Michigan, Ann Arbor, Michigan.

Comtrade (database). United Nations. Accessed on April 20, 2022. https://comtrade.un.org.

Dieppe, A., G. Georgiadis, M. Ricci, I. Van Robays, and B. van Roye. 2017. "ECB-Global: Introducing ECB's Global Macroeconomic Model for Spillover Analysis." Working Paper 2045, European Central Bank, Frankfurt.

Eberhardt, M., and A. Presbitero. 2021. "Commodity Prices and Banking Crisis." CEPR Discussion Paper 15959, Center for Economic Policy Research, London.

EC (European Commission). 2022. "Communication from the Commission to the European Parliament, the European Council, the Council, the European Economic and Social Committee and the Committee of the Regions." European Commission, Brussels.

EIA (Energy Information Administration). 2022. "Short-Term Energy Outlook." U.S. Energy Information, Administration, Washington, DC.

EPA (Environmental Protection Agency). 2007. "Summary of the Energy Independence and Security Act, Public Law 110-140." U.S. Environmental Protection Agency, Washington, DC.

Federle J., A. Meier, G. Müller, and V. Sehn. 2022. "Economic Spillovers from the War in Ukraine: The Proximity Penalty." VoxEU.org, CEPR Policy Portal, 18 April. https://voxeu.org/article/economic-spillovers-war-ukraine-proximity-penalty.

Feldkircher, M. and I. Korhonen. 2012. "The Rise of China and its Implications for Emerging Markets - Evidence from a GVAR Model." Institute for Economies in Transition Discussion Papers 2012-20, Bank of Finland.

Ferrara, L., M. Mogliani, and J.-G. Sahuc. 2022. "High-Frequency Macroeconomic Risk Measures in the Wake of the War in Ukraine." VoxEU.org, CEPR Policy Portal, April 7. https://voxeu.org/article/war-ukraine-and-high-frequency-macroeconomic-risk-measures.

Frankel, J. A. 2017. "How to Cope with Volatile Commodity Export Prices: Four Proposals." CID Faculty Working Paper 335, Center for International Development, Harvard University, Cambridge, MA.

Frankel, J. A., C. A. Végh, and G. Vuletin. 2013. "On Graduation from Fiscal Procyclicality." *Journal of Development Economics* 100 (1): 32-47.

Gervais, O. 2019. "How Oil Supply Shocks Affect the Global Economy: Evidence from Local Projections." Bank of Canada Staff Discussion Paper 2019-6, Bank of Canada, Ottawa.

Guénette, J. D., P. Kenworthy, and C. Wheeler. 2022. "Implications of the War in Ukraine for the Global Economy." Equitable Growth, Finance, And Institutions Policy Note, World Bank, Washington, DC.

Hamilton, J. 2009. "Causes and Consequences of the Oil Shock of 2007-08." NBER Working Paper, 15002, National Bureau of Economic Research, Cambridge, MA.

Hoffman, R. 2012. "Estimates of Oil Price Elasticities." IAEE Energy Forum Newsletter, 1st Quarter 2012, International Association for Energy Economics, Cleveland, Ohio.

Ilkenberry, G. 1988. *Reasons of State: Oil Politics and the Capacities of American Government.* Ithaca, NY: Cornell University Press.

IMF (International Monetary Fund). 2014. "2014 Spillover Report." International Monetary Fund, Washington, DC.

Jimenez-Rodriguez, R., and M. Sanchez. 2005. "Oil Price Shocks and Real GDP Growth: Empirical

Evidence for Some OECD Countries." *Applied Economics* 37 (2): 201-228.

Kilian, L. 2009. "Not All Oil Price Shocks Are Alike: Disentangling Demand and Supply Shocks in the Crude Oil Market." *American Economic Review* 99 (3): 1053-69.

Kilian, L. 2014. "Oil Price Shocks: Causes and Consequences." *Annual Review of Resource Economics* 6 (1): 133-154.

Kilian, L., and L. T. Lewis. 2011. "Does the FED Respond to Oil Price Shocks?" *The Economic Journal* 121 (555): 1047–72.

Kose, M. A., P. Nagle, F. Ohnsorge, and N. Sugawara. 2021. Global Waves of Debt: Causes and Consequences. Washington, DC: World Bank.

Lafrogne-Joussier, R., A. Levchenko, J. Martin, I. Mejean. 2022. "Beyond Macro: Firm-Level Effects of Cutting Off Russian Energy." VoxEU.org, CEPR Policy Portal, April 24. https://voxeu.org/article/firm-level-effects-cutting-russian-energy.

Mahlstein, K., C. McDaniel, S. Schropp, and M. Tsigas. 2022. "Potential Economic Effects of Sanctions on Russia: An Allied Trade Embargo." VoxEU.org, CEPR Policy Portal, May 6. https://voxeu.org/article/potential-economic-effects-allied-trade-embargo-russia.

McFee, I. 2022. "A Darker Economic Scenario from Russia's War." Global Research Briefing, Oxford Economics, Oxford, U.K.

Mendes, A., and S. Pennings. 2020. "One Rule Fits All? Heterogenous Fiscal Rules for Commodity Exporters when Price Shocks Can be Persistent: Theory and Evidence." Policy Research Working Paper 9400, World Bank, Washington, DC.

Millard, S. 2011. "An Estimated DSGE Model of Energy, Costs and Inflation in the United Kingdom." Working Paper 432, Bank of England, London.

OECD (Organisation for Economic Co-operation and Development). 2014. *OECD Economic Outlook: Volume 2014/2*. Paris: OECD.

OECD (Organisation for Economic Co-operation and Development). 2022. "Economic and Social Impacts and Policy Implications of the War in Ukraine." *OECD Economic Outlook, Interim Report*, Paris.

Oxford Economics. 2019. "Global Economic Model." July. Oxford Economics, Oxford, U.K.

Peersman, G., and I. Van Robays. 2012. "Cross-Country Differences in the Effects of Oil Shocks." *Energy Economics* 34 (5): 1532-1547.

Rahman, S., and A. Serletis. 2011. "The Asymmetric Effects of Oil Price Shocks." Macroeconomic Dynamics 15 (S3): 437-471.

Rasmussen, T. N., and A. Roitman. 2011. "Oil Shocks in a Global Perspective: Are they Really that Bad?" IMF Working Paper 11/194, International Monetary Fund, Washington, DC.

Reinhart, C. M., V. Reinhart, and C. Trebesch. 2016. "Global Cycles: Capital Flows, Commodities, and Sovereign Defaults." *American Economic Review* 106 (5): 574-580.

Riera-Crichton, D., C. Végh, and G. Vuletin. 2015. "Procyclical and Countercyclical Fiscal Multipliers: Evidence from OECD Countries." *Journal of International Money and Finance* 52 (C): 15-31.

Scott, R. 1994. "The History of the International Energy Agency. Volume Two. Major Policies and Actions." International Energy Agency, Paris.

Shibata, H. 1982. "The Energy Crises and Japanese Response." *Resources and Energy* 5 (2): 129-154.

U.S. Congress. 1975. "Public Law 94-163." Energy Policy and Conservation Act, 42 USC 6201 Note.

van de Ven, D. J. and R. Fouquet. 2017. "Historical Energy Price Shocks and Their Changing Effects on the Economy." *Energy Economics* 62 (February): 204–16.

World Bank. 2013. *Global Economic Prospects: Less Volatile, but Slower Growth*. June. Washington, DC: World Bank.

World Bank. 2021. *Commodity Markets Outlook: Urbanization and Commodity Demand*. October. Washington, DC: World Bank.

World Bank. 2022a. *Commodity Markets Outlook—The Impact of the War in Ukraine on Commodity* Markets . April. Washington, DC: World Bank.

World Bank. 2022b. *Global Economic Prospects*. January. Washington, DC: World Bank.

CHAPTER 2

REGIONAL OUTLOOKS

EAST ASIA and PACIFIC

Growth in the East Asia and Pacific (EAP) region is projected to decelerate to 4.4 percent in 2022 as slower growth in China more than offsets a rebound in the rest of the region. The region has so far been affected less than the rest of the world by the spillovers from the Russian Federation's invasion of Ukraine, in terms of both output and inflation; however, the war's effects on commodity prices and global demand are expected to dampen the recovery, especially in commodity-importing economies. Downside risks to the outlook include a lingering pandemic and resulting mobility restrictions, financial stress triggered by tightening global financial conditions, larger-than-expected spillovers from the war, and disruptions from natural disasters.

Recent developments

After rebounding to 7.2 percent in 2021, growth in the East Asia and Pacific (EAP) region has decelerated rapidly with a slowdown in China (table 2.1.1). In China, after a much stronger recovery from the initial phase of the pandemic than in the rest of the world, growth lost momentum amid recurrent COVID-19 outbreaks that were met with strict mobility restrictions (figure 2.1.1.A). To mitigate the impact of the pandemic on growth, China has relaxed some property and financial regulations and eased fiscal and monetary policies (figure 2.1.1.B). Infrastructure investment has rebounded and the pace of contraction in the real estate investment moderated at the start of the year, but it has deepened again as a result of pandemic-related restrictions (figure 2.1.1.C). The government has drafted a financial stability law to deal with systemic risks. It also committed to setting up a fund to assist troubled financial companies, including in the real estate sector, which remains under stress owing to squeezed margins and falling profits (figure 2.1.1.D).

In the rest of the region, growth reached 2.6 percent in 2021, about half its previous decade average trend rate. Weak rebound reflected the modest scale of fiscal and monetary policy support, slow progress with vaccinations, and significant disruptions from COVID-19 outbreaks (figure 2.1.2.A). The recovery has been uneven across the region, leaving output in almost two-thirds of economies below pre-pandemic levels. Growth has generally firmed this year, supported by higher commodity export prices in Indonesia and Malaysia, by a rebound of private consumption and investment in the Philippines, and by an incipient recovery of tourism in Thailand (figure 2.1.2.B). COVID-19 outbreaks and delayed broader reopenings have impeded the recovery in some tourism-dependent Pacific Island economies. Activity has also been disrupted by natural disasters, including the volcanic eruption in Tonga in January. Myanmar's economy appears to be stabilizing after a steep 18 percent contraction in fiscal year 2021. The near-term outlook remains fragile owing to sharply higher input prices, recurring electricity outages, escalating conflict, and the recent introduction of trade and foreign exchange restrictions.

Direct effects of the war on the EAP region have been limited because of modest trade and financial linkages with Russia and Ukraine. Consumer price inflation in the region has been contained until recently thanks to subdued prices for rice (due to record-high inventories) and pork (following the abatement of the African swine fever epidemic in China). The region, however, is now being affected by higher global commodity prices which

---

Note: This section was prepared by Ekaterine Vashakmadze.

FIGURE 2.1.1 China: Recent developments

China, which experienced a much stronger recovery from the initial stages of the COVID-19 pandemic than the rest of the world, has been experiencing slowing momentum due to recurrent COVID-19 flare-ups. The government has eased fiscal policy to mitigate the impact of outbreaks. Infrastructure investment has rebounded and the contraction in real estate investment moderated at the start of the year, but it has deepened again because of pandemic related restrictions. The real estate sector remains in financial distress.

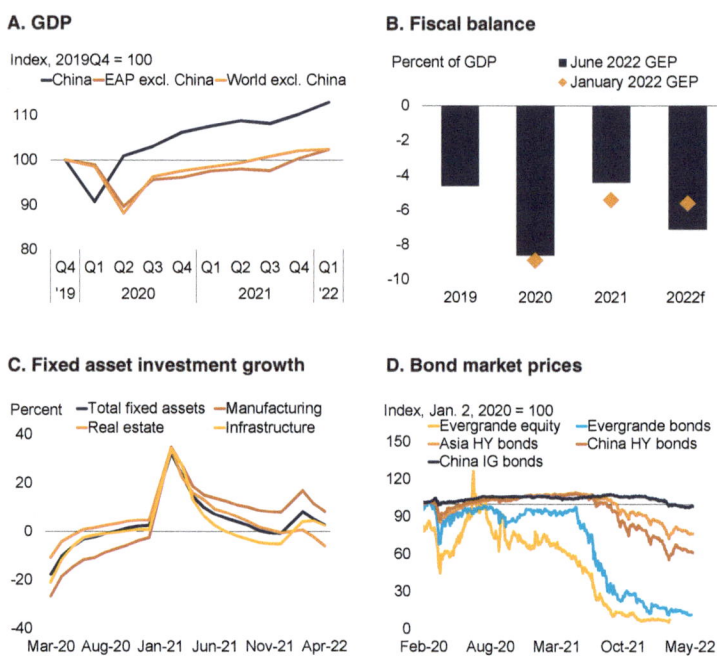

A. GDP

Index, 2019Q4 = 100
—China —EAP excl. China —World excl. China

B. Fiscal balance

Percent of GDP   ■ June 2022 GEP
                  ◆ January 2022 GEP

C. Fixed asset investment growth

Percent   —Total fixed assets —Manufacturing
           —Real estate   —Infrastructure

D. Bond market prices

Index, Jan. 2, 2020 = 100
—Evergrande equity   —Evergrande bonds
—Asia HY bonds   —China HY bonds
—China IG bonds

Sources: Bloomberg; Haver Analytics; Morgan Stanley Capital International; National Bureau of Statistics of China; World Bank.
Note: EAP = East Asia and Pacific.
A. GDP level indexed at 2019Q4 = 100. Last observation is 2022Q1. Aggregates are calculated using average 2010-19 GDP weights and market exchange rates.
B. f = forecast. The consolidated balance of the general public (excluding adjustments from the stabilization fund), government fund, state capital operation, and the social security fund budgets. World Bank staff calculations.
C. Figure shows 3-month moving average of real year-over-year growth. Last observation is April 2022.
D. "China IG bonds" refers to Bloomberg Asia Ex-Japan USD Credit China investment-grade bonds. "China HY bonds" refers to Bloomberg Asia Ex-Japan USD Credit China high-yield bonds. "Asia HY bonds" refers to Bloomberg Asia Ex-Japan USD Credit high-yield bonds. Evergrande's offshore bond price is weighted average by issuance amounts. Trading in Evergrande shares was halted on March 21, 2022. Last observation is May 31, 2022.

are contributing to inflation. Trade flows across the region have moderated because of disrupted supply chains and international trade resulting partly from the war but also from the lockdowns in parts of China (figure 2.1.2.C). Some countries with relatively high dependence on food and fuel imports, such as Mongolia, Thailand, and some Pacific Island economies, have recently experienced rapid increases in consumer price inflation (figure 2.1.2.D). Higher food and fuel prices are also increasing the budgetary costs of

government subsidies and price controls, limiting scope for further policy support amid depleted fiscal buffers (World Bank 2022a).

Several central banks in the region have kept their nominal policy rates unchanged amid relatively high real interest rates, low core inflation, and significant economic slack. Meanwhile, external financing conditions have tightened, and risk premiums have edged up following faster-than-expected monetary policy tightening in the United States and the war-related volatility in global financial markets. Net debt and equity flows to the region have turned negative since late-February, with pronounced outflows from China. Some of the region's major currencies have weakened against the U.S. dollar despite sustained current account surpluses and still-large real interest rate differentials (China, Malaysia).

Outlook

Growth in the region is projected to decelerate to 4.4 percent in 2022, with slowing activity in China more than offsetting a rebound in the rest of the region where the relaxation of pandemic-related restrictions boosts domestic demand (figure 2.1.3.A). Regional growth is projected to stabilize at an average of 5.2 percent in 2023-24, slightly above the estimated post-pandemic potential growth rate. Regional growth projection for 2022 is 0.7 percentage point below January forecast. Median annual headline consumer inflation in the region is expected to surpass 3 percent in 2022 (above previous expectations), with inflation now envisioned to overshoot the upper bound of inflation targets in several economies (Mongolia, the Philippines, Thailand).

In China, fiscal and monetary policy support for domestic demand and an easing of restrictions on the real estate sector are expected to partly offset the slowdown caused by COVID-19 resurgence and continued stress in the real estate sector (figure 2.1.3.B). Growth is projected to slow to 4.3 percent in 2022—0.8 percentage point below January forecast. The downgrade reflects the impact of costly lockdowns in parts of China, weaker-than-expected global trade, and weak business and consumer confidence. The outlook is subject to significant downside risks related to repeated COVID-19 outbreaks and renewed stress in the real estate sector (chapter 1). Growth is projected to rebound in the second half of this year and stabilize at 5.2 percent on average in 2023-24, led by private consumption.

In the rest of the region, growth is projected to pick up to 4.8 percent in 2022 as domestic demand recovers, and to 5.4 percent a year on average in 2023-24, assuming that the economic impact of Russia's invasion of Ukraine gradually fades. Projected growth in 2022 is 0.2 percentage point below previous forecasts, reflecting significant downgrades for commodity-importing economies. For commodity importers excluding China, the growth forecast for 2022 has been downgraded by 0.3 percentage point, the largest downward revisions being for Thailand and several Pacific Island economies (table 2.1.2). These reflect spillovers from the war via higher commodity prices, weaker international trade, and tighter financing conditions. Domestic demand is expected to be dampened by higher inflation and tighter monetary policy than envisaged in previous forecasts. In many tourism-dependent economies output is not expected to recover to pre-pandemic levels until after 2023 (Fiji, Palau).

Commodity-exporting economies are expected to outperform commodity importers because of improved terms of trade. Buoyant fiscal revenue amid higher commodity prices will allow Indonesia—the largest commodity exporting economy in the region—to adhere to the moderate fiscal tightening envisaged in its medium-term fiscal plan. More generally, fiscal policies in the region excluding China are expected to tighten even if recovery is incomplete. This will help to stabilize government debt, which has grown by more than 10 percentage points of GDP on average since 2019. Output in all countries is projected to remain below pre-pandemic trends until at least 2023, with the shortfall in about half of economies forecast exceeding 10 percent next year (figure 2.1.3.C).

The pandemic has caused major economic disruptions, including to human capital accumulation. Global uncertainties related to Russia's invasion of Ukraine will further depress

FIGURE 2.1.2 EAP excluding China: Recent developments

The region excluding China has experienced a weak recovery from the pandemic; however, growth has firmed this year. The war in Ukraine is affecting the region mainly through its impact on global trade and commodity prices. Higher food and fuel prices have already pushed inflation above central bank targets, notably in Mongolia and Thailand.

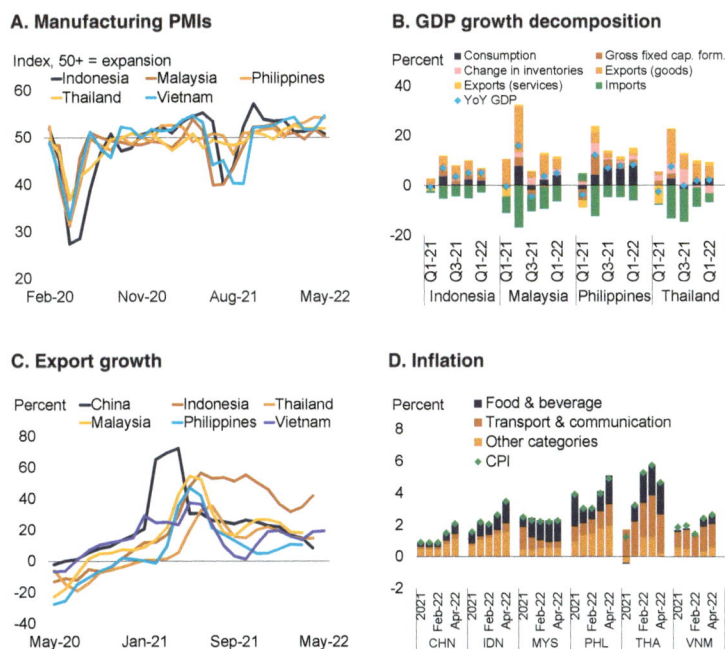

A. Manufacturing PMIs

B. GDP growth decomposition

C. Export growth

D. Inflation

Sources: Haver Analytics; International Monetary Fund; World Bank.
Note: EAP = East Asia and Pacific.
A. Above 50 indicates expansion. Last observation is May 2022.
B. Last observation is 2022Q1.
C. Value of goods exports in U.S. dollars. Figure shows 3-month moving average of year-on-year change. Last observation is May 2022 for Vietnam. Last observation is April 2022 for China, Indonesia, and Thailand. Last observation is March 2022 for Malaysia and the Philippines.
D. CHN = China; IDN = Indonesia; MYS = Malaysia; PHL = the Philippines; THA = Thailand; VNM = Vietnam. Based on the estimated weights of China's CPI basket. Last observation is April 2022.

investment. Weaker human and physical capital accumulation will weigh on medium- and long-term growth prospects for the region and accelerate the ongoing slowdown. Potential output in EAP is now projected to expand 4.6 percent a year over 2022-30—down from 6.5 percent in the decade preceding the pandemic (2011-19; figure 2.1.3.D). The most severe and long-lasting effects from the pandemic on growth are in countries that have suffered most from the COVID-19 outbreaks and the collapse of global tourism and trade amid the disruptions from natural disasters, domestic policy uncertainty, and the terms-of-trade shock (World Bank, forthcoming).

FIGURE 2.1.3 EAP: Outlook

Growth in the region is projected to decelerate to 4.4 percent in 2022 as slowing growth in China more than offsets a rebound elsewhere. In China, fiscal support and other policy measures are expected to partly mitigate the slowdown in 2022. Weaker human and physical capital accumulation will weigh on medium- and long-term growth prospects for the region. Output is projected to remain below pre-pandemic trends in all countries, with gaps still exceeding 10 percent in about half of the economies in 2023.

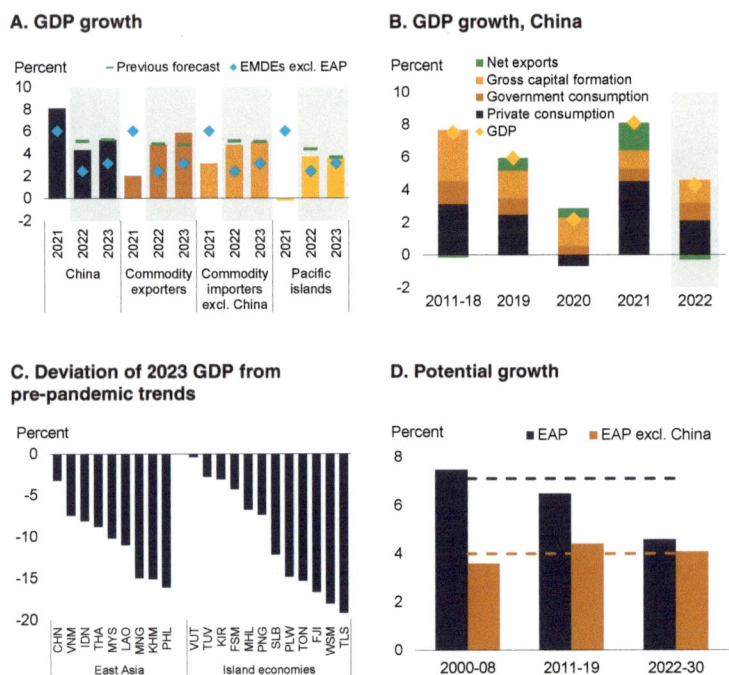

A. GDP growth

B. GDP growth, China

C. Deviation of 2023 GDP from pre-pandemic trends

D. Potential growth

Sources: Haver Analytics; World Bank.
Note: EAP = East Asia and Pacific; EMDEs = emerging market and developing economies; Commodity exporters include Fiji, Indonesia, Lao PDR, Mongolia, Myanmar, Papua New Guinea, Solomon Islands, and Timor-Leste. Commodity importers include Cambodia, China, Kiribati, Malaysia, Marshall Islands, Micronesia, Nauru, Palau, the Philippines, Samoa, Thailand, Tonga, Tuvalu, Vanuatu, and Vietnam. The International Organization for Standardization (ISO) three-digit alphabetic codes are used for the abbreviations of each economy (https://www.iso.org). Data in shaded areas indicate forecasts.
A. Year-on-year change of real GDP in 2010-19 average prices. Aggregate growth rates are calculated using average 2010-19 GDP weights and market exchange rates.
B. Figure shows year-on-year real GDP growth and expenditure contributions. Last observation is 2021. Data in shaded areas are forecasts.
C. Figure shows percent deviation between the levels of January 2020 and January 2022 baseline World Bank projections for 2020 to 2022. For 2023, the January 2020 baseline is extended using projected growth for 2022. Growth rates are calculated using GDP weights at average 2010-19 prices and market exchange rates.
D. Annual GDP-weighted averages for respective periods. Potential growth estimates based on production function approach. EAP sample includes six economies, including China, Indonesia, Malaysia, Mongolia, the Philippines, and Thailand. Dashed lines refer to 2000-19 period averages for respective aggregation.

Risks

Downside risks to the baseline growth forecast for the region predominate and include a lingering pandemic and resulting mobility restrictions, larger-than-expected spillovers from Russia's invasion of Ukraine, and financial stress triggered by global financial tightening. Small island countries remain particularly vulnerable to risks of

natural disasters and weather-related events, losing on average about 1 percent of GDP a year to damage caused by natural disasters (Scandurra et al. 2018).

A resurgence in COVID-19 in China and other large economies is a notable downside risk to the outlook. The impact of pandemic resurgence and associated restrictions could reduce China's growth relative to baseline by 0.5 percentage point in 2022 and 0.3 percentage point in 2023 (chapter 1). The lingering pandemic and associated impediments to activity at critical infrastructure facilities like ports could further disrupt production and supply chains. This would prolong shortages of vital inputs like semi-conductors, dampen investor and consumer confidence, and lower investment and growth outlooks.

There are also uncertainties about the size, composition, and effectiveness of policy stimulus in China where increased investment in the stock of public infrastructure faces diminishing returns. The pandemic has also led to persistently lower consumption, with the recovery up to mid-2021 heavily based on investment in industry, real estate, and infrastructure (World Bank 2021a). The return to investment-led support risks exacerbating economic and financial imbalances and could delay progress toward the government's objective of rebalancing growth away from exports and investment in favor of consumption.

Easing of regulatory policies could exacerbate risks in the real estate sector and fail to restore private investor confidence. Potential financial stress among property developers could spill over to upstream sectors and weigh on investment, employment, and consumption. Continued heavy reliance on highly leveraged state-owned enterprises to maintain economic growth may exacerbate distortions in credit allocation, hamper productivity growth, and accelerate the ongoing slowdown in China's potential output growth.

A prolonged war in Ukraine and intensifying geopolitical uncertainty could further reduce global confidence and lead to a sharper-than-projected slowdown in the region's export growth due to weaker global demand, further increases in shipping costs, and distorted trade flows. The shortages of essential commodities and inputs could disrupt production and dampen the recovery, especially in EAP countries with high dependance on food and fuel imports (Cambodia, Mongolia, the Philippines, Thailand, and many Pacific Island economies) (figures 2.1.4.A and 2.1.4.B). Further commodity price surges and higher-than-expected inflation could increase the risk of inflation expectations becoming de-anchored, particularly if countries, especially commodity exporters, engage in pro-cyclical fiscal policies (Ha et al., 2022; World Bank 2021b). Persistent price pressures from significantly higher food and fuel prices and sustained supply chain disruptions, could prompt substantially more monetary tightening than currently expected. Additional increases in food prices could also lead to food insecurity in several small Pacific Island economies and food shortages for the large vulnerable segments of populous EAP countries.

An unexpected tightening in major financial markets would lead to capital outflows from EAP. This would put pressure on regional currencies, thereby adding to inflation. This risk is particularly acute for countries that rely on short-term capital inflows (Mongolia, Thailand). The broad-based surge in debt across sectors and countries during the pandemic is an important source of vulnerability (figure 2.1.4.C; Kose, Ohnsorge, and Sugawara 2021). The ratio of public and publicly guaranteed debt to GDP has almost doubled in Fiji since end-2019 and has surpassed 80 percent in Fiji, the Lao People's Democratic Republic, and Mongolia, and 60 percent in Malaysia. The combination of high debt, rising interest rates, and weak economic recoveries risks magnifying damage from financial stress. The impact is likely to be concentrated in countries with elevated external debt levels (Lao PDR, Malaysia, Mongolia, Papua New Guinea), large external financing needs (Cambodia, Fiji, Malaysia, Mongolia, Timor-Leste; figure 2.1.4.D), deeper and more internationally integrated financial markets, and commodity-importing countries where higher commodity prices will significantly worsen current account deficits (many Pacific Island economies).

FIGURE 2.1.4 EAP: Risks

Cambodia and Thailand, among the larger economies, and Fiji, Palau, and Samoa, among the smaller ones, are most dependent on fuel imports. Small island countries are vulnerable to food insecurity. Risk of debt distress is an important vulnerability. The risk of financial stress is concentrated in countries with elevated external debt and high external financing needs.

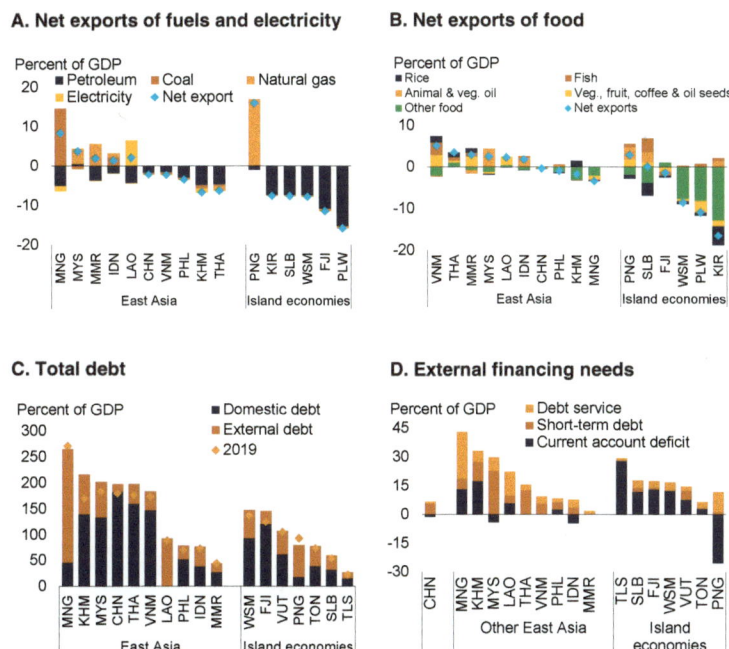

Sources: International Monetary Fund; Institute of International Finance; UN Comtrade; World Bank.
Note: EMDEs = emerging market and developing economies. The International Organization for Standardization (ISO) three-digit alphabetic codes are used for the abbreviations of each economy (https://www.iso.org).
A.B. Simple average of net exports from 2010 to 2020.
C. Chart shows an estimated stock of domestic and external debt. Domestic debt stock data are based on World Development Indicators data. Last observation is end-2020. External debt stock data for Cambodia, China, Fiji, Indonesia, Malaysia, Mongolia, Papua New Guinea, the Philippines, Solomon Islands, Tonga, and Thailand are calculated based on Quarterly External Debt Statistics (QEDS). Last observation is 2021Q4. External debt stock data for Lao PDR, Myanmar, Samoa, Timor-Leste, Vanuatu, and Vietnam are based on World Development Indicators (WDI) data. Last observation is end-2020. Revised GDP methodology is used for measuring Vietnam's debt-to-GDP ratio. Domestic debt includes foreign holdings of government bonds, estimated at 4.9 percent of GDP in China, 19.1 percent in Indonesia, 25.9 percent in Malaysia, and 13.4 percent in Thailand.
D. Figure shows the difference between debt obligations and current account balance for 2022. Debt obligations include: (1) the sum of principal repayments and interest (in currency, goods, or services) on long-term, and short-term debt, and repayments (repurchases and charges) to the IMF in corresponding year; (2) Short-term external debt stocks in corresponding year. External debt in 2022 is an estimate. Positive dark blue bars denote current account deficit.

TABLE 2.1.1 East Asia and Pacific forecast summary

(Real GDP growth at market prices in percent, unless indicated otherwise)

Percentage point differences from January 2022 projections

	2019	2020	2021e	2022f	2023f	2024f	2022f	2023f
EMDE EAP, GDP [1]	**5.8**	**1.2**	**7.2**	**4.4**	**5.2**	**5.2**	**-0.7**	**0.0**
GDP per capita (U.S. dollars)	5.2	0.6	6.6	3.9	4.7	4.7	-0.7	0.0
(Average including countries that report expenditure components in national accounts)[2]								
EMDE EAP, GDP [2]	5.8	1.2	7.4	4.4	5.2	5.1	-0.7	0.0
PPP GDP	5.7	0.8	7.0	4.5	5.2	5.1	-0.6	0.0
Private consumption	6.1	-2.1	10.0	3.9	6.2	6.2	-2.1	0.0
Public consumption	7.1	3.5	4.4	6.5	3.1	3.4	0.4	-2.8
Fixed investment	4.5	3.0	2.8	4.4	5.3	5.0	-0.1	1.0
Exports, GNFS [3]	3.1	-1.2	15.1	4.6	4.9	4.7	-0.3	0.2
Imports, GNFS [3]	0.3	-3.7	10.4	5.8	6.0	6.0	-0.2	0.1
Net exports, contribution to growth	0.7	0.6	1.3	-0.1	-0.1	-0.1	0.0	0.0
Memo items: GDP								
China	6.0	2.2	8.1	4.3	5.2	5.1	-0.8	-0.1
East Asia excluding China	4.8	-3.7	2.6	4.8	5.4	5.4	-0.2	0.4
Indonesia	5.0	-2.1	3.7	5.1	5.3	5.3	-0.1	0.2
Thailand	2.2	-6.2	1.6	2.9	4.3	3.9	-1.0	0.0
Commodity exporters	5.1	-1.8	2.0	4.8	5.9	6.0	-0.1	1.1
Commodity importers excl. China	4.6	-5.4	3.1	4.8	5.1	4.9	-0.3	0.0
Pacific Island Economies [4]	4.4	-5.3	-0.2	3.7	3.6	3.1	-0.7	-0.1

Source: World Bank.

Note: e = estimate; f = forecast; PPP = purchasing power parity; EMDE = emerging market and developing economy. World Bank forecasts are frequently updated based on new information and changing (global) circumstances. Consequently, projections presented here may differ from those contained in other Bank documents, even if basic assessments of countries' prospects do not differ at any given moment in time.

1. GDP and expenditure components are measured in average 2010-19 prices and market exchange rates. Excludes the Democratic People's Republic of Korea and dependent territories.
2. Subregion aggregate excludes the Democratic People's Republic of Korea, dependent territories, Fiji, Kiribati, the Marshall Islands, the Federated States of Micronesia, Myanmar, Palau, Papua New Guinea, Samoa, Timor-Leste, Tonga, and Tuvalu, for which data limitations prevent the forecasting of GDP components.
3. Exports and imports of goods and nonfactor services (GNFS).
4. Includes Fiji, Kiribati, the Marshall Islands, the Federated States of Micronesia, Nauru, Palau, Papua New Guinea, Samoa, the Solomon Islands, Tonga, Tuvalu, and Vanuatu.

TABLE 2.1.2 East Asia and Pacific country forecasts [1]

(Real GDP growth at market prices in percent, unless indicated otherwise)

Percentage point differences from January 2022 projections

	2019	2020	2021e	2022f	2023f	2024f	2022f	2023f
Cambodia	7.1	-3.1	3.0	4.5	5.8	6.6	0.0	0.3
China	6.0	2.2	8.1	4.3	5.2	5.1	-0.8	-0.1
Fiji	-0.4	-15.7	-4.1	6.3	7.7	5.6	-1.5	0.8
Indonesia	5.0	-2.1	3.7	5.1	5.3	5.3	-0.1	0.2
Kiribati	3.9	-0.5	1.5	1.8	2.5	2.3	-0.8	0.1
Lao PDR	5.5	0.5	2.5	3.8	4.0	4.2	-0.7	-0.8
Malaysia	4.4	-5.6	3.1	5.5	4.5	4.4	-0.3	0.0
Marshall Islands	6.6	-2.2	-2.5	3.0	2.4	2.6	-0.5	-0.1
Micronesia, Fed. Sts.	1.2	-1.8	-3.2	0.4	3.2	1.9	-0.6	0.2
Mongolia	5.0	-4.4	1.4	2.5	5.8	6.8	-2.6	-0.4
Myanmar [2]	6.8	3.2	-18.0	..	..	..	..	..
Nauru	1.0	1.1	1.5	0.9	2.6	2.4	0.0	1.8
Palau	-1.8	-9.7	-17.1	7.2	16.2	4.5	-4.8	2.2
Papua New Guinea	5.9	-3.5	1.0	4.0	2.7	2.5	0.0	-0.3
Philippines	6.1	-9.6	5.6	5.7	5.6	5.6	-0.2	-0.1
Samoa	4.4	-2.6	-8.1	-0.3	2.5	3.8	-1.8	-0.5
Solomon Islands	1.2	-4.3	0.1	-2.9	5.3	3.8	-7.4	0.9
Thailand	2.2	-6.2	1.6	2.9	4.3	3.9	-1.0	0.0
Timor-Leste	1.8	-8.6	1.6	2.4	2.8	3.0	-1.3	-1.5
Tonga	0.7	0.7	-2.7	-1.6	3.2	3.2	-4.2	-0.1
Tuvalu	13.9	4.4	2.5	3.5	3.8	4.0	0.0	0.0
Vanuatu	3.9	-6.8	1.2	2.0	4.1	3.7	-1.0	0.0
Vietnam	7.0	2.9	2.6	5.8	6.5	6.5	0.3	0.0

Source: World Bank.

Note: e = estimate; f = forecast. World Bank forecasts are frequently updated based on new information and changing (global) circumstances. Consequently, projections presented here may differ from those contained in other Bank documents, even if basic assessments of countries' prospects do not significantly differ at any given moment in time.

1. Data are based on GDP measured in average 2010-19 prices and market exchange rates. Values for Timor-Leste represent non-oil GDP. For the following countries, values correspond to the fiscal year: the Marshall Islands, the Federated States of Micronesia, Myanmar, and Palau (October 1– September 30); Nauru, Samoa, and Tonga (July 1–June 30).
2. Forecast for Myanmar beyond 2021 are excluded because of a high degree of uncertainty.

EUROPE and CENTRAL ASIA

The Russian Federation's invasion of Ukraine has triggered a humanitarian crisis in Ukraine, set back economic growth in Europe and Central Asia (ECA) and beyond, and heightened global geopolitical instability. The invasion has devastated Ukraine's economy, while output in Russia has plummeted. Output in ECA is forecast to shrink by about 3 percent in 2022, as the invasion and its repercussions reverberate through commodity and financial markets, trade and migration links, and business and consumer confidence. The largest regional spillovers of the war in Ukraine are likely to be through higher commodity prices and weaker external demand from the euro area. The invasion has increased the risks of widespread financial stress, a de-anchoring of inflation expectations, and food insecurity. A protracted war is likely to further heighten policy uncertainty and fragment regional trade and investment integration.

Recent developments

Since 2020, the Europe and Central Asia (ECA) economy has suffered two major adverse shocks—the COVID-19 pandemic and Russia's invasion of Ukraine. Prior to the invasion, the region's economic recovery from the pandemic had been losing momentum alongside waning external demand growth, tightening macroeconomic policies, and persistent supply-chain disruptions. The war has delivered a further, major blow to the recovery. It has also triggered a humanitarian crisis and the fastest growing refugee crisis in Europe since World War II, displacing about one-third of Ukraine's population, including about two-thirds of its children (figure 2.2.1.A; UNDP 2022; UNHCR 2022; UNOCHA 2022).

Economic activity in Ukraine has been rendered impossible in some areas, with the war destroying productive infrastructure and causing 50 percent of Ukrainian businesses to shut down completely (UNDP 2022). Ukraine's international trade in goods has virtually come to a halt, especially as the loss of access to the Black Sea cuts off all seaborne trade, which accounts for half of Ukraine's exports.

Activity in Russia—the region's largest economy—appears to have contracted, with the composite PMI shrinking in March and April this year. The manufacturing PMI for new export orders has also contracted, reaching its lowest reading since mid-2020. Financial restrictions encompass about three-quarters of Russia's banking sector (measured in terms of assets), with several Russian banks cut from the SWIFT network. About half of Russia's international reserves are frozen due to restrictions on the Central Bank of the Russian Federation (CBR). Financial markets and the banking sector have stabilized since March, after pronounced volatility prompted authorities to raise the policy interest rate from 9.5 to 20 percent, impose capital controls, restrict investor activity, and provide bank liquidity and broad forbearance measures. As a result of these measures, the ruble surpassed its prewar level against the U.S. dollar, allowing the CBR to cut its interest rate three times since April, to 11 percent.

Neighboring economies are facing adverse spillovers from the war, including through fractures in critical trade and transit routes, sharp falls in remittances, and higher commodity prices and inflation (figure 2.2.1.B). Maritime, air, rail, and road transit routes have been disrupted, while higher fuel prices and a surge in insurance premiums due to security concerns have pushed

Note: This section was prepared by Collette Mari Wheeler.

FIGURE 2.2.1 ECA: Recent developments

Russia's invasion of Ukraine has triggered the largest refugee crisis in Europe since World War II. Spillovers from the war are causing serious damage to ECA's economies due to tight trade, commodity, and financial linkages. The war has disrupted trade, especially maritime, which is feeding through regional supply chains.

A. Refugees from wars

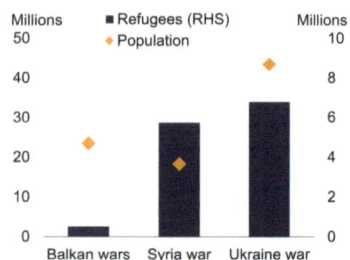

B. ECA exposure to Russia and Ukraine

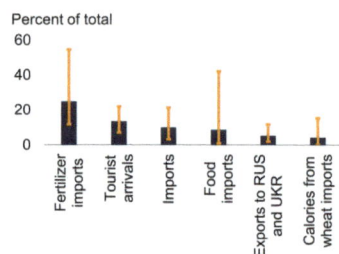

C. ECA dependence on imports from Russia

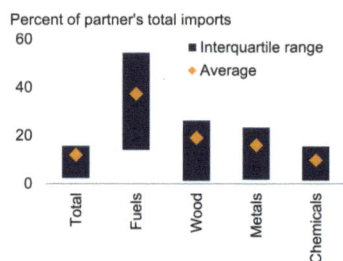

D. Maritime port calls

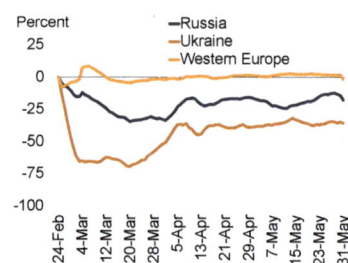

Sources: Barutciski (1994); Bloomberg; Ministry of Economy Armenia; United Nations; Comtrade (database); UNWTO (2021); United Nations High Commissioner for Refugees; U.S. Department of Agriculture; Winkler, Wuester, and Knight (2022); World Bank.
Note: ECA = Europe and Central Asia; RUS = Russian Federation; UKR = Ukraine.
A. Current estimate of Ukrainian refugees is 6.8 million as of May 29, 2022, based on UN data.
B. Bars shows goods exports/imports to/from the Russian Federation and Ukraine as a share of total goods exports/imports for ECA in 2019-20. Tourist arrivals refer to nonresident tourists at national borders by nationality. For countries where this data series is not available, estimates use number of nonresident visitors at national borders by nationality. Orange whiskers show the interquartile range.
C. Based on Winkler, Wuester, and Knight (2022).
D. Percent change in seven-day moving average of port calls compared to February 24, 2022. The last observation is May 31, 2022.

up shipping costs. Regional value chains have been interrupted, as many ECA economies heavily depend on both Russia and Ukraine for imports of key commodities and intermediate goods (figure 2.2.1.C; Winkler, Wuester, and Knight 2022). The war is also dampening regional trade by weighing on external demand from the euro area—ECA's largest trading partner—and Russia.

Transit disruptions, including airspace restrictions, have dented services trade in the region, as tourists from Russia and Ukraine account for more than 10 percent of arrivals in about half of ECA's economies, including those reliant on tourism such as Georgia, Montenegro, and Turkey. Yet, at

the same time, the influx of Ukrainian refugees and Russian migrants, particularly of educated and skilled workers, is likely to have positive effects in the near term on domestic demand and in the medium to long term on economic growth by expanding labor supply.

The region's food supplies rely on Belarus, Russia, and Ukraine for key agricultural products and inputs. Higher input costs—including for fertilizers from rising energy prices—are posing constraints to agricultural production. The war continues to disrupt planting and harvest seasons in Ukraine; threaten critical wheat stores, infrastructure, and production, especially in eastern Ukraine; and halt shipping from the Black Sea, from which about 90 percent of Ukraine's grains are traded (figure 2.2.1.D). Russia's trade restrictions on agricultural products, including tighter licensing quotas and export bans announced in March, are putting further strain on food prices. As a result, a rise in commodity prices is passing through to inflation and worsening food security for vulnerable households in the region (Artuc et al. 2022).

Inflationary pressures have intensified, with median inflation in the region accelerating to over 12 percent in April—its fastest pace since 2008, despite tightening monetary conditions in nearly all economies over the past year. Since the start of the year, two-thirds of the region have continued to hike policy interest rates amid upside risks to inflation from mounting geopolitical tensions and marked uncertainty. Higher energy prices have translated directly into larger import bills and wider current account deficits. They have also generated sizable fiscal costs in several countries because of fossil fuel subsidies.

Outlook

Regional output had nearly returned to its pre-pandemic trend at the start of 2022. Russia's invasion of Ukraine, however, has largely reversed the recovery, with output in 2022 forecast to contract by about 3 percent—about a 6 percentage point downgrade relative to January forecasts (figures 2.2.2.A-C). In addition to Russia and Ukraine, four other ECA economies are expected to shrink this year—Belarus, Kyrgyz Republic, Moldova, and Tajikistan—while most of the rest are projected to experience a sharp growth deceleration (tables 2.2.1 and 2.2.2). Excluding Russia and Ukraine, ECA GDP in 2022 is projected to grow 2.8 percent. Growth projections for 2022 have been downgraded throughout most of the region because of spillovers from the war in Ukraine, weaker-than-expected growth in the euro area, tighter-than-anticipated macroeconomic policy, and commodity and financial market shocks.

The baseline projections assume that the war in Ukraine persists in the near term but becomes increasingly contained to the eastern part of the country. They also assume that uncertainty remains elevated relative to historical norms and that sanctions on Belarus and Russia remain in place over the forecast horizon. The forecast is also predicated on commodity prices moderating (but remain at high levels), as well as a global environment characterized by tighter global financing conditions, softening external demand, and lingering supply chain bottlenecks. On that basis, ECA GDP is projected to expand at a tepid rate of 1.5 percent in 2023. If the war escalates such that Russian energy exports are further disrupted, regional output could be far weaker (figure 2.2.2.D; World Bank 2022b).

In *Ukraine*, GDP is projected to contract by about 45 percent in 2022. Poverty rates below the $5.50 per day threshold is projected to increase from about 2 percent to 20 percent of the population in 2022 (World Bank 2022b). Growth is expected to resume in 2023 but remain weak, with reconstruction efforts gathering momentum toward the end of the forecast period. The repercussions of the war are expected to reverberate beyond the short term, with economic activity scarred by the destruction of productive capacity, damage to arable land, and reduced labor supply—especially if refugees do not return. Wars inflict particularly severe damage to productivity for several years, through reducing and disrupting the labor force, weakening capital deepening, disrupting value chains, and hindering innovation (Dieppe, Kilic-Celik, and Okou 2020). Learning losses stemming from the pandemic are expected

FIGURE 2.2.2 ECA: Outlook

Regional output is forecast to contract around 3 percent in 2022, reflecting a deep recession in Russia and steep economic contraction in Ukraine, with most other regional economies expected to grow at a weakened pace. An escalation in the war could worsen the outlook.

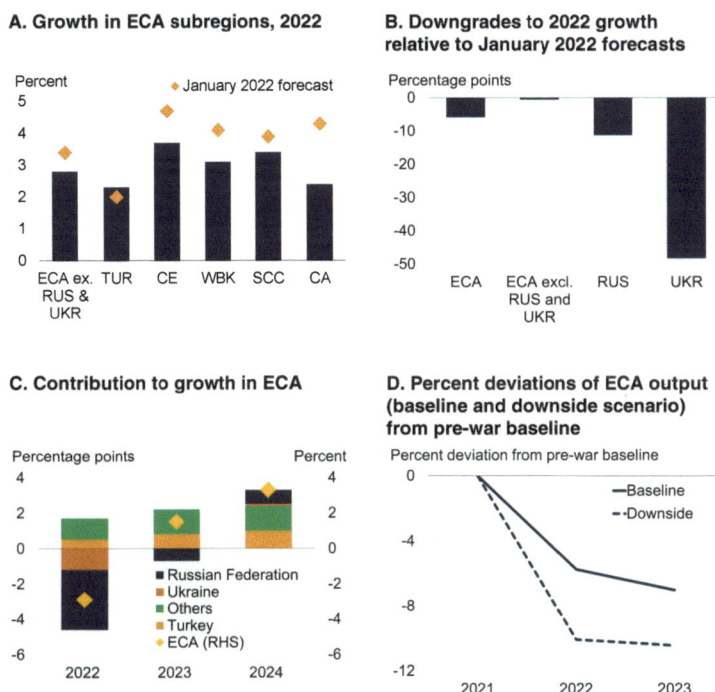

A. Growth in ECA subregions, 2022

B. Downgrades to 2022 growth relative to January 2022 forecasts

C. Contribution to growth in ECA

D. Percent deviations of ECA output (baseline and downside scenario) from pre-war baseline

Sources: International Monetary Fund; Oxford Economics; United Nations World Tourism Organization (UNWTO); World Bank.
Note: CA = Central Asia; CE = Central Europe; RUS = Russian Federation; SCC = South Caucasus; TUR = Turkey; UKR = Ukraine; WBK = Western Balkans.
A. Bars denote latest forecast; diamonds correspond to January 2022 forecasts in the *Global Economic Prospects* report.
B. Figure shows the percentage point difference between the latest projections and forecasts released in the January 2022 edition of the *Global Economic Prospects* report (World Bank 2022).
C. Aggregates calculated using constant GDP weights at average 2010-19 prices and market exchange rates. The sample includes 23 ECA countries.
D. Figure shows the percent deviation from the prewar baseline in ECA output as a result of the Russian invasion of Ukraine. Prewar is defined as projections published in the January 2022 edition of the *Global Economic Prospects* report. "Baseline" entails current projections as reflected in table 2.2.2. "Downside" entails a scenario in which the war's impact is much more severe, as outlined in World Bank (2022). It assumes that an escalation of the war triggers additional sanctions and reduces Russian exports to the euro area. The downside scenario also assumes a shock to financial confidence, a 20 percent contraction in Russian GDP, and a 75 percent contraction in Ukrainian GDP. The Oxford Global Economic Model (GEM)—a large-scale global semi-structural projection model—is used to conduct the simulations described here (Oxford Economics 2019).

to be amplified by the war given the destruction of schools and disruption to schooling.

Russian output is forecast to contract by 8.9 percent in 2022, reflecting a sharp fall in domestic demand and declining exports. GDP is expected to continue to contract in 2023, by 2 percent, as the impact of a partial oil embargo on Russia's oil exports to the EU dampens net exports. Although fiscal support to households has helped stave off a larger fall in 2022, private consumption is expected to remain depressed as income losses and supply shortages mount. Private fixed investment is expected to continue to fall amid lower foreign investment, input shortages, weakened economic prospects, and high credit costs. Import compression from the fall in domestic demand and export bans to Russia will ameliorate external financing pressures. Over the medium term, there is the possibility that Russia can manage to reroute some of its trade and investment from countries imposing sanctions to others, notably China and India. The decision by many countries to ban exports of key high-tech goods to Russia— including software, semiconductors, and avionics—will deprive Russian industry of critical inputs and exacerbate regional supply chain disruptions. As a result of the war, oil production will be curtailed due to the exit of foreign oil companies, investment will weaken, and access to foreign technology will shrink.

In *Turkey*—the region's second largest economy— growth is projected to slow sharply in 2022, to 2.3 percent, after surging last year. The war in Ukraine is exacerbating domestic headwinds that predated the war, including high inflation and weakening investor sentiment. Following multiple policy rate cuts, annual consumer price inflation has more than tripled to 70 percent in April, a 20-year high, with the lira hovering near last year's record lows against the U.S. dollar (World Bank 2022b). Higher commodity prices from the Ukraine war are expected to add to inflation, widen the current account deficit, and weigh on consumption. On the other hand, growth could be stronger if fiscal policy or tourism prove to be more supportive this year.

In *Eastern Europe excluding Ukraine*, GDP is projected to contract by 5.6 percent in 2022 as the recession deepens in Belarus. Private consumption will be set back by recessions in Russia and Ukraine, as 50 percent and 15 percent of remittances are sourced from Russia and Ukraine, respectively. The influx of refugees to Moldova has at times exceeded 15 percent of Moldova's population; although a large share have transited to the EU, the remaining refugees will likely have high fiscal costs, squeezing resources for long-term development priorities.

In ECA countries outside Eastern Europe, growth is expected to be weakened in most countries in *Central Asia* and the *South Caucasus* because of tight economic linkages with the Russian economy. In both subregions, growth is projected to about halve in 2022 from 2021, falling to 2.4 percent in Central Asia and 3.4 percent in the South Caucasus. Although higher global commodity prices should provide windfalls that help cushion activity in some economies (Azerbaijan, Kazakhstan, Uzbekistan), these benefits are likely to be limited. An important reason is supply constraints, with the oil sector already operating close to capacity in Azerbaijan and an earlier disruption to a major pipeline in Kazakhstan. More broadly, sharp reductions in external demand and remittances from Russia are likely to form a larger drag on some of these economies than the gains from higher commodity prices. In Central Asia, sanctions on Russia imposed in response to Russia's invasion of Ukraine pose challenges to financial intermediation. The war is magnifying other vulnerabilities also, including risks of debt distress in the Kyrgyz Republic and Tajikistan. Both countries are expected to experience output contractions this year, wider fiscal and external current account deficits, and sharp currency depreciations.

In *Central Europe*, the key economic transmission channels from the Ukraine war are the influx of refugees, higher commodity prices, and lower external demand from the euro area. Energy supply disruptions could put additional strains on production and exacerbate upward pressures on prices, especially in light of Russia's cutting off direct natural gas exports to Poland and Bulgaria and the EU's announced plans to ban or phase out fossil fuel imports from Russia by 2027 (Special Focus 2). Growth in Central Europe is forecast to weaken in 2022 alongside that in the euro area, slipping to 3.7 percent, as external demand slows and higher inflation, tighter monetary policies, and greater policy uncertainty dampen domestic demand. The large inflow of displaced people from Ukraine—who are predominantly women, children, and the elderly—is increasing demand for public services and housing, putting pressure on public finances. The influx has been especially large in Poland, with arriving Ukrainian refugees amounting to about 10 percent of Poland's population. Over the medium term, the Central European economies will benefit from funding from the European Union (EU) Recovery and Resilience Facility—the centerpiece of the Next Generation EU funds.

In the *Western Balkans*, GDP growth is forecast to slow to 3.1 percent in 2022, reflecting higher commodity prices and weaker euro area growth from the war, and to continue at about that annual rate in 2023-24. Over the medium term, the subregion is expected to benefit from the EU's recently adopted Economic and Investment Plan for the Western Balkans, which will mobilize funding to support competitiveness and inclusive growth, as well as the green and digital transition.

Risks

Risks to the ECA outlook remain heavily skewed to the downside. Prolonged or intensified war or armed conflict could cause significantly larger economic damage and greater potential for fragmentation of international trade and investment, especially as it comes on the heels of heightened tensions in the region (figure 2.2.3.A). There would also be a further deterioration of the humanitarian situation, which is already dire in the baseline outlook (figure 2.2.3.B).

The outlook remains vulnerable to financial stress, especially given high debt levels and elevated inflation (figure 2.2.3.C). Russia's sizable macroeconomic buffers are now impaired, increasing the risk of a credit crunch in the banking sector—additional restrictions could cause further dysfunction in domestic financial markets and greater macroeconomic destabilization. There are unknown risks that could materialize in the regional financial system, potentially arising from under-appreciated exposures to Russia, such as leveraged over-the-counter products that depend on underlying Russian assets.

Additional war-driven disruptions in energy imports from Russia could materially worsen the growth outlook, especially for the euro area—ECA's largest trading partner—and Russia, which would further damage ECA's economy. Possible

FIGURE 2.2.3 ECA: Risks

The war comes on the heels of heightened tensions. It is expected to push millions into poverty in Ukraine, but sharply higher commodity prices could cause poverty rates to rise across the region. The war has increased the risk of financial stress, especially given high inflation and debt. Continued disruptions to regional trade could worsen food insecurity for the most vulnerable.

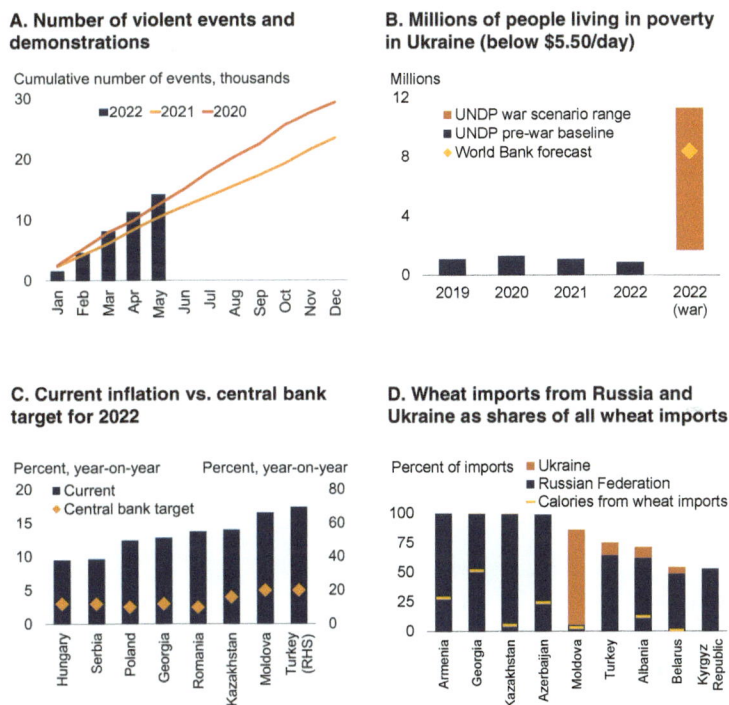

A. Number of violent events and demonstrations

B. Millions of people living in poverty in Ukraine (below $5.50/day)

C. Current inflation vs. central bank target for 2022

D. Wheat imports from Russia and Ukraine as shares of all wheat imports

Sources: Armed Conflict Location & Event Data Project (ACLED), https://www.acleddata.com; Central bank websites; Food and Agriculture Organization of the United Nations; Haver Analytics; International Monetary Fund; Comtrade (database); U.S. Department of Agriculture; World Bank.
Note: ECA = Europe and Central Asia.
A. Cumulative number of violent events and demonstrations reported across 23 ECA EMDEs. Violent events include violence against civilians, riots, protests, battles, and explosions/remote violence. Last observation is May 27, 2022.
B. The range shows estimates based on four scenarios using previous armed conflict as benchmarks, as presented in UNDP (2022). The four scenarios simulated are economic contractions of 7, 15, 20, and 60 percent. The yellow diamond is the World Bank Ukraine poverty estimate.
C. "Current" indicates most recently available monthly year-on-year inflation data. "Current" data are right-hand side (RHS) and "Central bank target" data are left-hand side for Turkey. Data are through May 31, 2022.
D. Data as of 2020.

disruptions to supplies of natural gas and oil are acute risks in Central Europe and the Western Balkans. Available stocks of natural gas vary, with limited storage capacity in smaller countries, such as Bosnia and Herzegovina, while in Serbia existing inventory could help mitigate the immediate supply shock.

If record-high food prices persist, monetary policy tightening could be accelerated and a significantly higher number of people than currently expected could be pushed into extreme poverty and experience food insecurity, especially in those countries reliant on Russia and Ukraine for grains (figure 2.2.3.D). The spike in commodity prices and subsequently higher inflation could also contribute to social unrest in some countries (Kammer et al. 2022). Vulnerable countries typically have weaker governance and social safety nets, fewer job opportunities, less fiscal space, and elevated political tensions.

TABLE 2.2.1 Europe and Central Asia forecast summary

(Real GDP growth at market prices in percent, unless indicated otherwise)

Percentage point differences from January 2022 projections

	2019	2020	2021e	2022f	2023f	2024f	2022f	2023f
EMDE ECA, GDP[1]	2.7	-1.9	6.5	-2.9	1.5	3.3	-5.9	-1.4
GDP per capita (U.S. dollars)	2.3	-2.2	6.3	-3.1	1.4	3.2	-5.9	-1.4
EMDE ECA, GDP excl. Russian Federation and Ukraine	3.1	-1.3	7.9	2.8	3.5	3.8	-0.6	-0.1
EMDE ECA, GDP excl. Turkey	3.2	-2.9	5.3	-4.5	1.0	3.0	-7.8	-1.9
(Average including countries that report expenditure components in national accounts)[2]								
EMDE ECA, GDP[2]	2.6	-1.9	6.6	-3.5	1.3	3.2	-6.4	-1.4
PPP GDP	2.5	-1.9	6.6	-4.5	1.3	3.2	-7.3	-1.4
Private consumption	3.7	-3.1	9.7	-4.3	2.4	2.8	-7.4	-0.7
Public consumption	3.0	2.5	2.2	2.7	2.2	1.7	1.2	0.1
Fixed investment	-0.8	-1.5	7.1	-9.7	0.1	8.6	-12.5	-3.9
Exports, GNFS[3]	3.6	-6.6	9.5	-8.1	4.5	4.8	-13.8	-0.4
Imports, GNFS[3]	3.0	-4.5	10.0	-4.7	5.3	5.9	-10.2	-0.8
Net exports, contribution to growth	0.4	-1.0	0.2	-1.5	-0.2	-0.3	-1.8	0.0
Memo items: GDP								
Commodity exporters[4]	2.6	-2.7	4.7	-9.0	-0.7	2.7	-11.7	-3.1
Commodity exporters excl. Russian Federation and Ukraine	4.6	-2.1	5.3	2.5	4.0	3.8	-1.6	-0.7
Commodity importers[5]	2.8	-1.1	8.3	2.8	3.4	3.7	-0.5	0.0
Central Europe[6]	4.5	-3.3	6.2	3.7	3.7	3.7	-1.0	0.0
Western Balkans[7]	3.7	-3.3	7.5	3.1	3.1	3.2	-1.0	-0.7
Eastern Europe[8]	2.7	-3.1	3.6	-30.6	1.9	3.9	-32.0	-1.3
South Caucasus[9]	3.8	-5.3	6.7	3.4	3.3	3.3	-0.5	-0.3
Central Asia[10]	4.9	-1.3	5.1	2.4	4.3	4.1	-1.9	-0.8
Russian Federation	2.2	-2.7	4.7	-8.9	-2.0	2.2	-11.3	-3.8
Turkey	0.9	1.8	11.0	2.3	3.2	4.0	0.3	0.2
Poland	4.7	-2.2	5.9	3.9	3.6	3.7	-0.8	0.2

Source: World Bank.

Note: e = estimate; f = forecast; PPP = purchasing power parity; EMDE = emerging market and developing economy. World Bank forecasts are frequently updated based on new information and changing (global) circumstances. Consequently, projections presented here may differ from those contained in other Bank documents, even if basic assessments of countries' prospects do not differ at any given moment in time. The World Bank is currently not publishing economic output, income, or growth data for Turkmenistan owing to a lack of reliable data of adequate quality. Turkmenistan is excluded from cross-country macroeconomic aggregates.

1. GDP and expenditure components are measured in average 2010-19 prices and market exchange rates, thus aggregates presented here may differ from other World Bank documents.

2. Aggregates presented here exclude Azerbaijan, Bosnia and Herzegovina, Kazakhstan, Kosovo, the Kyrgyz Republic, Montenegro, Serbia, Tajikistan, Turkmenistan, and Uzbekistan, for which data limitations prevent the forecasting of GDP components.

3. Exports and imports of goods and nonfactor services (GNFS).

4. Includes Armenia, Azerbaijan, Kazakhstan, the Kyrgyz Republic, Kosovo, the Russian Federation, Tajikistan, Ukraine, and Uzbekistan.

5. Includes Albania, Belarus, Bosnia and Herzegovina, Bulgaria, Croatia, Georgia, Hungary, Moldova, Montenegro, North Macedonia, Poland, Romania, Serbia, and Turkey.

6. Includes Bulgaria, Croatia, Hungary, Poland, and Romania.

7. Includes Albania, Bosnia and Herzegovina, Kosovo, Montenegro, North Macedonia, and Serbia.

8. Includes Belarus, Moldova, and Ukraine.

9. Includes Armenia, Azerbaijan, and Georgia.

10. Includes Kazakhstan, the Kyrgyz Republic, Tajikistan, and Uzbekistan.

TABLE 2.2.2 Europe and Central Asia country forecasts[1]

(Real GDP growth at market prices in percent, unless indicated otherwise)

Percentage point differences from January 2022 projections

	2019	2020	2021e	2022f	2023f	2024f	2022f	2023f
Albania	2.2	-3.5	8.5	3.2	3.5	3.5	-0.6	-0.2
Armenia	7.6	-7.2	5.7	3.5	4.6	4.9	-1.3	-0.8
Azerbaijan	2.5	-4.3	5.6	2.7	2.2	2.3	-0.4	-0.5
Belarus	1.4	-0.9	2.3	-6.5	1.5	1.6	-3.7	-0.8
Bosnia and Herzegovina[2]	2.8	-3.1	7.1	2.7	3.1	3.5	-0.3	-0.1
Bulgaria	4.0	-4.4	4.2	2.6	4.3	3.7	-1.2	0.7
Croatia	3.5	-8.1	10.4	3.8	3.4	3.1	-1.6	-1.0
Georgia	5.0	-6.8	10.6	5.5	5.5	5.0	0.0	0.5
Hungary	4.6	-4.5	7.1	4.6	3.8	3.4	-0.4	-0.5
Kazakhstan	4.5	-2.5	4.0	2.0	4.0	3.5	-1.7	-0.8
Kosovo	4.8	-5.3	9.1	3.9	4.3	4.2	-0.2	-0.1
Kyrgyz Republic	4.6	-8.4	3.6	-2.0	3.4	4.0	-6.7	-0.9
Moldova	3.7	-7.4	13.9	-0.4	2.7	4.2	-4.3	-1.7
Montenegro	4.1	-15.3	12.4	3.6	4.7	3.7	-2.0	-0.1
North Macedonia	3.9	-6.1	4.0	2.7	3.1	3.2	-1.0	-0.3
Poland	4.7	-2.2	5.9	3.9	3.6	3.7	-0.8	0.2
Romania	4.2	-3.7	5.9	2.9	3.7	3.9	-1.4	-0.1
Russian Federation	2.2	-2.7	4.7	-8.9	-2.0	2.2	-11.3	-3.8
Serbia	4.3	-0.9	7.4	3.2	2.7	2.8	-1.3	-1.3
Tajikistan	7.4	4.4	9.2	-0.4	3.3	4.3	-5.9	-1.2
Turkey	0.9	1.8	11.0	2.3	3.2	4.0	0.3	0.2
Ukraine	3.2	-3.8	3.4	-45.1	2.1	5.8	-48.3	-1.4
Uzbekistan	5.7	1.9	7.4	4.3	5.3	5.5	-1.3	-0.5

Source: World Bank.

Note: e = estimate; f = forecast. World Bank forecasts are frequently updated based on new information and changing (global) circumstances. Consequently, projections presented here may differ from those contained in other Bank documents, even if basic assessments of countries' prospects do not significantly differ at any given moment in time. The World Bank is currently not publishing economic output, income, or growth data for Turkmenistan owing to a lack of reliable data of adequate quality. Turkmenistan is excluded from cross-country macroeconomic aggregates.

1. Data are based on GDP measured in average 2010-19 prices and market exchange rates, unless indicated otherwise.

2. GDP growth rate at constant prices is based on production approach.

LATIN AMERICA and THE CARIBBEAN

Growth in Latin America and the Caribbean (LAC) is forecast to slow sharply in 2022 and remain weak in the following two years. Elevated inflation, tighter financial conditions, and policy uncertainty are expected to take a toll domestically, while slowing growth in key export markets, U.S. monetary tightening, and global supply bottlenecks impart negative spillovers to the region. The largest economies in LAC will be some of the slowest growing this year, dragging region-wide growth down to 2.5 percent. Growth is set to slow further in 2023 to just 1.9 percent. The Russian Federation's invasion of Ukraine has raised prices for many regional exports, but is likely to have a negative net effect on growth in LAC via weaker global trade and increases in input costs and consumer prices. Recent high inflation is likely to extend monetary policy tightening cycles. Risks to the baseline projections are tilted to the downside, and include further shocks to global growth, domestic stagflation, financial stress, and social unrest linked to sharply higher prices for food and energy.

Recent developments

The war in Ukraine has limited direct effects on Latin America and the Caribbean (LAC), given the region's modest trade and financial linkages with eastern Europe and central Asia, but there are substantial indirect spillovers via commodity prices and global growth. Current account and fiscal balances of some LAC commodity exporters are benefitting from high commodity prices (figure 2.3.1.A). However, positive effects on economic activity are being outweighed by rising consumer prices, higher policy interest rates to rein in inflation and weaker sentiment (World Bank 2022c). The net negative effect on growth compounds a slowdown already underway across the region. Even before the war, headwinds from high inflation, rising interest rates, and protracted supply chain disruptions had been weighing on activity. The recovery from the pandemic remains incomplete, hampered by structural impediments such as low productivity growth and high inequality (Dieppe 2021; World Bank 2022b).

Inflation across LAC has risen well above central bank targets. Increases in food and fuel prices have been a major driver, but recent data show price acceleration broadening across consumption baskets. Adding to the pressures are supply chain bottlenecks in some countries (Brazil, Mexico) and above-trend domestic demand following stimulative policies in others (Chile, Colombia). In Argentina, amid rising international food and energy prices, continued, albeit declining, monetary financing of the fiscal deficit has contributed to pushing monthly inflation to about 6 percent. Monetary authorities in LAC have raised policy interest rates significantly and signaled further increases this year, even as activity indicators have remained soft in some countries (figure 2.3.1.B). Governments across the region (Chile, Colombia, Mexico, Suriname) have increased subsidies or cut taxes on fuel to limit the impact of high oil prices on consumers, while the government of Mexico has also introduced voluntary price agreements with the private sector, while suspending import tariffs for staple goods and facilitating access to fertilizer for small food producers.

Financial conditions in LAC have tightened notably in recent months, largely as a result of rising U.S. and domestic interest rates. Across Brazil, Chile, Colombia, Mexico, and Peru, the average ten-year government bond yield has increased by about 150 basis points year-to-date. LAC financial markets showed resilience early in

Note: This section was prepared by Phil Kenworthy.

FIGURE 2.3.1 **LAC: Recent developments**

Higher commodity prices will benefit fiscal and current account balances in much of LAC, but positive effects will be offset by sharply higher inflation and rapidly rising interest rates. High vaccination rates have led to substantial reductions in deaths from COVID-19, but supply chain disruptions continue to curb manufacturing output.

A. Commodity trade balances

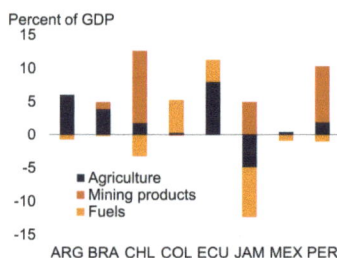

B. Central bank interest rates

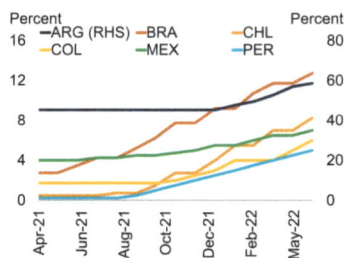

C. COVID-19 deaths and vaccinations

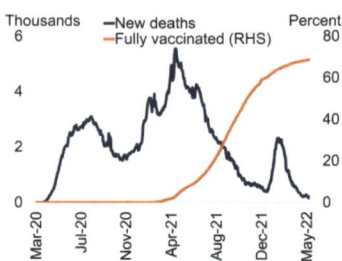

D. Auto production and prices in Mexico and Brazil

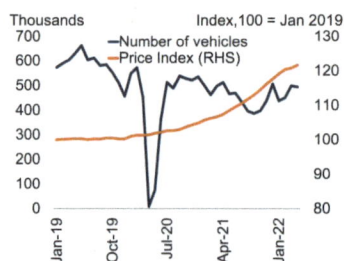

Sources: Federal Reserve Bank of St. Louis (database); Haver Analytics; national sources; Our World in Data (database); WTO stats (database); World Bank.
A. B. ARG = Argentina; BRA = Brazil; CHL = Chile; COL = Colombia; ECU = Ecuador; JAM = Jamaica; MEX = Mexico; PER = Peru.
A. Average of annual net exports as a percent of GDP for 2015-19.
B. Policy rates at the end of the reference month. Last observation is May 2022.
C. New deaths show seven-day moving average. Fully vaccinated is the number of people in LAC fully vaccinated as a percent of the LAC population. Last observation is May 30, 2022.
D. Sum of production of vehicles in Mexico and Brazil. Last observation is April 2022. Price index is an average of auto prices in Brazil, Mexico, and the United States.

the year, but reversed course in April as nonresident debt and equity flows turned negative and South American currencies depreciated swiftly. Sovereign spreads also widened, though they generally remain contained compared to historical episodes of financial stress in the region.

The spread of the Omicron variant of COVID-19 caused a sharp but brief spike in case rates in LAC in 2022Q1. The regional rise in deaths was muted by relatively high vaccination levels, though vaccination rates in several Caribbean countries remain below 40 percent, reflecting vaccine hesitancy and insufficient health infrastructure (figure 2.3.1.C; PAHO 2022). Successive COVID

-19 waves around the world have exacerbated bottlenecks in LAC supply chains, weighing on manufacturing. For example, auto production in Mexico and Brazil remains far below 2019 levels despite high prices, illustrating the extent of supply chain frictions (figure 2.3.1.D).

Outlook

Growth in LAC is projected to slow sharply to 2.5 percent in 2022, after a post-pandemic rebound of 6.7 percent in 2021. The region's growth is expected to decelerate further in 2023, to 1.9 percent, before picking up slightly to 2.4 percent in 2024. This slowdown reflects the maturing of the recovery from the pandemic-recession, tighter financial conditions, in part because of faster-than-anticipated U.S. monetary tightening, weakening external demand growth, increased inflation, and high policy uncertainty in some countries. Regional growth in 2022 has been downgraded marginally from previous projections, by 0.1 percentage point. Growth in 2023 has been downgraded by 0.8 percentage point. This largely corresponds to the lagged effects on investment from rising interest rates. The growth outlook underscores the challenge to deliver rising living standards in LAC. Per capita GDP is set to increase just 0.6 percent between 2019 and 2023, compared to 1.3 percent per year in the preceding 20 years.

All large LAC economies except Mexico are net commodity exporters, so higher commodity prices will generally improve terms of trade and export earnings. Prices of several key exports are expected to be substantially higher on average in 2022, including oil, coal, agricultural commodities, copper, and gold. However, benefits to growth will take time to materialize and be dampened by factors such as adverse weather, which is impacting crop yields, and long lags in the response of metals production to higher prices (Boer, Pescatori, and Stuermer 2021). Further, commodity price developments are not as favorable for LAC as for predominantly energy-exporting regions. Surging energy prices instead represent sharply increasing input costs in many countries, while higher fertilizer costs will curb benefits from elevated agricultural export prices.

Brazil imports about 80 percent of its fertilizer, while Argentina imports close to 70 percent.

The ongoing monetary tightening cycle has seen real policy interest rates climb sharply in some LAC economies, but inflation is expected to remain above central bank targets throughout 2022, prompting further tightening (figure 2.3.2.A). In this context, investment in LAC is expected to rise only modestly, by 2.2 percent in 2022 and 1.6 percent in 2023. The projections assume fiscal consolidation in about three-quarters of LAC economies in 2022 and 2023. New policies to shield consumers from food and energy price rises in about 40 percent of LAC countries have reduced the pace of consolidation, but fiscal policy is still expected to exert a modest drag on growth (Acosta-Ormaechea, Goldfajn, and Roldos 2022). The regionwide primary fiscal deficit is expected to narrow to less than 1 percent of GDP in 2022 (figure 2.3.2.B).

In *Brazil*, growth is expected to fall sharply to 1.5 percent in 2022, from 4.6 percent in 2021, and then slow further to just 0.8 percent in 2023. After a solid start to 2022, growth is expected to wane over the year, owing to the squeeze on real incomes from double-digit inflation, stalling investment growth, and heightened domestic policy uncertainty. Recently announced programs to allow extraordinary withdrawals from unemployment insurance funds, accelerate social security payments, and extend concessional loans will offer some relief to households, but possibly at the cost of further stoking inflation. In 2023, weak momentum and the ongoing effects of tighter monetary policy on investment and activity are expected to limit growth.

Growth in *Mexico* is forecast to weaken to 1.7 percent in 2022, from 4.8 percent in 2021, before picking up slightly to 1.9 percent in 2023. Given above-target and broad-based inflation, the central bank is expected to continue raising interest rates throughout 2022, which will weigh on investment. Weaker output growth is also a consequence of supply bottlenecks, which have disrupted Mexico's globally integrated manufacturing sector and are expected to abate only gradually. Regulatory uncertainty in sectors

FIGURE 2.3.2 LAC: Outlook

Real interest rates have risen sharply in some LAC economies, and monetary policies are expected to tighten further, dampening demand. Fiscal policy will also exert a modest drag on growth in 2022. With tighter macroeconomic policies and weakening growth, much of projected growth in 2022 is due to carryover effects. Caribbean tourism is expected to continue to recover in coming years.

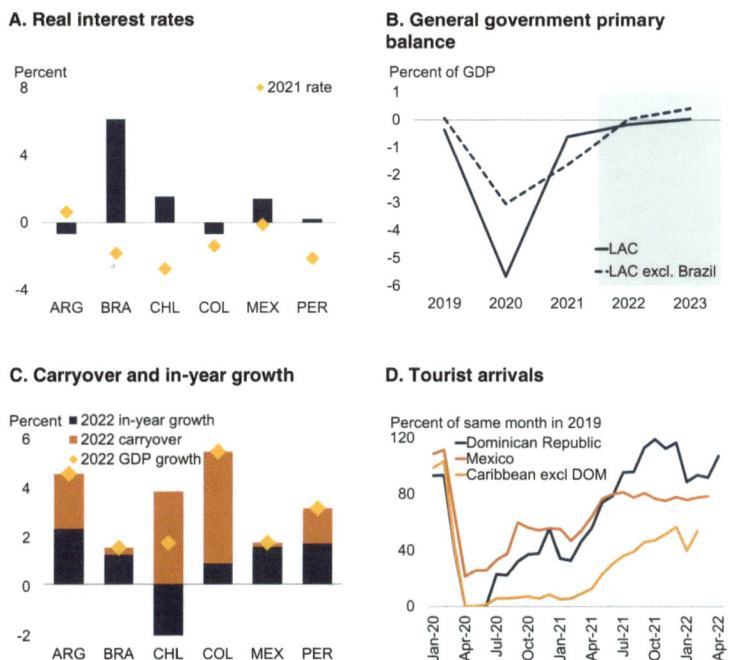

A. Real interest rates

B. General government primary balance

C. Carryover and in-year growth

D. Tourist arrivals

Sources: Consensus Economics; Haver Analytics; International Monetary Fund; national sources; World Bank.
A. Real interest rate is the central bank policy rate minus one-year-ahead inflation expectations constructed from 2022 and 2023 Consensus Economics estimates for consumer price inflation. Transformation is via the method used in Ruch (2021), Bordo and Siklos (2017), and Siklos (2013). "2021 rate" is the equivalent value for June 2021.
A. B. ARG = Argentina; BRA = Brazil; CHL = Chile; COL = Colombia; MEX = Mexico; PER = Peru.
B. Figure shows the GDP-weighted general government primary balance. Gray shading indicates forecasts. Sample includes 29 LAC economies.
C. Carryover assumes that real GDP is the same in every quarter of 2022 as it was in 2021Q4.
D. Data are international tourist arrivals. Caribbean includes Antigua and Barbuda, The Bahamas, Barbados, Belize, Jamaica, and St. Lucia. Last observation is February 2022 for tourism to the Caribbean, April 2022 the Dominican Republic and March 2022 for tourism to Mexico. DOM = the Dominican Republic.

such as energy and extractives may dampen investment, despite supportive prices. Tax cuts intended to limit fuel price increases will provide some relief for households, but are not targeted to those most in need.

Output in *Argentina* is expected to grow 4.5 percent in 2022 and 2.5 percent in both 2023 and 2024. The projected expansion in 2022 represents a 1.9 percentage point upgrade from previous forecasts, which is close to the statistical carryover effect from strong growth momentum (figure 2.3.2.C). Net trade is forecast to be broadly neutral for growth, while the rising cost of imported energy compared to 2021 is expected to limit current account benefits from higher prices for agricultural exports. High energy prices will put pressure on spending, given large energy subsidies. Control of inflation remains elusive, which will continue to weigh on activity.

Growth in *Colombia* is projected to reach 5.4 percent in 2022, mostly owing to carryover effects, and 3.2 percent in 2023. Monetary policy is expected to tighten this year, while the primary fiscal deficit is envisioned to decline rapidly over the forecast horizon as the yield from recent tax reforms kicks in and pandemic-related spending declines. Colombia's current account balance will benefit substantially from higher prices for oil, coal, and metals.

Chile is forecast to grow 1.7 percent in 2022 owing to carryover effects from strong consumption growth. Rapid tightening of fiscal and monetary policies in light of elevated inflation is projected to slow activity in 2022, though the current account balance is expected to improve markedly as imports fall. Annual growth is forecast to slow further in 2023 to 0.8 percent, as export growth declines and investment remains subdued.

Peru is projected to grow by 3.1 percent in 2022 and 2.9 percent in 2023, bolstered by increasing mining output, though heightened policy uncertainty will curb investment. The ongoing normalization of labor markets will support steady expansion of consumption, as will growth in government spending.

Growth in *Central America* is forecast at 3.9 percent in 2022 (on a GDP-weighted basis), moderating to 3.5 percent in 2023. Growth and consumption will slow more than previously forecast in 2022-23, broadly tracking activity in the United States, the main source of export demand and remittances. Fiscal policy is expected to be contractionary in much of Central America, as pandemic-related spending is withdrawn, and governments seek to stabilize debt, though in *Guatemala*, public spending is expected to increase, supporting growth in 2022. Across most of Central America oil imports will weigh on

terms of trade, while sharply rising food prices will cut into real household spending. *Panama* is a set to outperform the surrounding region, with growth of 6.3 percent in 2022 thanks to rising mining output and a pick-up in tourism.

For the *Caribbean*, robust growth of 6.9 percent is forecast for 2022, slowing slightly to 6.5 percent in 2023. The continued, but incomplete, recovery of tourism towards pre-pandemic levels is an important driver of growth, supporting exports, employment, and investment (figure 2.3.2.D). In addition, *Guyana's* economy is forecast to double in size in 2022-23, on account of the rapid development of the offshore oil and gas industry. In *Jamaica*, increasing alumina production will boost exports, though dependence on imported oil will weigh on the current account.

Risks

Risks to the forecast are to the downside. In the context of unusually high uncertainty over the global outlook, there is a significant risk that weaker-than-expected growth in major trading partners could result in softer exports and investment in LAC. China is the largest export market for most South American countries, while for Mexico and Central America, the United States provides the majority of export demand and remittances (figure 2.3.3.A). A sharper slowdown in China would likely lead to lower prices for LAC exports such as copper, soybeans, and iron ore. Given sluggish domestic demand, a negative external shock would further increase the chances of recession in some large LAC economies.

Russia's invasion of Ukraine has exacerbated the rise in fertilizer prices. The largest agricultural producers in LAC depend on fertilizer imports, as the region has limited production capacity. In 2019, LAC countries sourced about one-quarter of these fertilizer imports from Belarus and Russia (figure 2.3.3.B). So far, fertilizer inventories and planting schedules have prevented rising fertilizer costs from substantially impacting crop yields. However, if war-related disruptions, recession in Russia, and continued high energy prices cause fertilizer shortages, future harvests could be impacted (World Bank 2022d). As a direct consequence, agricultural output in LAC could fall. Indirect reverberations could be more severe. Food prices could rise further, increasing food insecurity and poverty—high food prices could contribute to an additional 3 million people in LAC experiencing extreme poverty in 2022, versus pre-pandemic projections (Mahler et al. 2022). Social unrest could follow, dampening investment and sentiment. In response, governments might be tempted to pursue ultimately counterproductive policies such as price controls and export restrictions (World Bank 2020).

Given the history of inflation problems and macroeconomic instability in LAC, there is a serious risk that high inflation becomes embedded in inflation expectations. Though medium-term measures of inflation expectations appear relatively well-anchored, core inflation in the region's largest economies has risen swiftly alongside food and fuel prices (figure 2.3.3.C). If inflation does not decline substantially in the coming months, the region's central banks may be forced to raise interest rates significantly more than expected, even in the context of slowing growth, possibly resulting in a sharp slowdown or recession.

Another risk, especially given rising U.S. interest rates, is that negative sentiment and regional vulnerabilities combine to generate financial stress. The pandemic has weakened long-term growth prospects and public debt-to-GDP ratios in the largest LAC economies are expected to be on average 18 percentage points higher in 2022 than they were in 2015 (figure 2.3.3.D). Sovereign spreads remain contained, but further shocks to activity or sentiment could see investors reappraise growth outlooks and debt-carrying capacity in LAC. Capital outflows and increases in risk premia could follow. Countries with elevated public debt or lacking strong fiscal frameworks could be at particular risk, especially where high levels of uncertainty and fractious politics make it challenging for policy makers to credibly commit to necessary reforms. Debt management strategies that lean towards excessive short-term or external debt could exacerbate vulnerabilities in some countries in the region.

FIGURE 2.3.3 LAC: Risks

Slower-than-forecast growth in major trading partners would pose risks to export demand in LAC. Dependence on imported fertilizer could compromise food production. Increases in core inflation may necessitate faster-than-expected monetary tightening. Public debt has risen considerably across the region in recent years, eroding financial buffers.

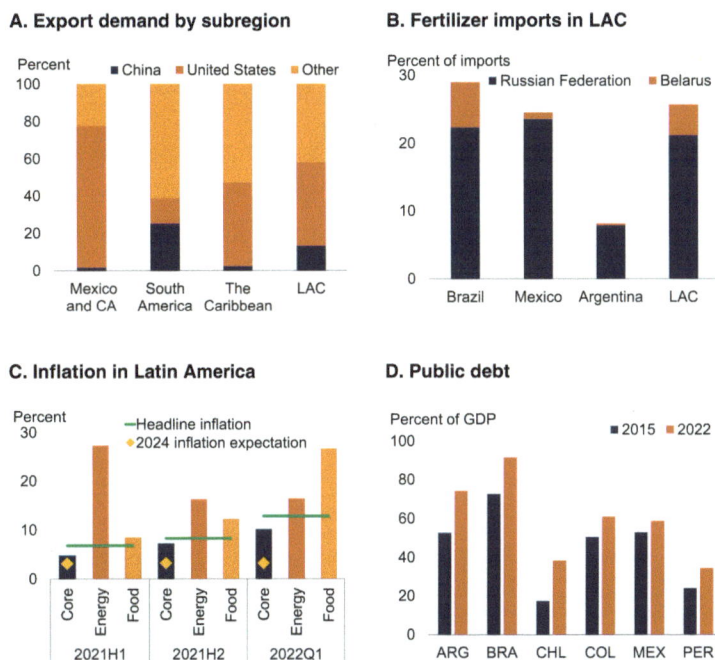

A. Export demand by subregion

B. Fertilizer imports in LAC

C. Inflation in Latin America

D. Public debt

Sources: Comtrade (database); Consensus Economics; Haver Analytics; International Monetary Fund; World Bank.

A. CA = Central America. Shows the source of export demand for 2019 and 2020 exports. "Other" includes intraregional exports.

B. Percent of imports. LAC sample includes 18 economies.

C. Data represent averages for Brazil, Chile, Colombia, and Mexico. Rates of inflation in each category and time period are annualized for comparability. Data are seasonally adjusted. 2024 inflation expectation is the Consensus Economics inflation forecast for 2024. Categories contain some common elements and category definitions vary by country.

D. General government gross debt as a percentage of GDP. ARG = Argentina; BRA = Brazil; CHL = Chile; COL = Colombia; MEX = Mexico; PER = Peru.

TABLE 2.3.1 Latin America and the Caribbean forecast summary

(Real GDP growth at market prices in percent, unless indicated otherwise)

Percentage point differences from January 2022 projections

	2019	2020	2021e	2022f	2023f	2024f	2022f	2023f
EMDE LAC, GDP[1]	0.8	-6.4	6.7	2.5	1.9	2.4	-0.1	-0.8
GDP per capita (U.S. dollars)	-0.3	-7.4	5.7	1.7	1.1	1.6	0.0	-0.8
(Average including countries that report expenditure components in national accounts)[2]								
EMDE LAC, GDP[2]	0.8	-6.5	6.7	2.4	1.8	2.4	-0.1	-0.8
PPP GDP	0.8	-6.7	6.9	2.5	1.9	2.4	-0.1	-0.7
Private consumption	1.1	-7.9	7.3	2.8	2.1	2.4	0.1	-0.8
Public consumption	0.0	-2.4	3.7	0.8	0.5	0.5	-1.0	0.3
Fixed investment	-0.7	-11.0	17.4	2.2	1.6	3.5	0.7	-2.1
Exports, GNFS[3]	0.8	-8.9	8.2	4.9	4.7	4.2	-0.4	0.1
Imports, GNFS[3]	-0.8	-13.9	17.7	4.3	4.3	4.2	0.2	-0.6
Net exports, contribution to growth	0.4	1.2	-2.0	0.1	0.0	0.0	-0.1	0.1
Memo items: GDP								
South America[4]	0.9	-5.8	7.0	2.5	1.6	2.3	0.4	-1.0
Central America[5]	2.7	-7.6	10.3	3.9	3.5	3.6	-0.8	-0.2
Caribbean[6]	3.2	-6.7	8.9	6.9	6.5	4.0	-0.4	0.6
Brazil	1.2	-3.9	4.6	1.5	0.8	2.0	0.1	-1.9
Mexico	-0.2	-8.2	4.8	1.7	1.9	2.0	-1.3	-0.3
Argentina	-2.0	-9.9	10.3	4.5	2.5	2.5	1.9	0.4

Source: World Bank.

Note: e = estimate; f = forecast; PPP = purchasing power parity; EMDE = emerging market and developing economy. World Bank forecasts are frequently updated based on new information and changing (global) circumstances. Consequently, projections presented here may differ from those contained in other Bank documents, even if basic assessments of countries' prospects do not differ at any given moment in time. The World Bank is currently not publishing economic output, income, or growth data for República Bolivariana de Venezuela owing to a lack of reliable data of adequate quality. República Bolivariana de Venezuela is excluded from cross-country macroeconomic aggregates.

1. GDP and expenditure components are measured in average 2010-19 prices and market exchange rates.

2. Aggregate includes all countries in notes 4, 5, and 6, plus Mexico, except Antigua and Barbuda, Barbados, Dominica, Grenada, Guyana, Haiti, St. Kitts and Nevis, St. Lucia, St. Vincent and the Grenadines, and Suriname.

3. Exports and imports of goods and nonfactor services (GNFS).

4. Includes Argentina, Bolivia, Brazil, Chile, Colombia, Ecuador, Paraguay, Peru, and Uruguay.

5. Includes Costa Rica, El Salvador, Guatemala, Honduras, Nicaragua, and Panama.

6. Includes Antigua and Barbuda, The Bahamas, Barbados, Belize, Dominica, the Dominican Republic, Grenada, Guyana, Haiti, Jamaica, St. Kitts and Nevis, St. Lucia, St. Vincent and the Grenadines, and Suriname.

TABLE 2.3.2 Latin America and the Caribbean country forecasts [1]

(Real GDP growth at market prices in percent, unless indicated otherwise)

Percentage point differences from January 2022 projections

	2019	2020	2021e	2022f	2023f	2024f	2022f	2023f
Argentina	-2.0	-9.9	10.3	4.5	2.5	2.5	1.9	0.4
Bahamas, The	0.7	-14.5	5.6	6.0	4.1	3.0	-2.0	0.1
Barbados	-1.3	-13.7	1.4	11.2	4.9	3.0	2.7	0.1
Belize	2.0	-16.7	9.8	5.7	3.4	2.0	1.7	1.6
Bolivia	2.2	-8.7	6.1	3.9	2.8	2.7	0.4	0.1
Brazil	1.2	-3.9	4.6	1.5	0.8	2.0	0.1	-1.9
Chile	0.8	-6.0	11.7	1.7	0.8	2.0	-0.5	-1.0
Colombia	3.2	-7.0	10.6	5.4	3.2	3.3	1.3	-0.3
Costa Rica	2.4	-4.1	7.6	3.4	3.2	3.2	-0.1	0.0
Dominica	5.5	-11.0	3.7	6.8	5.0	4.6	-1.3	-0.9
Dominican Republic	5.1	-6.7	12.3	5.0	5.0	5.0	0.0	0.0
Ecuador	0.0	-7.8	4.4	3.7	3.1	2.9	0.6	0.6
El Salvador	2.6	-8.0	10.7	2.7	1.9	2.0	-1.3	-0.6
Grenada	0.7	-13.8	5.3	3.8	3.4	3.1	-0.6	-0.4
Guatemala	4.0	-1.8	8.0	3.4	3.4	3.5	-0.5	-0.1
Guyana	5.4	43.5	19.9	47.9	34.3	3.8	-1.8	9.3
Haiti [2]	-1.7	-3.3	-1.8	-0.4	1.4	2.0	-0.4	-0.1
Honduras	2.7	-9.0	12.5	3.1	3.6	3.7	-1.3	-0.2
Jamaica	0.9	-10.0	4.6	3.2	2.3	1.2	0.2	0.3
Mexico	-0.2	-8.2	4.8	1.7	1.9	2.0	-1.3	-0.3
Nicaragua	-3.8	-1.8	10.3	2.9	2.3	2.5	-0.1	-0.2
Panama	3.0	-17.9	15.3	6.3	5.0	5.0	-1.5	0.0
Paraguay	-0.4	-0.8	4.2	0.7	4.7	3.8	-3.3	0.8
Peru	2.2	-11.0	13.3	3.1	2.9	3.0	-0.1	-0.1
St. Lucia	-0.1	-20.4	6.6	6.4	5.2	3.3	-3.2	-1.9
St. Vincent and the Grenadines	0.4	-5.3	-2.8	3.7	6.4	3.2	-4.6	0.3
Suriname	1.1	-15.9	-3.5	1.8	2.1	2.7	0.0	0.0
Uruguay	0.4	-6.1	4.4	3.3	2.6	2.5	0.2	0.1

Source: World Bank.

Note: e = estimate; f = forecast. World Bank forecasts are frequently updated based on new information and changing (global) circumstances. Consequently, projections presented here may differ from those contained in other Bank documents, even if basic assessments of countries' prospects do not significantly differ at any given moment in time.

1. Data are based on GDP measured in average 2010-19 prices and market exchange rates.
2. GDP is based on fiscal year, which runs from October to September of next year.

MIDDLE EAST and NORTH AFRICA

Output in the Middle East and North Africa region is expected to expand by 5.3 percent in 2022—0.9 percentage point above previous projections, in part reflecting higher oil prices. This would be the region's fastest growth in a decade; however, this rebound is expected to be short-lived. The region faces a growing divide between oil exporters—which on net should benefit from elevated oil prices and high COVID-19 vaccination rates—and oil importers, which face higher food and energy prices, deteriorating external balances, and still-limited vaccination rates. Risks to the outlook are predominantly to the downside, with drought conditions, policy uncertainty, new outbreaks of COVID-19, and geopolitical tensions threatening to raise prices further, erode real incomes, and aggravate social tensions.

Recent developments

The economic recovery in the Middle East and North Africa (MNA) slowed briefly at the turn of the year as Omicron outbreaks sapped growth momentum (figure 2.4.1.A). New confirmed cases of COVID-19 have since abated with broad-based declines across all economies. The pandemic-induced slowdown was followed by the Russian Federation's invasion of Ukraine, leading to higher commodity prices, tighter financing conditions (amid reduced monetary accommodation in both advanced economies and in the region), and a further deceleration in global growth. The impact on the region is, however, notably divergent. On the one hand, oil exporters are benefiting from higher energy prices only partly offset by higher food prices and borrowing costs, even for large wheat importers like Algeria. On the other, oil importers face further headwinds to growth.

Oil exporters are benefiting from robust growth in the oil sector, with increasing oil production and higher prices—Brent crude oil prices have increased by about one-half since the start of the year—helping to bolster growth in the non-oil sector through improved government revenue and other spillovers to the broader economy (figure 2.4.1.B). In April 2022, oil production in the member countries of the Gulf Cooperation Council (GCC)[1] was about 3 million barrels a day higher than a year earlier, a 20 percent increase, and back above its pre-pandemic levels (IEA 2022). In other MNA oil producers (Algeria, the Islamic Republic of Iran, Iraq, Libya), oil production has expanded by 6 percent from a year earlier. Not all oil exporters have fully benefitted, with ongoing conflict in the Republic of Yemen constraining production and prolonging an unprecedented humanitarian and economic crisis.

Oil importers are facing multiple headwinds. In the Arab Republic of Egypt, growth slowed in early 2022 following a boom in the first half of the fiscal year. Export revenues in March soared about 80 percent above pre-pandemic highs. In Morocco, growth has also slowed significantly. The country's worst drought in decades reduced output in the agriculture sector (accounting for about one-tenth of GDP and one-third of employment) with rising inflation eroding real incomes. In Tunisia, the recovery is modest and unemployment, while edging down, remains elevated. The country faces challenging economic conditions, with high policy uncertainty, weak reform implementation, and large fiscal and current account deficits.

Note: This section was prepared by Franz Ulrich Ruch.

[1] GCC economies include Bahrain, Kuwait, Oman, Qatar, Saudi Arabia, and the United Arab Emirates.

FIGURE 2.4.1 MNA: Recent developments

Economic activity in the Middle East and North Africa has remained robust despite a short-lived hit from Omicron outbreaks and the net losses to oil importers due to the war in Ukraine. Oil exporters are benefiting from rising oil revenues and recovering non-oil sectors. Consumer inflation has been rising in oil importers and exporters, with an increasing contribution from food prices. Oil-importing economies are heavily reliant on cereal imports from the Russian Federation and Ukraine.

A. Purchasing Managers Index

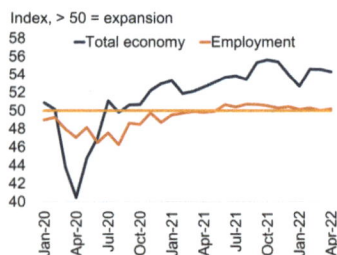

B. Oil exporters: Contributions to growth

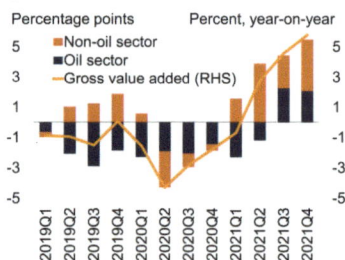

C. Contributions to consumer inflation

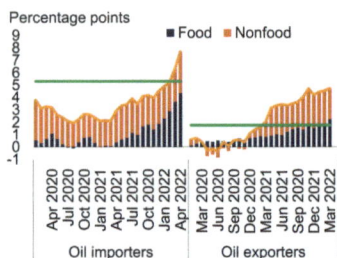

D. Cereal imports

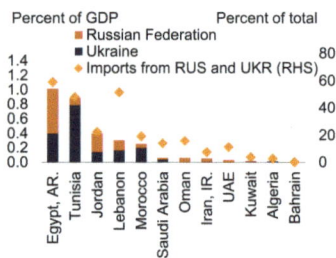

Sources: Haver Analytics; United Nations Comtrade.
Note: Egypt, AR. = the Arab Republic of Egypt; EMDEs = emerging market and developing economies; Iran, IR. = the Islamic Republic of Iran; RUS = Russian Federation; UAE = United Arab Emirates; UKR = Ukraine
A. GDP-weighted average of six economies.
B. Based on data for the Islamic Republic of Iran, Qatar, and Saudi Arabia. Weighted using 2021 constant GDP in U.S. dollars.
C. Data for oil importers based on four economies and seven oil exporters. Unweighted averages. Long-run averages (green lines) refer to 2012-19 or where available. Excludes data for the Islamic Republic of Iran and Lebanon.
D. Based on data from 2017-19.

Inflation in the region has been rising, surpassing average inflation in the decade prior to the pandemic in most economies, as the war in Ukraine has further increased food and energy prices (figure 2.4.1.C). Among oil importers, consumer price inflation averaged 7.7 percent in April 2022, but with wide variation. In Egypt, depreciation of the pound and heavy dependence on food imports have driven inflation to double-digit annual rates. In Lebanon, consumer prices recently increased by over 200 percent from a year earlier, partly owing to a collapsing exchange rate and economic mismanagement (World Bank

2022e). Among oil exporters, consumer inflation has averaged 4.7 percent, more than double its longer-run average. In the Islamic Republic of Iran, inflation remained elevated at 39 percent in May 2022.

With 70 percent of the region's agricultural production being rain-fed, below-average rainfall, along with unusually high temperatures, markedly weakened wheat yields in many parts of the region in early 2022 (the Islamic Republic of Iran, Iraq, the Maghreb region, and the Syrian Arab Republic; World Bank 2014). With dwindling domestic supplies due to drought, the war in Ukraine has also upended access to wheat imports. Oil importers are particularly vulnerable to rising food prices and shortages as imports of cereals (including wheat) from Russia and Ukraine averaged four-tenths of their cereal imports during 2017-19 (figure 2.4.1.D). Egypt, Lebanon, and Tunisia are most exposed, given their heavy reliance on food imports from Russia and Ukraine, but countries facing fragility and conflict (Syria, Republic of Yemen) are also vulnerable given their already high levels of food insecurity and poverty (FAO et al. 2020; FAO-WFP 2022). One-third of the calories people consume in the region are from subsidized wheat products (Belhaj and Soliman 2021).

Outlook

Growth in the region is expected to firm to 5.3 percent in 2022, assisted by rising oil revenues, structural reforms in some economies (Egypt, Saudi Arabia, United Arab Emirates), and a general waning of the pandemic's adverse impacts (figure 2.4.2.A). These growth projections represent an upward revision of 0.9 percentage point from the January forecast, mainly accounted for by improved prospects among the GCC economies (figure 2.4.2.B). Regional growth is expected to reach its fastest rate in a decade in 2022, but the rebound could have been even stronger had it not been for the detrimental impact of Russia's invasion of Ukraine on oil importers. The war has undermined external demand, increased uncertainty, and lifted food and energy prices. Activity in MNA is expected to slow through 2024, with growth in the region returning to 3.2 percent as services activity stabilizes and policy support is withdrawn.

Although output in the region remains below pre-pandemic trends, the gap is projected to have roughly halved by 2023 relative to 2020 (figure 2.4.2.C). This projected narrowing of the gap, however, is more than fully accounted for by faster growth in oil exporters—particularly in 2022. In oil importers, the effects of the pandemic and the war in Ukraine will further widen the gap.

In oil exporters, the support to activity from higher oil revenues, as well as waning pandemic effects amid high vaccination rates in the GCC, will help growth reach a peak of 5.6 percent in 2022—1.2 percentage points higher than previously projected. Upward revisions are broad-based, with Saudi Arabia and Oman seeing the largest upgrades, at over 2 percentage points. The rebound among oil exporters, however, is expected to be short-lived, with growth in 2023 falling back to below the average in the 2000-2019 period.

In *Saudi Arabia*, strong oil production growth and a robust recovery in the non-oil sector is expected to drive 2022 growth to a decade high of 7.0 percent, before slowing to 3.8 percent in 2023. Non-oil activity will benefit from robust private consumption growth and capital spending, partly because of the impact of higher oil prices on government revenue and the broader economy. The *United Arab Emirates* will also benefit in the near term from rising oil prices, while in the medium term, reforms to deepen capital markets, increase labor market flexibility, and accelerate technological innovation will support growth. Output in the *Islamic Republic of Iran* is expected to grow by 3.7 percent in 2022, boosted by the waning of the pandemic and higher oil prices. Growth is expected to slow subsequently, however, as unresolved structural challenges and feeble fixed investment limit the country's growth potential. In the *Republic of Yemen*, after two years of contraction, growth is expected to turn positive this year, benefiting from increased remittance inflows and base effects. The outlook, however, depends crucially on the course of the armed conflict and its resolution.

FIGURE 2.4.2 MNA: Outlook

Growth is expected to rebound to a decade high in 2022, with a marked improvement in prospects for oil-exporting economies outweighing a deterioration in the outlook for oil importers. Oil exporters are gradually catching up to their pre-pandemic output trends, while the gap for oil importers is expected to remain wide. Increased fiscal revenues and reduced expenditures have resulted in a large reduction of fiscal deficits in oil exporters. Oil importers' fiscal deficits are expected to widen because of higher expenditures.

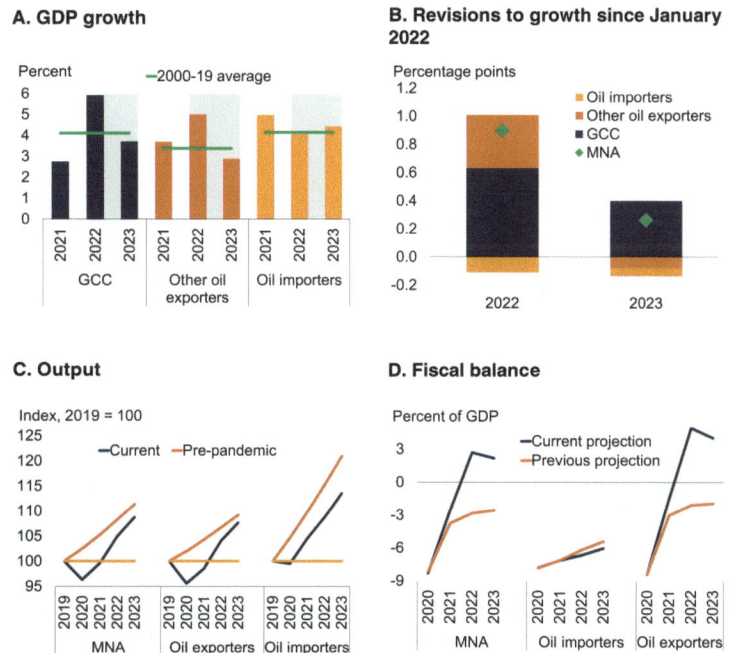

A. GDP growth

B. Revisions to growth since January 2022

C. Output

D. Fiscal balance

Sources: International Monetary Fund; World Bank.
Note: EMDEs = emerging market and developing economies; GCC = Gulf Cooperation Council; MNA = Middle East and North Africa.
A.B. GDP at average 2010-19 prices and market exchange rates. GCC economies include Bahrain, Kuwait, Oman, Qatar, Saudi Arabia, and the United Arab Emirates.
C. The pre-pandemic trend is based on the January 2020 *Global Economic Prospects* Report. For 2023, growth is equal to the 2022 forecast at the time.
D. Based on a GDP-weighted average of 13 economies: 4 oil importers, and 9 oil exporters. "Previous projection" reflects forecast made in October 2021.

Output in oil importers is expected to grow by 4.1 percent in 2022 before accelerating to 4.4 percent in 2023. Growth prospects for 2022, however, have been revised down by 0.5 percentage point as the impact of the war in Ukraine worsens terms of trade, and rising food and energy prices weigh on consumption. In *Egypt*, stronger-than-expected activity for the first half of the fiscal year, only partly offset by repercussions from the war in Ukraine, saw growth revised up to 6.1 percent in FY2021/22. Growth is expected to moderate to 4.8 percent in FY2022/23, a 0.7 percentage point downgrade, as rising food and energy inflation

FIGURE 2.4.3 MNA: Risks

Increasing uncertainty, including through oil price and financial market volatility, could undermine consumption and investment in the region. Further increases in food inflation, already at decade highs, could erode real incomes, undermining food security and increasing the incidence of under-nourishment. Government stability has deteriorated in the Middle East and North Africa. Energy subsidies have decreased in recent years but remain a significant portion of government expenditure.

A. Financial market and oil price volatility

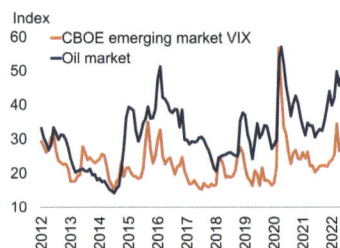

B. Undernourishment

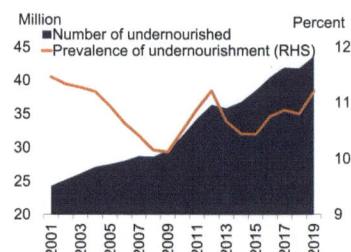

C. Government stability

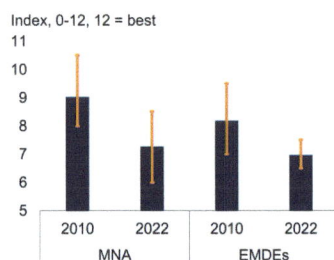

D. Energy subsidies

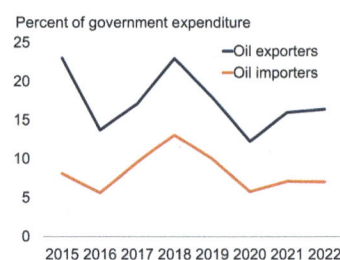

Sources: Bloomberg; Food and Agricultural Organization of the United Nations; Haver Analytics; International Monetary Fund; PRS Group; World Bank.
Note: CBOE = Chicago Board Options Exchange; EMDEs = emerging market and developing economies; MNA = Middle East and North Africa; VIX = Volatility Index.
A. Oil price volatility defined as implied volatility of at-the-money 6-month forward option prices.
B. "Number of undernourished" based on data for 12 economies. "Prevalence of undernourishment" is the unweighted average for 14 economies. Data for Libya, the Syrian Arab Republic, and the West Bank and Gaza are excluded.
C. Based on the "Government stability" subindex of the International Country Risk Guide. Unweighted average of 17 MNA economies and 103 EMDEs. Orange whiskers indicate interquartile range.
D. Explicit energy subsides. Unweighted averages. Based on data for 7 oil importers and 11 oil exporters.

slows income growth and raise input costs in key sectors, and tourism flows moderate. Growth in Egypt will still be supported by the gas extractives sector, as it benefits from elevated prices, by remittances from the GCC, and by continued reform momentum. In *Djibouti*, spillovers from conflict in Ethiopia have undermined the outlook, amid a high risk of external debt distress. Growth has been revised 1.0 percentage point lower in 2022, to 3.3 precent. In *Morocco*, growth is expected to slow significantly, to 1.1 percent in 2022, as persistent drought conditions and the impact of the war in Ukraine outweigh the expected services sector recovery.

Fiscal support is expected to be withdrawn over the forecast horizon, with higher oil prices assisting faster consolidation in oil exporters (figure 2.4.2.D). Oil exporters may have space to provide relief to households suffering from higher inflation by improving social safety nets and providing temporary targeted support measures. Oil importers, that face increasing fiscal pressures, may need to accelerate fiscal consolidation. In Egypt and Tunisia, food and fuel subsidies will contribute to deteriorating fiscal balances, whereas in Lebanon limited foreign-currency reserves may undermine the sustainability of importing cereals at the official exchange rate (Breisinger et al. 2021). Monetary policy authorities are expected to continue with the tightening cycle that began in early 2022 and raise policy rates.

Risks

Risks to the baseline projections remain tilted to the downside and include even sharper increases in food prices than assumed, further financial and oil market volatility, more rapidly tightening global financing conditions, growing social tensions, and new adverse pandemic developments. The war in Ukraine could potentially further disrupt the travel and tourism sectors on which several economies in the region rely heavily; inbound tourism revenues averaged 6 percent of GDP in the region in 2019 and was double digits in Bahrain, Jordan, and Lebanon.

High and volatile oil prices pose risks to the region, but with differing impacts on oil importers and exporters (figure 2.4.3.A). Among oil importers, further increases in oil prices could raise inflation, undermine growth, increase poverty, limit social spending by governments (because of costly energy subsidies), and further widen current account deficits. For oil exporters, sustained high oil prices may improve fiscal and current account balances and incentivize increased production. High price volatility, however, may continue to undermine investment in the sector while production quotas under OPEC+, if not relaxed, limit upside benefits to real activity (World Bank 2017). The repercussions of the war in Ukraine, and ongoing lockdowns in China, could cause a more abrupt slowdown in economic activity and reduce global oil demand.

Rising food inflation in an environment of limited political stability, and inadequate resources to maintain subsidies, may increase social tensions and could undermine growth and food security in the region (figures 2.4.3.B and 2.4.3.C). The war in Ukraine may further disrupt food supply chains and increase already high agriculture prices. Pressure on fiscal balances could force governments to reverse food subsidies, increasing the vulnerability of the poor and adding to already high levels of food insecurity (FAO et al. 2020). In the past, rising food prices have also sparked social unrest in the region, most notably during the Arab Spring in the early 2010s, with negative impacts on output, confidence, and uncertainty (Hadzi-Vaskov, Pienknagura, and Ricci 2021). Securing sufficient food supplies will be an ongoing challenge for the region as climate change is increasing the frequency and intensity of drought (IMF 2022a).

While both oil importers and exporters have made meaningful progress in lowering energy subsidies, they remain high and could undermine fiscal sustainability among oil importers if oil prices remain elevated (figure 2.4.3.D). Explicit energy subsidies accounted for 16 percent of government expenditure in 2021 in the region's oil exporters, and 7 percent in oil importers (Parry, Black, and Vernon 2021). In some economies, food subsidies remain significant and will widen fiscal imbalances absent a change in government policies. The combination of rising food and energy prices, falling real incomes, less fiscal support, and social unrest could significantly increase deprivation among the poor and push more people below the poverty line.

Financial conditions have tightened globally since the start of the year because of faster monetary policy tightening in response to rising inflation in advanced economies while the war in Ukraine led to a repricing of assets. With the cost of borrowing rising, some oil importers, particularly those with elevated external debt positions, are vulnerable to further bouts of market retrenchment that could depreciate their exchange rates or drawdown foreign exchange reserves, further raise borrowing costs, and increase import bills. In Tunisia, for example, the spread on foreign currency government borrowing (over U.S. rates) almost doubled since the invasion of Ukraine peaking at over 30 percent in May. More abrupt monetary policy tightening may also be needed in the region—particularly if inflation persists at elevated levels—putting further pressure on government finances and household consumption. This pressure may be acute for economies with elevated gross government debt (Bahrain, Djibouti, Egypt, Jordan, Lebanon, Morocco, Tunisia).

Renewed COVID-19 outbreaks, and the continued risk of new emerging variants, may require the reimposition of mobility restrictions to slow community spread and preserve healthcare capacity, further damaging economic activity in vulnerable sectors and undermining external demand. Vaccination rates among MNA economies remain low except in the GCC and a few other economies (Morocco, Tunisia). In one-third of MNA economies, the share of the population that is fully vaccinated is below 30 percent. Urgent investment in the health sector and health surveillance can mitigate the health and economic impacts of future outbreaks (World Bank 2021c).

TABLE 2.4.1 Middle East and North Africa forecast summary

(Real GDP growth at market prices in percent, unless indicated otherwise)

Percentage point differences from January 2022 projections

	2019	2020	2021e	2022f	2023f	2024f	2022f	2023f
EMDE MNA, GDP[1]	**0.9**	**-3.7**	**3.4**	**5.3**	**3.6**	**3.2**	**0.9**	**0.2**
GDP per capita (U.S. dollars)	-0.9	-5.3	1.8	3.7	2.1	1.8	0.9	0.2
(Average including countries that report expenditure components in national accounts)[2]								
EMDE MNA, GDP[2]	0.4	-2.9	3.6	5.0	3.5	3.1	0.9	0.5
PPP GDP	0.3	-1.9	3.8	5.0	3.5	3.2	0.9	0.4
Private consumption	2.5	-2.4	5.9	3.6	3.3	3.1	0.5	0.3
Public consumption	0.6	1.1	1.4	2.0	1.8	1.6	1.2	1.0
Fixed investment	-1.1	-6.3	4.2	5.4	5.1	4.3	1.7	0.9
Exports, GNFS[3]	-5.9	-9.7	5.2	9.7	6.1	5.4	2.2	1.1
Imports, GNFS[3]	-6.1	-12.7	7.1	7.3	5.7	4.9	2.6	1.4
Net exports, contribution to growth	-0.5	0.2	-0.1	1.8	0.8	0.8	0.1	0.0
Memo items: GDP								
Oil exporters[4]	0.3	-4.4	3.1	5.6	3.4	2.9	1.2	0.4
GCC countries[5]	1.1	-5.0	2.7	5.9	3.7	3.2	1.2	0.7
Saudi Arabia	0.3	-4.1	3.2	7.0	3.8	3.0	2.1	1.5
Iran, Islamic Rep.[6]	-6.8	3.4	4.1	3.7	2.7	2.3	1.3	0.5
Oil importers[7]	3.6	-0.5	5.0	4.1	4.4	4.3	-0.5	-0.3
Egypt, Arab Rep.[6]	5.6	3.6	3.3	6.1	4.8	5.0	0.6	-0.7

Source: World Bank.

Note: e = estimate; f = forecast; PPP = purchasing power parity; EMDE = emerging market and developing economy. World Bank forecasts are frequently updated based on new information and changing (global) circumstances. Consequently, projections presented here may differ from those contained in other Bank documents, even if basic assessments of countries' prospects do not differ at any given moment in time.

1. GDP and expenditure components are measured in average 2010-19 prices and market exchange rates. Excludes Lebanon, Libya, the Syrian Arab Republic, and the Republic of Yemen as a result of the high degree of uncertainty.
2. Aggregate includes all economies in notes 4 and 7 except Djibouti, Iraq, Qatar, and West Bank and Gaza, for which data limitations prevent the forecasting of GDP components.
3. Exports and imports of goods and nonfactor services (GNFS).
4. Oil exporters include Algeria, Bahrain, the Islamic Republic of Iran, Iraq, Kuwait, Oman, Qatar, Saudi Arabia, and the United Arab Emirates.
5. The Gulf Cooperation Council (GCC) includes Bahrain, Kuwait, Oman, Qatar, Saudi Arabia, and the United Arab Emirates.
6. Fiscal-year based numbers. The fiscal year runs from July 1 to June 30 in the Arab Republic of Egypt, with 2020 reflecting FY2019/20. For the Islamic Republic of Iran, it runs from March 21 through March 20, with 2020 reflecting FY2020/21.
7. Oil importers include Djibouti, Egypt, Jordan, Morocco, Tunisia, and West Bank and Gaza.

TABLE 2.4.2 Middle East and North Africa economy forecasts[1]

(Real GDP growth at market prices in percent, unless indicated otherwise)

Percentage point differences from January 2022 projections

	2019	2020	2021e	2022f	2023f	2024f	2022f	2023f
Algeria	1.0	-5.1	3.9	3.2	1.3	1.4	1.2	-0.2
Bahrain	2.2	-4.9	2.2	3.5	3.1	3.1	0.3	0.2
Djibouti	7.8	0.5	4.3	3.3	5.2	6.2	-1.0	-0.3
Egypt, Arab Rep.[2]	5.6	3.6	3.3	6.1	4.8	5.0	0.6	-0.7
Iran, Islamic Rep.[2]	-6.8	3.4	4.1	3.7	2.7	2.3	1.3	0.5
Iraq	5.5	-11.3	2.8	8.8	4.5	3.0	1.5	-1.8
Jordan	2.0	-1.6	2.2	2.1	2.3	2.3	-0.2	0.0
Kuwait	-0.6	-8.9	2.3	5.7	3.6	2.5	0.4	0.6
Lebanon[3]	-7.2	-21.4	-10.5	-6.5	..	..	..	..
Libya[3]	2.5	-31.3	99.3	..	..	..	..	..
Morocco	2.6	-6.3	7.4	1.1	4.3	3.6	-2.1	0.8
Oman	-0.8	-2.8	2.1	5.6	2.8	2.6	2.2	-1.3
Qatar	0.8	-3.6	1.5	4.9	4.5	4.4	0.1	-0.4
Saudi Arabia	0.3	-4.1	3.2	7.0	3.8	3.0	2.1	1.5
Syrian Arab Republic[3]	3.7	1.3	-2.1	-2.6	..	..	..	..
Tunisia	1.3	-8.7	3.1	3.0	3.5	3.3	-0.5	0.2
United Arab Emirates	3.4	-6.1	2.8	4.7	3.4	3.6	0.1	0.5
West Bank and Gaza	1.4	-11.3	7.1	3.7	3.2	3.1	0.3	-0.2
Yemen, Rep.[3]	1.4	-8.5	-2.1	0.8	2.5	..	..	..

Source: World Bank.

Note: e = estimate; f = forecast. World Bank forecasts are frequently updated based on new information and changing (global) circumstances. Consequently, projections presented here may differ from those contained in other Bank documents, even if basic assessments of economies' prospects do not significantly differ at any given moment in time.

1. Data are based on GDP measured in average 2010-19 prices and market exchange rates.

2. Fiscal-year based numbers. The fiscal year runs from July 1 to June 30 in the Arab Republic of Egypt, with 2020 reflecting FY2019/20. For the Islamic Republic of Iran, it runs from March 21 through March 20, with 2020 reflecting FY2020/21.

3. Forecasts for Lebanon and the Syrian Arab Republic (beyond 2022), Libya (beyond 2021), and the Republic of Yemen (beyond 2023) are excluded because of a high degree of uncertainty.

SOUTH ASIA

South Asia has endured significant adverse spillovers from the Russian Federation's invasion of Ukraine. Growth is expected to slow from 7.6 percent in 2021 to 6.8 percent in 2022—0.8 percentage points below previous projections. The external environment has worsened markedly, with soaring energy and agricultural prices, slowing global growth, and rising financing costs. While domestic conditions remain solid in many economies, Afghanistan is facing a humanitarian crisis, and Sri Lanka is facing dual balance of payments and sovereign debt crises. Surging food costs in a region populated by more than one-third of the global poor and where one-fifth of calories come from wheat products pose significant challenges to poverty alleviation and food security. Downside risks to the outlook relate to adverse geopolitical developments, the possibility of even-higher inflation, tighter financing conditions, the re-emergence of stress in the financial sector, and the resurgence of the COVID-19 pandemic, all in an environment of high debt levels and worsening current account positions.

Recent developments

The Russian Federation's invasion of Ukraine has dampened the recovery in the South Asia region (SAR) and amplified pre-existing vulnerabilities. The region entered 2022 with robust economic growth, despite some softening because of an Omicron-driven pandemic resurgence and its attendant restrictions (figure 2.5.1.A). The Omicron wave has since abated across the region, leading to the loosening of restrictions.

The war in Ukraine has had a small direct impact on the region as trade and financial exposure to Russia and Ukraine is limited. Nonetheless, the indirect impact has been significant, mainly through much higher commodity prices, tighter financial conditions, and weaker external demand. Rising commodity prices are worsening the terms of trade and increasing trade deficits (figure 2.5.1.B). Wheat products account for about one-fifth of calorie intake in the region, however much of the supply comes from within the region. Financial conditions have tightened globally and in SAR (figure 2.5.1.C). The war has also

increased global risk aversion, leading to capital outflows, depreciating currencies, falling equity prices, and rising bond yields. Foreign exchange reserves have been under pressure and are dwindling in some economies, eliciting import restrictions (Nepal, Pakistan, Sri Lanka). External demand growth is also slowing as advanced economies face substantial spillovers from the war. In Sri Lanka, with international reserves down to one-fourth of their pre-pandemic level, the government abandoned its exchange rate peg in early March, leading to a close to 80 percent depreciation against the U.S. dollar. Policy rates have been raised by 7 percentage points in response. In India, rising inflationary pressures led to an unscheduled policy rate hike in May. In Pakistan, the central bank has raised rates by 4 percentage points since April.

Some authorities have implemented policies to cushion the impact of high inflation. In Pakistan, for example, the government announced an energy price reduction package in February (World Bank 2022f). However, gasoline and diesel pump prices were recently increased. In India, the government has extended a food scheme to support poor households, reduced taxes on fuels, and reduced import duties on several products. In Bangladesh, the government reduced the value added tax on

Note: This section was prepared by Franz Ulrich Ruch.

FIGURE 2.5.1 **SAR: Recent developments**

Growth momentum this year has slowed because of the Omicron wave following a robust recovery in the second half of 2021. Increased energy and food prices are raising import bills and worsening terms of trade. Financing conditions have tightened as central banks in advanced economies and the region have reduced policy support, and geopolitical developments have heightened risk aversion. South Asia is seeing broad-based increases in consumer inflation, to rates above central bank targets, on rising food and energy prices.

A. Economic activity

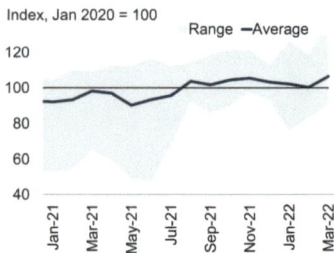

B. Trade

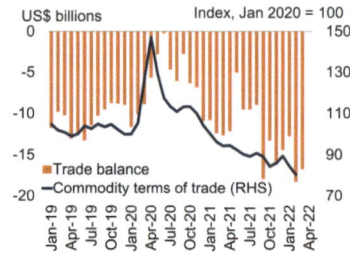

C. Financing conditions

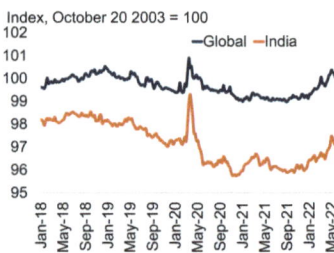

D. Contributions to inflation

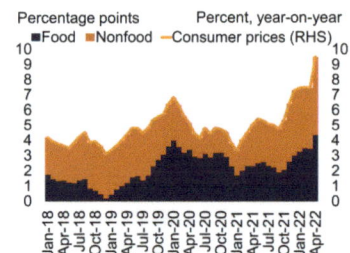

Sources: Bloomberg; Haver Analytics; International Monetary Fund.
Note: EMDEs = emerging market and developing economies.
A. Unweighted average of industrial production in Bangladesh, India, Pakistan, and Sri Lanka, and tourist arrivals in Maldives. "Range" reflects country minimum and maximum outcomes. Last observation is March 2022.
B. GDP weighted. "Terms of trade" excludes data for Afghanistan. "Trade balance" based on data for Bangladesh, India, Nepal, Pakistan, and Sri Lanka.
C. Based on Goldman Sachs Financial Conditions Index for the Brazil, Euro Area, India, Indonesia, Japan, Mexico, Turkey, United Kingdom, and United States. Weighted using constant 2010-19 U.S. dollar GDP for 2021. Last observation is May 27, 2022.
D. Unweighted average. Based on data for six economies. Urban consumer prices in Pakistan, Colombo prices in Sri Lanka. Last observation is April 2022.

the import of edible oils (soybean and palm) to dampen price increases.

In India, growth slowed in the first half of 2022 as activity was disrupted both by a surge in COVID-19 cases, accompanied by more-targeted mobility restrictions, and by the war in Ukraine. The recovery is facing headwinds from rising inflation. The unemployment rate has declined to levels seen prior to the pandemic, but the labor force participation rate remains below pre-pandemic levels and workers have shifted to lower-paying

and less-secure jobs. India's growth in fiscal year 2021/22, which ended in March 2022, was 8.7 percent, with the release of pent-up demand late last year following the mid-2021 wave of the pandemic offset by weakness in early 2022.

For the region excluding India, stronger-than-expected rebounds from the pandemic in Bangladesh and Pakistan helped to boost activity through early 2022, helping to maintain robust growth during their fiscal year 2021/22, ending June 2022. In Bangladesh and Pakistan, goods exports have grown by over 25 percent so far this fiscal year (to April), and manufacturing production in both countries has expanded at its fastest pace in at least four years. But the war in Ukraine has dampened activity, as rising food and energy prices have stunted purchasing power, and increased uncertainty. Conditions are particularly dire in Sri Lanka, where the government announced a cessation of external debt repayments and the country faces dual balance of payments and sovereign debt crises (World Bank 2022g). In Bhutan, after two years of contraction, growth is expected to have returned to positive territory because of an easing of mobility restrictions and ongoing fiscal support, with the fiscal deficit reaching 10.1 percent of GDP in FY2021/22.

Economic and social conditions in Afghanistan remain dire, despite increasing international humanitarian support following the abrupt cessation of aid inflows in August 2021. The economy has collapsed, employment and imports—including food and energy—are estimated to have halved, and government spending has likely fallen by three-fourths since August 2021 (World Bank 2022h). Recent surveys show that three-fourths of households report insufficient incomes to meet basic needs.

Consumer price inflation in South Asia has been rising rapidly and now exceeds central banks' targets (figure 2.5.1.D). In Pakistan and Sri Lanka, annual headline consumer inflation reached double digits by late last year and have accelerated further during 2022; in the latter to close to over 30 percent. In India, both headline and core consumer inflation have breached the upper end of the central bank's headline inflation target range of 2-6 percent. In Maldives, unlike the rest of the region, consumer inflation has remained low at about 1 percent, reflecting a fixed exchange rate and substantial food and energy-related subsidies. Inflation expectations have risen in the region. Higher inflation, especially for food prices, are a significant concern given the region's large share of the global poor, who spend a substantial proportion of their income on food.

Outlook

Growth in South Asia is projected to moderate to 6.8 and 5.8 percent in 2022 and 2023, respectively, as the momentum of the recovery wanes, and the war in Ukraine undermines external demand and erodes real incomes through higher food and energy prices (figure 2.5.2.A). Weakening net exports and eroded consumer demand amid higher prices are expected to remain a significant drag on activity, the former reducing growth in 2022 by 2 percentage points (figure 2.5.2.B). As the recovery from the pandemic recession matures, growth will be supported by private consumption, which is projected to contribute about 4 percentage points a year to GDP growth over 2022-24. The contribution to growth from government consumption will peak in 2022 and wane thereafter as fiscal support is withdrawn (figure 2.5.2.C).

In *India*, growth is forecast to edge down to 7.5 percent in fiscal year 2022/23, with headwinds from rising inflation, supply chain disruptions, and geopolitical tensions offsetting buoyancy in the recovery of services consumption from the pandemic. Growth will also be supported by fixed investment undertaken by the private sector and by the government, which has introduced incentives and reforms to improve the business climate. This forecast reflects a 1.2 percentage point downward revision of growth from the January projection. Growth is expected to slow further to 7.1 percent in 2023/24 back towards its longer-run potential.

In the region excluding India, GDP growth, after peaking at 5.7 percent in fiscal year 2021/22 (ending June 2022), is projected to slow to 4.0 percent in 2022/23 on account of policy consolidation, rising inflation, and weakening

FIGURE 2.5.2 SAR: Outlook

Economic prospects for the region have deteriorated since January, and growth in 2022 is now expected to slow to a rate equal to the average of the decade before the pandemic. Private consumption is forecast to remain the largest driver of growth, but its contribution is projected to wane while net exports remain a significant drag. Average real interest rates reflect rapid tightening of policy rates in Pakistan and Sri Lanka and a surprise policy hike in India. Fiscal policy remains accommodative but is gradually tightening. The external current account deficit is projected to widen on geopolitical tensions, and gross government debt remains high but is expected to stabilize over the forecast horizon.

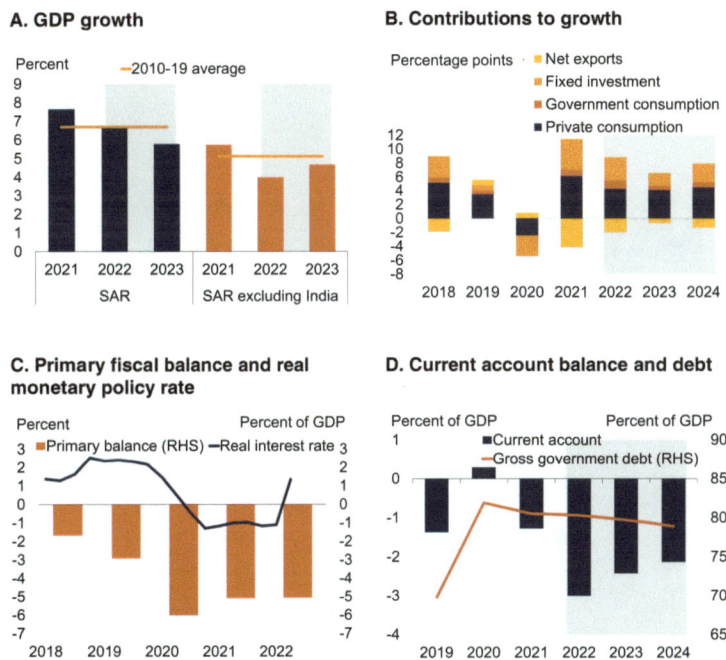

A. GDP growth

B. Contributions to growth

C. Primary fiscal balance and real monetary policy rate

D. Current account balance and debt

Sources: Consensus Economics; Haver Analytics; World Bank.
Note: EMDEs = emerging market and developing economies; SAR = South Asia.
A.B. GDP at average 2010-19 prices and market exchange rates.
C. Unweighted average. "Real interest rate" is the nominal policy rate less inflation forecasts at a one-year fixed horizon for Bangladesh, India, Pakistan, and Sri Lanka. "Primary balance" excludes Afghanistan.
D. GDP-weighted average. Data exclude Afghanistan.

external growth. In *Pakistan*, growth is expected to slow from 5.7 percent in FY2020/21 to 4.0 percent in 2022/23 as foreign demand slows significantly and policy support is withdrawn to contain external and fiscal imbalances.[1] The current account deficit for the region as a whole is forecast to widen to levels last seen a decade ago (figure 2.5.2.D). In *Bangladesh*, growth is forecast

---

[1] The Government's preliminary estimate for real GDP (factor cost) growth for 2021/22 is 6.0 percent.

FIGURE 2.5.3 SAR: Risks

Risks of financial stress have been exacerbated by tightening financing conditions in an environment of high debt, the possibility of hidden public debt, and increased exposure of commercial banks to sovereign debt. Agricultural commodity prices have risen on account of geopolitical tensions, with producer and wholesale prices showing double-digit annual increases for almost a year. Further increases in energy prices could undermine income growth and widen fiscal deficits through rising energy subsidies. School closures in South Asia owing to the pandemic were significantly higher than in other regions and could undermine future growth prospects.

A. Bank holdings of government debt and 10-year government bond yields

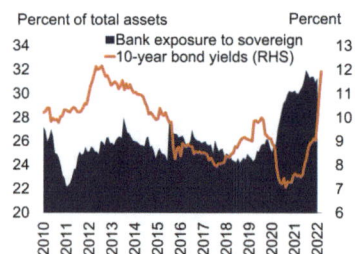

B. Food inflation

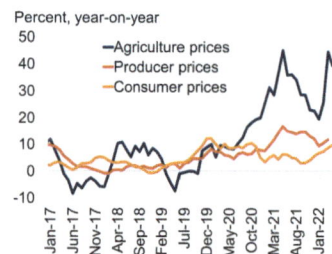

C. Energy dependence

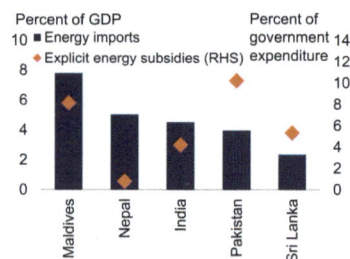

D. School closures

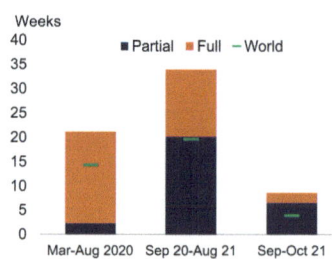

Sources: Bloomberg; Haver Analytics; International Monetary Fund; United Nations Comtrade; UNESCO Global Dataset; World Bank.
A. Unweighted averages. "Bank exposure to sovereign" is credit to government as a ratio to total domestic credit of the banking system or commercial banks in net or gross terms (based on availability) in Bangladesh, Bhutan, India, Maldives, Nepal, Pakistan, and Sri Lanka. "10-year bond yields" data for Bangladesh, India, Pakistan, and Sri Lanka.
B. GDP-weighted average of consumer and producer/wholesale food inflation. "Agriculture prices" based on the World Bank's food index adjusted to local currencies.
C. Import value of petroleum and gas as a share of GDP and of explicit energy subsidies as a share of government expenditure. Based on data for 2017-19.
D. Unweighted averages of 8 economies for South Asia and 210 economies for global. "World" reflects both partial and full school closures.

to slow to 6.4 percent in FY2021/22, as pent-up demand subsides, and to pick up to 6.7 percent in 2022/23 as investment recovers and remittance inflows rise as a result of higher growth in the Gulf Cooperation Council countries (particularly Saudi Arabia and the United Arab Emirates). In *Maldives,* projected growth in 2022 has been revised down by 3.4 percentage points to 7.6 percent, reflecting the expected effects of the war in Ukraine on tourist inflows, in a stagnating

investment environment. In *Nepal,* growth is forecast to accelerate to 4.1 percent and 5.8 percent, respectively, in the next two fiscal years as pent-up demand boosts the services sector, and hydropower production increases at the recently completed Upper Tamakoshi plant. Growth in *Bhutan* is also expected to benefit from the recovery of services and should see hydropower generation double in the medium term driven by the completion of several projects (World Bank 2022i).

A balance of payments crisis and the cessation of external debt repayments in *Sri Lanka* have significantly deteriorated growth prospects, which are highly uncertain and subject to significant downside risks. The economy is expected to contract by 7.8 percent in 2022 and 3.7 percent in 2023. The contraction can be greater in case of protracted delays in actions by the authorities to restore macroeconomic stability and in debt restructuring. The country faces severe economic difficulties and rising policy uncertainty—with ongoing electricity blackouts and an inability to import sufficient essentials including food and energy. Debt restructuring will be necessary to start the process of fiscal rehabilitation.

Some economies in the region have prioritized structural reforms to strengthen economic growth. In *Pakistan,* the government has enhanced its monetary policy framework by strengthening the functional and administrative autonomy of the central bank, prohibiting government borrowing from the central bank, and entrenching price stability as monetary policy's primary objective (World Bank 2022f). In *Nepal,* reforms will focus on improving governance and transparency; upgrading the tax system and improving spending efficiency; upgrading public debt management; strengthening financial regulation and supervision; ensuring the transition to a green, resilient, and inclusive development path; and integrating digital services (IMF 2022b; World Bank 2022j). In *India,* the focus of government spending has shifted toward infrastructure investment, labor regulations are being simplified, underperforming state-owned assets are being privatized, and the logistics sector is expected to be modernized and integrated.

Risks

Geopolitical developments have magnified downside risks to the regional outlook. Risks include private sector retrenchment resulting from tightening domestic financing conditions, widening current account deficits, eroding real incomes because of further increases in food and energy prices, and new flare-ups of COVID-19.

South Asia is facing an environment of tightening global financing conditions with significantly elevated debt levels, a combination that increases the likelihood of financial stress. Yields on local-currency debt have increased by 290 basis points, on average, since the beginning of 2022 (figure 2.5.3.A). Conditions in Sri Lanka are deteriorating rapidly, with 10-year government bond yields recently at over 20 percent, among the highest in EMDEs. South Asian banks are particularly exposed to sovereigns, with government debt having risen to one-third of bank's assets, on average, from one-fourth before the pandemic. This raises spillover risks from the government sector to the financial sector. Compounding these financial sector risks, the region is also vulnerable because of hidden public debt, including contingent liabilities, given the outsized roles of state-owned enterprises and off-balance-sheet operations (Melecky 2021). State-owned banks, for example, account for the largest share of total bank assets among EMDE regions.

With geopolitical developments affecting the supply of wheat, edible oils, and input costs of fertilizer and energy, agricultural prices (in domestic currency terms) have risen by more than one-fourth since the beginning of 2022 (figure 2.5.3.B). Additional increases in commodity prices may put further upward pressure on food inflation, which is already high, eroding real incomes and reducing consumption. The region is particularly vulnerable to the impact of higher food prices, with food accounting for 43 percent of the consumption basket on average, compared to 33 percent across EMDEs.

Rising energy prices, given the region's high dependence on energy imports and elevated energy subsidies in some economies, could further undermine growth and threaten a widening of fiscal imbalances (figure 2.5.3.C). Energy subsidies as a share of income and government expenditure are lower in SAR than the average EMDE but still account for 5 percent of government expenditure on average in 2021 (Parry, Black, and Vernon 2021). Energy subsidies as a share of government expenditure are highest in Bangladesh, Maldives, and Pakistan. With already high energy costs and the uncertain outlook, the region could face additional pressure on inflation—despite the dampening effect of subsidies—and larger current account deficits. This pressure could undermine growth, increase poverty, and divert budgetary resources away from productivity-enhancing investment and social protection.

While the direct economic impact of new waves of COVID-19 has moderated, pandemic developments remain an ongoing downside risk. The emergence of new variants in the presence of waning vaccine effectiveness could overwhelm health systems unless mobility restrictions are imposed. The longer-term consequences of the pandemic will also be significant. Pandemic-related school closures have averaged 64 weeks in South Asia—much higher than the global average of 38 weeks—and kept nearly 400 million children out of school (figure 2.5.3.D; UNESCO and UNICEF 2021). This outsized damage to human capital accumulation could undermine the pace of poverty reduction and significantly impair lifetime earnings (Azevedo et al. 2021; World Bank 2021d).

TABLE 2.5.1 South Asia forecast summary

(Real GDP growth at market prices in percent, unless indicated otherwise)

Percentage point differences from January 2022 projections

	2019	2020	2021e	2022f	2023f	2024f	2022f	2023f
EMDE South Asia, GDP[1,2]	4.1	-4.5	7.6	6.8	5.8	6.5	-0.8	-0.2
GDP per capita (U.S. dollars)	3.0	-5.6	6.5	5.6	4.7	5.4	-0.9	-0.2
(Average including countries that report expenditure components in national accounts)[3]								
EMDE South Asia, GDP[3]	4.1	-4.5	7.6	6.8	5.8	6.5	-0.8	-0.2
PPP GDP	4.1	-4.6	7.6	6.8	5.8	6.5	-0.8	-0.2
Private consumption	4.9	-3.4	8.5	5.8	5.6	6.1	-1.7	0.0
Public consumption	3.9	0.2	7.4	10.5	4.7	6.2	1.0	-0.5
Fixed investment	2.6	-9.6	14.8	10.5	5.9	8.3	0.5	-1.2
Exports, GNFS[4]	1.5	-9.2	18.4	8.9	8.3	7.9	1.3	-0.3
Imports, GNFS[4]	-1.5	-8.6	26.1	11.3	6.9	8.5	2.9	-2.3
Net exports, contribution to growth	0.8	0.8	-4.2	-2.0	-0.7	-1.3	-1.2	0.2
Memo items: GDP[2]	**2018/19**	**2019/20**	**2020/21e**	**2021/22f**	**2022/23f**	**2023/24f**	**2021/22f**	**2022/23f**
South Asia excluding India	5.7	3.0	2.6	5.7	4.0	4.7	1.3	-0.8
India	6.5	3.7	-6.6	8.7	7.5	7.1	0.4	-1.2
Pakistan (factor cost)	3.1	-0.9	5.7	4.3	4.0	4.2	0.9	0.0
Bangladesh	7.9	3.4	6.9	6.4	6.7	6.9	0.0	-0.2

Source: World Bank.

Note: e = estimate; f = forecast; PPP = purchasing power parity; EMDE = emerging market and developing economy. World Bank forecasts are frequently updated based on new information and changing (global) circumstances. Consequently, projections presented here may differ from those contained in other Bank documents, even if basic assessments of countries' prospects do not differ at any given moment in time.

1. GDP and expenditure components are measured in average 2010-19 prices and market exchange rates. Excludes Afghanistan because of the high degree of uncertainty.

2. National income and product account data refer to fiscal years (FY) while aggregates are presented in calendar year (CY) terms. (For example, aggregate under 2020/21 refers to CY 2020). The fiscal year runs from July 1 through June 30 in Bangladesh, Bhutan, and Pakistan; from July 16 through July 15 in Nepal; and April 1 through March 31 in India.

3. Subregion aggregate excludes Afghanistan, Bhutan, and Maldives, for which data limitations prevent the forecasting of GDP components.

4. Exports and imports of goods and nonfactor services (GNFS).

TABLE 2.5.2 South Asia country forecasts

(Real GDP growth at market prices in percent, unless indicated otherwise)

Percentage point differences from January 2022 projections

	2019	2020	2021e	2022f	2023f	2024f	2022f	2023f
Calendar year basis[1]								
Afghanistan[2]	3.9	-1.9	..	..	..	..	..	..
Maldives	6.9	-33.5	31.0	7.6	10.2	7.1	-3.4	-1.8
Sri Lanka	2.3	-3.6	3.7	-7.8	-3.7	1.0	-9.9	-5.9
Fiscal year basis[1]	**2018/19**	**2019/20**	**2020/21e**	**2021/22f**	**2022/23f**	**2023/24f**	**2021/22f**	**2022/23f**
Bangladesh	7.9	3.4	6.9	6.4	6.7	6.9	0.0	-0.2
Bhutan	4.4	-2.4	-3.7	4.4	4.7	6.7	-0.7	-0.1
India	6.5	3.7	-6.6	8.7	7.5	7.1	0.4	-1.2
Nepal	6.7	-2.1	1.8	3.7	4.1	5.8	-0.2	-0.6
Pakistan (factor cost)	3.1	-0.9	5.7	4.3	4.0	4.2	0.9	0.0

Source: World Bank.

Note: e = estimate; f = forecast. World Bank forecasts are frequently updated based on new information and changing (global) circumstances. Consequently, projections presented here may differ from those contained in other Bank documents, even if basic assessments of countries' prospects do not significantly differ at any given moment in time.

1. Historical data are reported on a market price basis. National income and product account data refer to fiscal years (FY) with the exception of Afghanistan, Maldives, and Sri Lanka, which report in calendar year. The fiscal year runs from July 1 through June 30 in Bangladesh, Bhutan, and Pakistan; from July 16 through July 15 in Nepal; and April 1 through March 31 in India.

2. Forecast for Afghanistan (beyond 2020) are excluded because of a high degree of uncertainty.

SUB-SAHARAN AFRICA

Growth in Sub-Saharan Africa (SSA) is projected to slow to 3.7 percent this year, reflecting forecast downgrades in over 60 percent of regional economies. Price pressures, partly induced by the Russian Federation's invasion of Ukraine, are sharply reducing food affordability and real incomes across the region. At just above 1 percent, per capita income growth in SSA is projected to remain much lower than in other EMDEs. More people in SSA are expected to fall into extreme poverty, especially in countries reliant on imports of foods and fuel. Fiscal space is narrowing further as governments ramp up spending on subsidies, support to farmers, and, in some countries, security. However, the impact of the war will vary across countries, as elevated commodity prices will help soften the damaging effects of high inflation in some large commodity exporters. Among the risks to the forecast, prolonged disruptions to the food supply across the region could significantly increase poverty, hunger, and malnutrition, while persistent inflation could ignite stagflation risks and further limit policy space to support recoveries. An elevated cost of living could increase the risk of social unrest, especially in low-income countries.

Recent developments

Limited direct trade and financial linkages with Europe and Central Asia have helped contain some of the adverse effects of the Russian Federation's invasion of Ukraine on Sub-Saharan Africa (SSA). However, the deceleration of global growth and war-induced increases in food and fuel prices are creating headwinds for the region. Although some large exporters of metals and energy are benefiting from elevated commodity prices, surging prices of staple foods and farming inputs are stoking inflation across the region and sharply reducing food affordability (WFP 2022).

Food insecurity is worsening in SSA, especially in countries dependent on food imports and where the poor account for a large share of net food buying households (Simler 2010; Wodon and Zaman 2008). On average, food imports account for 20 percent of total imports in SSA countries—almost twice as high as in other emerging markets and developing economies (EMDEs; figure 2.6.1.A). Almost three-quarters of SSA economies were already classified as food-deficit countries before the current food price surge (FAO 2021).

SSA is facing these shocks as it continues to endure pandemic-induced increases in poverty and food insecurity (figure 2.6.1.B). Even before Russia's invasion of Ukraine, prices were already accelerating rapidly in many SSA countries amid large currency depreciations, conflict, and adverse weather. A recent surge in global food prices has pushed food price inflation in SSA even higher, with annual food inflation exceeding 20 percent in some countries (figure 2.6.1.C). With SSA households spending a disproportionately large share of their incomes on food, the sharp rise in food prices has eroded domestic demand and weakened recoveries in nonresource sectors (FAO et al. 2021; OECD/FAO 2020, 2021; Wodon et al. 2008; World Bank 2022k). Even in SSA commodity exporters, increased living costs and shortages of food and fuel have begun weighing on activity (figure 2.6.1.D).

In the three largest SSA economies—Angola, Nigeria, and South Africa—the boost from favorable commodity prices is being offset by rising inflation and policy tightening. Elevated oil prices are supporting activity in Angola and Nigeria—the two biggest oil producing economies in the region. Growth in Nigeria strengthened in the first half of the year, driven by increased oil revenues and a strong recovery in non-oil sectors,

Note: This section was prepared by Sergiy Kasyanenko.

FIGURE 2.6.1. SSA: Recent developments

The surge in global food prices resulting from the Russia's invasion of Ukraine is weighing on recoveries across Sub-Saharan Africa (SSA), especially in countries heavily reliant on food imports. Surging living costs are tempering the boost to recoveries from high prices of metals and energy.

A. Imports of food in SSA

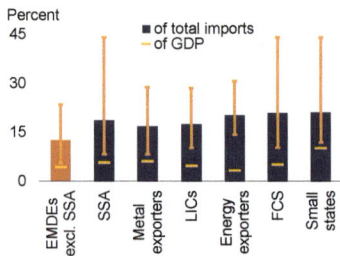

B. Extreme poverty in 2022

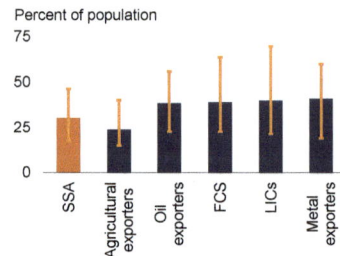

C. Food inflation

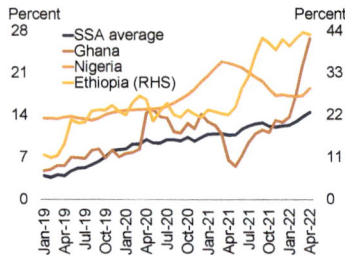

D. Purchasing managers indexes

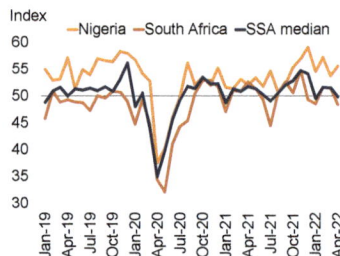

Sources: Comtrade (database); Haver Analytics; World Bank.
Note: EMDEs = emerging market and developing economies; FCS = fragile and conflict-affected situations; LICs = low-income countries; SSA = Sub-Saharan Africa.
A. Based on a sample of 52 EMDEs, including 32 SSA countries. Last observation 2021 or earliest available year. Vertical lines indicate the min-max range for imports of food in total imports.
B. Extreme poverty is measured as the number of people living on less than $1.90 per day. 2022 extreme poverty projections are based on growth forecasts from April 2022 Macro and Poverty Outlooks. Bars indicate medians; vertical lines indicate the 25-75 percentile range.
C. Unweighted average for the sample of 17 SSA EMDEs.
D. A value above 50 indicates expansion. Composite PMI covers manufacturing and services. Sample includes Ghana, Kenya, Mozambique, Nigeria, South Africa, Uganda, and Zambia. Last observation is April 2022.

despite the drag from recurring fuel shortages and power blackouts. High and persistent inflation, however, is starting to weigh on consumer purchasing power, especially of poor and vulnerable households. In Angola, stabilizing oil production and strong activity in agriculture are helping to put the economy on a track of recovery, though persistent inflationary pressures are restraining growth. In South Africa, growth has moderated substantially because of the growth-dampening effects of high unemployment; infrastructure bottlenecks, including recurring power shortages; slow progress with reforms; and weak private investment. Infrastructure damage to

the country's main port following severe floods has exacerbated supply chain disruptions related to Russia's invasion of Ukraine and mobility restrictions in China in response to pandemic outbreaks. Although the fiscal position has improved somewhat, high public debt constrains public spending, particularly investment.

Elsewhere in the region, tourism-reliant economies (Kenya, Madagascar, Mauritius, Namibia, Tanzania, Seychelles) are benefiting from returning international visitors, though war-related disruptions to global travel are holding back the pace of recovery. In some countries, elevated levels of violence and insecurity continue to dampen recoveries (Burkina Faso, Eswatini, Mali, Mozambique, Niger, Sudan), even though violence has abated somewhat in others (Central African Republic, Democratic Republic of Congo, Ethiopia).

Fiscal policy, already constrained by high public debt and tightening global financial conditions, have become even less accommodative. Spending pressures to curb the impact of rising prices have been building in many countries (for example, fuel subsidies in Cameroon, Kenya, and Nigeria; a fuel levy reduction in South Africa), further straining fiscal positions. Sovereign credit spreads have already widened and currencies weakened in countries perceived to be at high risk of debt distress (Ghana). The tightening of monetary policy to combat rising inflation has also gathered pace in several SSA economies (Ghana, Namibia, Nigeria, Rwanda, Sierra Leone, South Africa). Moreover, rising core inflation in several countries (Cameroon, Nigeria, Uganda) points to broadening price pressures, further reducing room for accommodative policies.

Outlook

Growth in SSA is projected to decelerate from 4.2 percent in 2021 to 3.7 percent in 2022, as high inflation and policy tightening weaken domestic demand. The growth deceleration in major trading partners is compounding these headwinds. Growth is projected to firm slightly to an average of 3.9 percent in 2023-24, assuming further progress with pandemic containment, favorable terms of trade in commodity exporters, and a gradual easing of global food price pressures.

Although forecasts for both 2022 and 2023 have been unchanged—mainly on account of upward revisions for Nigeria—regional growth excluding the three largest economies (Angola, Nigeria, and South Africa) has been revised down by 0.4 percentage points this year. This reflects slower-than-expected growth in 30 countries, or over 60 percent of SSA economies, which together account for more than one-quarter of the regional GDP (figure 2.6.2.A). Similarly for 2023, excluding the three largest economies, SSA growth has been revised down by 0.4 percent since January.

High inflation is anticipated to depress real incomes and domestic demand across the region. The accompanying increase in poverty is especially concerning in countries where many people are already at high risk of falling into food insecurity (Democratic Republic of Congo, Ethiopia, Liberia, Madagascar, Nigeria, Sierra Leone). Slowing reform momentum, elevated levels of violence and insecurity, and policy uncertainty are envisioned to continue to deter private investment in many countries. Lingering pandemic uncertainties are expected to continue to weigh on growth in nonresource sectors, especially in countries with low vaccination rates. Vaccination rates in SSA are anticipated to continue lagging other EMDEs, complicating pandemic management (Agarwal et al. 2022).

The growth slowdown could also intensify pandemic-induced losses in per capita incomes. In about 45 percent of the region's economies and a half of its fragile and conflict-affected countries, per capita incomes are forecast to remain below pre-pandemic levels in 2023. Only about 40 percent of SSA economies and 39 percent of the region's fragile and conflict-affected countries were expected to be in this position in January. SSA as a whole is now expected to remain the only EMDE region where per capita incomes will not return to their 2019 levels even next year.

In *Nigeria*, growth is projected to edge up to 3.4 percent in 2022, but will soften to 3.2 percent in both 2023 and 2024. Stronger growth this year

FIGURE 2.6.2 SSA: Outlook

Growth in SSA is projected to stay below long-term averages as surging food prices dent recoveries in consumer spending, especially in countries with large vulnerable populations. The recovery in tourism is projected to continue, albeit pandemic-related uncertainties will linger. While commodity exporters stand to benefit from higher global prices, growth in some countries is expected to be constrained in the short term by rising prices of farm inputs, such as fuel and fertilizers. Tighter global financial conditions are expected to restrain access to financing for many countries.

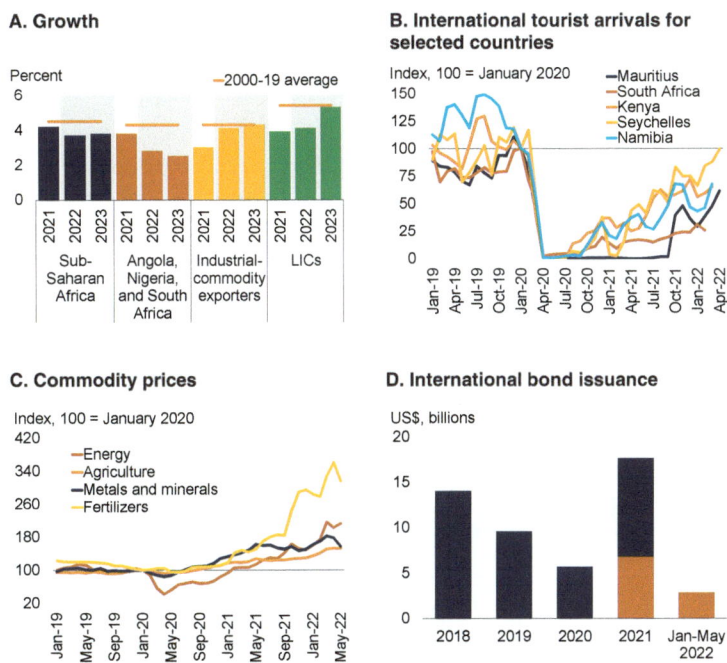

A. Growth

B. International tourist arrivals for selected countries

C. Commodity prices

D. International bond issuance

Sources: Dealogic; Haver Analytics; Namibia Statistics Agency; World Bank.
Note: EMDEs = emerging market and developing economies; LICs = low-income countries; SSA = Sub-Saharan Africa.
A. "Industrial-commodity exporters" represents oil and metal exporting countries. Aggregate growth rates calculated using constant GDP weights at average 2010-19 prices and market exchange rates. "Industrial commodity exporters" excludes Angola, Nigeria, and South Africa.
D. Cumulative issuance of international bonds by SSA governments and corporations, excluding Angola and South Africa. Red bar indicates the amount of bonds issued during the first five months of 2021 and 2022.

reflects support from elevated oil prices, the further recovery in agriculture and manufacturing, and structural reforms (for example, the Petroleum Industry Act of 2021). Production challenges in the oil sector are expected to persist, weighing on growth. The recovery in non-oil sectors is envisioned to continue, although shortages of fuel and higher food prices would restrain growth. Four in ten Nigerians live below the poverty line, with many more at risk of falling into poverty and becoming food insecure. Increases in food prices would further erode domestic demand.

Growth in *South Africa* is forecast to fall back to 2.1 percent this year and an average of 1.7 percent in 2023-24. High unemployment, power shortages, and slow reform momentum are expected to continue discouraging private investments. High government debt, along with elevated debt service costs, are expected to constrain much-needed public investment. The policy interest rate has already been raised four times during the current hiking cycle, with further increases likely in order to cool rising inflation.

Growth in *Angola* is projected to pick up to 3.1 percent this year, strengthening further to 3.3 percent in 2023 and 3.2 percent on in 2024. Oil production is expected to increase, as production challenges ease somewhat and investment in the oil sector increases. Higher oil revenues are expected to yield positive spillovers to the non-oil economy, help improve the fiscal position, and support increased spending on social protection. Elevated food price inflation is, however, anticipated to persist, slowing progress in reducing poverty and food insecurity.

Elsewhere in the region, growth is expected to average 5.3 percent in 2023-24—0.4 percentage points below January's forecast. Although increased commodity prices are projected to underpin recoveries in extractive sectors and strengthen export and fiscal revenues in some exporters of energy and industrial metals (Botswana, Democratic Republic of Congo, Republic of Congo, Guinea, Mozambique, Sudan), other producers are expected to struggle in ramping up mining production because of aging facilities and elevated security risks (Chad, South Sudan). Agricultural commodity exporters stand to benefit from higher global food prices as well; however, agricultural production will be constrained in the short term by surging costs of farm inputs (fertilizer, fuel), irregular rainfall, and high levels of violence in some countries (figure 2.6.2.C). More diversified economies (most WAEMU[1] countries, Rwanda) are nevertheless expected to grow on average by nearly 7 percent annually in 2023-24.

[1] Members of the West African Economic and Monetary Union (WAEMU) are Benin, Burkina Faso, Côte d'Ivoire, Guinea-Bissau, Mali, Niger, Senegal, and Togo.

Across the region, surging food and fuel prices are expected to reverse recent progress in poverty alleviation, especially in countries where vulnerable populations are sizable (Democratic Republic of Congo, Nigeria), and dependence on imported food is high (Benin, Comoros, The Gambia, Mozambique). Food imports represent about one-fifth of total SSA imports and 6 percent of GDP—over 10 percent of GDP in small and tourism-reliant SSA economies—higher than about 4 percent of GDP in other EMDEs.

Over 60 percent of countries in the region are in, or at a high risk of, debt distress following marked deteriorations in fiscal balances and increased indebtedness caused by the COVID-19 shock. Tighter global financial conditions are expected to significantly curtail access to financing in the region, compounding the negative impact of war-induced capital outflows (figure 2.6.2.D). This, together with pressures to improve debt sustainability, is likely to severely limit the scope for fiscal policy to stimulate demand, including support for food availability for vulnerable populations. Several countries already need to accelerate fiscal consolidation to stabilize public debt (Ethiopia, Ghana, South Africa).

Risks

Risks to the outlook are firmly to the downside, with much uncertainty emanating from Russia's invasion of Ukraine. Further disruption to global supplies of staple crops would lead to even higher food prices in SSA and increased spending on food imports. One in seven SSA countries—including several large economies that already have a high incidence of food insecurity (Democratic Republic of Congo, Nigeria, Sudan)—depend on Russia and Ukraine for over 45 percent of their wheat imports, while almost all of the region's economies are net importers of wheat (figure 2.6.3.A).

Higher prices for farming inputs—such as seeds, fuel, and fertilizers—would also prolong food price pressures in the region. The Russia's invasion of Ukraine has already amplified existing supply constraints in global fertilizer markets. Costlier farming inputs could reduce productivity in SSA agriculture and further deepen food shortages.

Higher fertilizer prices could also worsen fiscal pressures across the region, given that in many countries, government spending on subsidized fertilizers accounts for a large portion of public spending on agriculture (Ghana, Malawi, Zambia; Pernechele et al. 2021).

Reduced food supplies amplify the risk that extreme weather events could cause food prices to soar even further. Farming activities in SSA are already stressed because of climate change-induced shifts in rainfall patterns (Maino and Emrullahu 2022). Delayed and below-average rainfall and above-average temperatures have intensified drought severity in some areas (southern Ethiopia, Kenya, Uganda), while planting delays could reduce harvests and livestock (Burundi, Madagascar, Malawi, Mozambique). Multiple consecutive droughts in some areas (Madagascar) could push even more people into extreme food insecurity. Dry conditions are also threatening cocoa harvests in Côte d'Ivoire and Ghana.

Levels of violence and conflict remain elevated in SSA, particularly in the Sahel region. A rapid increase in the cost of living could trigger a wave of civil unrest across the region, further dampening growth in many countries (Hadzi-Vaskov, Pienknagura, and Ricci 2021; Weinberg and Bakker 2015).

A faster-than-expected deceleration of the global economy and increased volatility of commodity prices could hurt many SSA commodity exporters. Exporters of industrial metals, crude oil, and ores (Angola, Democratic Republic of Congo, Republic of Congo, South Africa, Zambia) could suffer from a substantial deceleration of activity in China (figure 2.6.3.B). A sharp contraction of growth in the euro area could hurt exporters of agricultural products—such as coffee, tea, tobacco, cotton, and textiles (Ethiopia, Madagascar, Malawi).

With financial conditions in EMDEs expected to continue to tighten, a sustained period of risk aversion and capital outflows triggered by global geopolitical tensions could sharply raise borrowing costs and rekindle currency depreciations, further elevating debt sustainability risks and fueling inflation in many economies. Higher borrowing

FIGURE 2.6.3 SSA: Risks

Disruptions in global food supplies from the Russia's invasion of Ukraine could significantly worsen poverty and food security in SSA. A sharper-than-expected deceleration of the global economy would have adverse effects on the region's exporters of industrial commodities. High and rising inflation could lead to an accelerated tightening of monetary policies. Low vaccination rates elevate the risk of recurrent outbreaks of new and more dangerous variants of COVID-19.

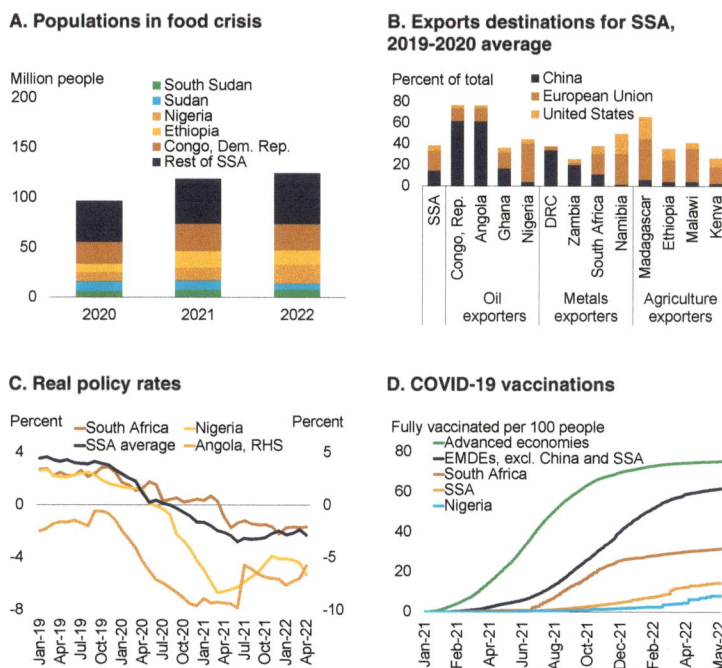

A. Populations in food crisis

B. Exports destinations for SSA, 2019-2020 average

C. Real policy rates

D. COVID-19 vaccinations

Sources: Comtrade (database); Global Network Against Food Crises; Haver Analytics; Our World in Data (database); World Bank.
Note: EMDEs = emerging market and developing economies; SSA = Sub-Saharan Africa; DRC = Democratic Republic of Congo.
A. Bars show the number of people in food crisis as classified by the Integrated Food Security Phase Classification (IPC/CH) Phase 3, that is, in acute food insecurity crisis or worse. Data for 2022 are estimates.
C. Policy rates adjusted for consumer price inflation. SSA aggregates is a simple average of nine countries. Last observation April 2022.
D. Total number of people who are fully vaccinated. Last observation is May 31, 2022.

costs and a decline in donor financing would put a squeeze on public spending, jeopardizing infrastructure and other development needs. Persistent increases in inflation could lead to much faster policy tightening in many SSA countries (figure 2.6.3.C). Accelerated policy tightening could also escalate stagflation risks across the region (World Bank 2022k).

Pandemic-related risks remain high. South Africa has already experienced a fifth wave of COVID-19 infections, though above-average vaccination rates helped keep it much milder compared to previous outbreaks. Recurring outbreaks of new and more dangerous variants of COVID-19 could lead to lasting and more serious disruptions to economic activity in countries where vaccination rates remain low. As of end-May, only 15 percent of SSA's population had been fully vaccinated against COVID-19, compared to an average of over 60 percent across other EMDEs (figure 2.6.3.D). In some of the region's most populous countries, such as the Democratic Republic of Congo and Nigeria—less than one in 10 people have been fully vaccinated.

TABLE 2.6.1 Sub-Saharan Africa forecast summary

(Real GDP growth at market prices in percent, unless indicated otherwise)

	2019	2020	2021e	2022f	2023f	2024f	Percentage point differences from January 2022 projections 2022f	Percentage point differences from January 2022 projections 2023f
EMDE SSA, GDP [1]	**2.6**	**-2.0**	**4.2**	**3.7**	**3.8**	**4.0**	**0.1**	**0.0**
GDP per capita (U.S. dollars)	-0.1	-4.5	1.6	1.1	1.3	1.5	0.1	0.0
(Average including countries that report expenditure components in national accounts) [2]								
EMDE SSA, GDP [2,3]	2.6	-2.1	4.2	3.7	3.8	4.0	0.1	0.0
PPP GDP	2.7	-1.8	4.2	3.7	3.9	4.1	0.0	-0.1
Private consumption	1.5	-1.2	3.7	3.3	3.6	3.6	0.2	0.4
Public consumption	4.1	3.0	2.6	3.0	0.9	2.7	3.1	0.8
Fixed investment	4.1	2.0	7.6	5.4	7.2	8.1	-1.4	-1.5
Exports, GNFS [4]	3.4	-12.8	7.2	6.0	6.2	5.8	0.5	0.7
Imports, GNFS [4]	5.1	-10.5	9.7	6.5	6.2	6.2	0.2	0.5
Net exports, contribution to growth	-0.5	-0.3	-0.9	-0.3	-0.2	-0.3	0.1	0.0
Memo items: GDP								
Eastern and Southern Africa	2.0	-3.0	4.4	3.4	3.6	3.8	-0.2	-0.2
Western and Central Africa	3.3	-0.8	3.9	4.0	4.1	4.3	0.4	0.2
SSA excluding Nigeria, South Africa, and Angola	4.3	0.2	4.6	4.5	5.1	5.4	-0.4	-0.4
Oil exporters [5]	2.1	-2.0	3.0	3.6	3.4	3.4	0.7	0.4
CFA countries [6]	4.2	0.5	4.1	4.5	5.3	5.8	-0.4	-0.2
CEMAC	1.8	-1.7	1.0	3.4	2.9	3.4	0.3	-0.2
WAEMU	5.7	1.8	5.9	5.1	6.7	7.2	-0.9	-0.1
SSA3	1.0	-4.1	3.8	2.8	2.5	2.7	0.4	0.2
Nigeria	2.2	-1.8	3.6	3.4	3.2	3.2	0.9	0.4
South Africa	0.1	-6.4	4.9	2.1	1.5	1.8	0.0	0.0
Angola	-0.7	-5.2	0.7	3.1	3.3	3.2	0.0	0.5

Source: World Bank.

Note: e = estimate; f = forecast; PPP = purchasing power parity; EMDE = emerging market and developing economy. World Bank forecasts are frequently updated based on new information and changing (global) circumstances. Consequently, projections presented here may differ from those contained in other Bank documents, even if basic assessments of countries' prospects do not differ at any given moment in time.

1. GDP and expenditure components are measured in average 2010-19 prices and market exchange rates.

2. Subregion aggregate excludes the Central African Republic, Eritrea, Guinea, São Tomé and Príncipe, Somalia, and South Sudan, for which data limitations prevent the forecasting of GDP components.

3. Subregion growth rates may differ from the most recent edition of Africa's Pulse (https://www.worldbank.org/en/region/afr/publication/africas-pulse) because of data revisions and the inclusion of the Central African Republic and São Tomé and Príncipe in the subregion aggregate of that publication.

4. Exports and imports of goods and nonfactor services (GNFS).

5. Includes Angola, Cameroon, Chad, the Republic of Congo, Equatorial Guinea, Gabon, Ghana, Nigeria, and South Sudan.

6. The Financial Community of Africa (CFA) franc zone consists of 14 countries in Sub-Saharan Africa, each affiliated with one of two monetary unions. The Central African Economic and Monetary Union (CEMAC) comprises Cameroon, the Central African Republic, Chad, the Republic of Congo, Equatorial Guinea, and Gabon; the West African Economic and Monetary Union (WAEMU) comprises Benin, Burkina Faso, Côte d'Ivoire, Guinea-Bissau, Mali, Niger, Senegal, and Togo.

TABLE 2.6.2 Sub-Saharan Africa country forecasts[1]

(Real GDP growth at market prices in percent, unless indicated otherwise)

Percentage point differences from January 2022 projections

	2019	2020	2021e	2022f	2023f	2024f	2022f	2023f
Angola	-0.7	-5.2	0.7	3.1	3.3	3.2	0.0	0.5
Benin	6.9	3.8	7.2	5.9	6.1	6.0	-0.6	-0.4
Botswana	3.0	-8.5	12.1	4.1	4.0	4.0	-1.8	-0.4
Burkina Faso	5.7	1.9	7.0	4.8	5.4	5.3	-0.8	0.1
Burundi	1.8	0.3	1.8	2.5	3.3	4.1	0.0	0.3
Central African Republic	3.1	0.9	0.9	3.2	3.4	4.0	-0.3	-1.1
Cabo Verde	5.7	-14.8	7.1	5.5	6.1	6.0	0.3	0.0
Cameroon	3.7	0.5	3.5	4.0	4.3	4.4	0.0	-0.1
Chad	3.2	-1.6	-1.2	2.8	3.5	3.9	1.0	0.6
Comoros	1.8	-0.3	2.4	2.8	3.1	3.7	-0.4	0.2
Congo, Dem. Rep.	4.4	1.7	5.7	6.0	6.4	6.1	1.2	1.3
Congo, Rep.	-0.1	-6.2	-3.5	3.5	3.0	4.5	0.3	0.0
Côte d'Ivoire	6.2	2.0	7.0	5.7	6.8	6.6	-0.8	0.4
Equatorial Guinea	-6.0	-4.9	-1.6	1.8	-2.6	-2.1	0.3	-1.7
Eritrea	3.8	-0.6	2.9	4.7	3.6	3.7	-0.1	-0.2
Eswatini	2.6	-1.9	3.1	2.0	1.8	1.8	0.2	-0.1
Ethiopia [2]	9.0	6.1	6.3	3.3	5.2	5.9	-1.0	-1.3
Gabon	3.9	-1.8	1.5	3.3	2.6	3.0	0.5	-0.4
Gambia, The	6.2	-0.2	5.6	5.6	6.2	6.5	-0.4	-0.3
Ghana	6.5	0.4	5.4	5.5	5.2	5.0	0.0	0.2
Guinea	5.6	4.6	3.1	4.3	5.9	5.8	-1.8	0.0
Guinea-Bissau	4.5	1.5	3.8	3.5	4.5	4.5	-0.5	-0.5
Kenya	5.0	-0.3	7.5	5.5	5.0	5.3	0.8	-0.1
Lesotho	2.6	-6.5	1.6	2.3	2.1	2.0	-0.7	-0.7
Liberia	-2.9	-3.0	4.0	4.4	4.8	5.2	-0.3	-0.2
Madagascar	4.4	-7.1	4.4	2.6	4.2	4.6	-2.8	-0.9
Malawi	5.4	0.8	2.8	2.1	4.3	4.2	-0.9	-0.1
Mali	4.8	-1.2	3.1	3.3	5.3	5.0	-1.9	0.3
Mauritania	5.3	-0.9	2.4	4.5	5.3	7.7	0.4	-1.1
Mauritius	3.0	-14.9	3.9	5.9	6.0	3.9	-0.7	1.8
Mozambique	2.3	-1.2	2.2	3.6	6.0	5.8	-1.5	-3.6
Namibia	-0.9	-8.5	0.8	2.9	2.1	2.0	0.5	0.6
Niger	5.9	3.6	1.4	5.2	7.1	10.4	-1.0	-2.3
Nigeria	2.2	-1.8	3.6	3.4	3.2	3.2	0.9	0.4
Rwanda	9.5	-3.4	10.9	6.8	7.2	7.4	-0.3	-0.6
São Tomé and Príncipe	2.2	3.1	1.8	2.8	3.0	3.3	-0.1	-0.3
Senegal	4.6	1.3	6.1	4.4	8.5	10.6	-1.1	-0.7
Seychelles	2.0	-13.3	7.9	4.6	5.7	5.0	-3.1	-1.1
Sierra Leone	5.3	-2.0	3.1	3.9	4.4	4.8	-2.1	0.1
South Africa	0.1	-6.4	4.9	2.1	1.5	1.8	0.0	0.0
Sudan	-2.2	-3.6	0.1	0.7	2.0	2.5	-2.8	-3.0
South Sudan [2]	3.2	9.5	-5.1	-0.8	2.5	4.0	-2.0	-1.0
Tanzania	5.8	2.0	4.3	5.3	5.7	6.1	-0.1	-0.2
Togo [3]	5.5	1.8	5.1	5.0	5.8	6.4	-0.6	-0.4
Uganda [2]	6.4	3.0	3.4	3.7	5.1	6.5	0.0	-0.4
Zambia	1.4	-3.0	3.6	3.3	3.6	4.0	0.4	-0.9
Zimbabwe	-6.1	-6.2	5.8	3.7	3.6	3.6	-0.6	-0.6

Source: World Bank.

Note: e = estimate; f = forecast. World Bank forecasts are frequently updated based on new information and changing (global) circumstances. Consequently, projections presented here may differ from those contained in other Bank documents, even if basic assessments of countries' prospects do not significantly differ at any given moment in time.

1. Data are based on GDP measured in average 2010-19 prices and market exchange rates.
2. Fiscal-year based numbers.
3. For Togo, growth figure in 2019 is based on pre-2020 rebasing GDP estimates.

References

Acosta-Ormaechea, S., I. Goldfajn, and J. Roldos. 2022. "Latin America Faces Unusually High Risks." *IMF Blog* (blog). April 26. https://blogs.imf.org /2022/04/26/latin-america-faces-unusually-high-risks.

Agarwal, R., G. Gopinath, J. Farrar, R. Hatchett, and P. Sands. 2022. "A Global Strategy to Manage the Long-Term Risks of COVID-19." IMF Working Paper 68, International Monetary Fund, Washington, DC.

Artuc, E., G. Falcone, G. Porto, and B. Rijkers. 2022. "War-Induced Food Price Inflation Imperils the Poor." VoxEU.org, CEPR Policy Portal, April 1. https:// voxeu.org/article/war-induced-food-price-inflation-imperils-poor.

Azevedo, J. P. W. D., F. H. Rogers, S. E. Ahlgren, M. H. Cloutier, B. Chakroun, G. Chang, S. Mizunoya, N. J. Reuge, M. Brossard, and J. L. Bergmann. 2021. *The State of the Global Education Crisis: A Path to Recovery.* Washington, DC: World Bank.

Barutciski, M. 1994. "EU States and the Refugee Crisis in the Former the Yugoslavia." Refuge: Canada's Journal on Refugees, 32–36.

Belhaj, F., and A. Soliman. 2021. "MENA Has a Food Security Problem, But There Are Ways to Address It." September 25. https://www.worldbank.org/en/news/ opinion/2021/09/24/mena-has-a-food-security-problem-but-there-are-ways-to-address-it.

Boer, L., A. Pescatori, and M. Stuermer. 2021. "Energy Transition Metals." IMF Working Paper 243, International Monetary Fund, Washington, DC.

Bordo, M. D., and P. L. Siklos. 2017. "Central Bank Credibility Before and After the Crisis." *Open Economies Review* 28 (1): 19–45.

Breisinger, C., Y. Kassim, S. Kurdi, J. Randriamamonjy, and J. Thurlow. "Food Subsidies and Cash Transfers in Egypt: Evaluating General Equilibrium Benefits and Trade-offs." MENA Working Paper 34, International Food Policy Research Institute, Washington, DC.

Comtrade (database). United Nations. Accessed on March 15, 2022. https://comtrade.un.org.

Dieppe, A., ed. 2021. *Global Productivity: Trends, Drivers, and Policies.* Washington, DC: World Bank.

Dieppe, A., S. Kilic-Celik, and C. Okou. 2020. "Implications of Major Adverse Events on Productivity." Policy Research Working Paper 9411, World Bank, Washington, DC.

FAO (Food and Agriculture Organization of the United Nations). 2021. "Low-Income Food-Deficit Countries (LIFDCs) - List updated June 2021." https:// www.fao.org/countryprofiles/lifdc/en.

FAO (Food and Agriculture Organization), IFAD (International Fund for Agricultural Development), UNICEF (United Nations Children's Fund), WFP (World Food Programme), and WHO (World Health Organization). 2021. *The State of Food Security and Nutrition in the World 2021. Transforming Food Systems for Food Security, Improved Nutrition, and Affordable Healthy Diets for All.* Rome: Food and Agriculture Organization of the United Nations.

FAO (Food and Agriculture Organization), IFAD (International Fund for Agricultural Development), UNICEF (United Nations Children's Fund), WFP (World Food Programme), and WHO (World Health Organization). 2020. *Regional Overview of Food Security and Nutrition in the Near East and North Africa 2019 – Rethinking food systems for healthy diets and improved nutrition.* Rome: Food and Agriculture Organization of the United Nations.

FAO-WFP (Food and Agricultural Organization of the United Nations and World Food Programme). 2022. *Hunger Hotspots: FAO-WFP Early Warnings of Acute Food Insecurity.* https://doi.org/10.4060/cb8376en.

Ha, J., M. A. Kose, H. Matsuoka, U. Panizza, and D. Vorisek. 2022. "Anchoring Inflation Expectations in Emerging and Developing Economies." VoxEU.org, CEPR Policy, February 8, https://voxeu.org/article/ anchoring-inflation-expectations-emerging-and-developing-economies.

Hadzi-Vaskov, M., S. Pienknagura, and L. Ricci. 2021. "The Macroeconomic Impact of Social Unrest." IMF Working Paper 135, International Monetary Fund, Washington, DC.

IEA (International Energy Agency). 2022. *Oil Market Report.* May. Paris: International Energy Agency.

IMF (International Monetary Fund). 2022a. *Feeling the Heat: Adapting to Climate Change in the Middle East and Central Asia.* Washington, DC: International Monetary Fund.

IMF (International Monetary Fund). 2022b. "Nepal: Request for an Arrangement Under the Extended Credit Facility." IMF Country Report 24, International Monetary Fund, Washington, DC.

Kammer, A., J. Azour, A. A. Selassie, I. Goldfajn, and C. Rhee. 2022. "How War in Ukraine Is Reverberating across World's Regions." *IMF Blog* (blog), March 15. https://blogs.imf.org/2022/03/15/how-war-in-ukraine-is-reverberating-across-worlds-regions.

Kose, M. A., F. Ohnsorge, and N. Sugawara. 2021. "A Mountain of Debt: Navigating the Legacy of the Pandemic." Policy Research Working Paper 9800, World Bank, Washington, DC.

Mahler, D. G., N. Yonzan, R. Hill, C. Lakner, H. Wu, and N. Yoshida. 2022. "Pandemic, Prices and Poverty." *Data Blog* (blog). April 26. https://blogs.worldbank.org/opendata/pandemic-prices-and-poverty.

Maino, R., and D. Emrullahu. 2022. "Climate Change in SubSaharan Africa's Fragile States. Evidence from Panel Estimations." IMF Working Paper 54, International Monetary Fund, Washington, DC.

Melecky, M. 2021. *Hidden Debt: Solutions to Avert the Next Financial Crisis in South Asia*. Washington, DC: World Bank.

OECD/FAO (Organisation for Economic Co-operation and Development / Food and Agriculture Organization of the United Nations). 2020. *OECD-FAO Agricultural Outlook 2020-2029*. Paris: OECD Publishing.

OECD/FAO (Organisation for Economic Co-operation and Development / Food and Agriculture Organization of the United Nations). 2021. *OECD-FAO Agricultural Outlook 2021-2030*. Paris: OECD Publishing.

Oxford Economics. 2019. "Global Economic Model." July, Oxford Economics, Oxford, UK.

PAHO (Pan American Health Organization). 2022. "Weekly Press Briefing on COVID-19 Director's Remarks." February 23. https://www.paho.org/en/documents/weekly-press-briefing-covid-19-directors-opening-remarks-february-23-2022.

Parry, I., S. Black, and N. Vernon. 2021. *Still Not Getting Energy Prices Right: A Global and Country Update of Fossil Fuel Subsidies*. IMF Working Paper 236, International Monetary Fund, Washington, DC.

Pernechele, V., F. Fontes, R. Baborska, J. Nkuingoua, X. Pan, and C. Tuyishime. 2021. *Public Expenditure on Food and Agriculture in Sub-Saharan Africa: Trends, Challenges and Priorities*. Rome: Food and Agriculture Organization of the United Nations.

Ruch, F. U. 2021. "Neutral Real Interest Rates in Inflation Targeting Emerging and Developing Economies." Policy Research Working Paper 9711, World Bank, Washington, DC.

Scandurra, G., A. Romanoa, M.Ronghia, and A. Carforab. 2018. "On the Vulnerability of Small Island Developing States: A Dynamic Analysis." *Ecological Indicators* 84 (January): 382-392.

Siklos, P. L. 2013. "Sources of Disagreement in Inflation Forecasts: An International Empirical Investigation." *Journal of International Economics* 90 (1): 218–231.

Simler, R. 2010. "The Short-Term Impact of Higher Food Prices on Poverty in Uganda." IMF Working Paper 5210, International Monetary Fund, Washington, DC.

UNDP (United Nations Development Programme). 2022. "The Development Impact of the War in Ukraine: Initial Projections." March 16. https://www.undp.org/publications/development-impact-war-ukraine-initial-projections.

UNESCO and UNICEF (United Nations Educational, Scientific and Cultural Organization and United Nations International Children's Emergency Fund). 2021. *Situation Analysis on the Effects of and Responses to COVID-19 on the Education Sector in South Asia. Regional Synthesis Report*. https://www.unicef.org/rosa/media/16436/file/Regional Situation Analysis Report.pdf.

UNHCR (United Nations High Commissioner for Refugees). 2022. "Ukraine Situation: Flash Update #8." UNHCR Regional Bureau for Europe. April 13. https://data2.unhcr.org/en/documents/details/92011.

UNOCHA (United Nations Office for the Coordination of Humanitarian Affairs). 2022. "Ukraine: Humanitarian Impact Situation Report." March 30. https://reliefweb.int/report/ukraine/ukraine-humanitarian-impact-situation-report-1200-pm-eet-30-march-2022.

Weinberg, J., and R. Bakker. 2015. "Let Them Eat Cake: Food Prices, Domestic Policy and Social Unrest." *Conflict Management and Peace Science* 32 (3): 309-26.

Winkler, D., L. Wuester, and D. Knight. 2022a. "Russia's Global Value Chain Participation: Implications of Russia's Invasion of Ukraine for its Trade Partners and Key Value Chains." World Bank, Washington, DC.

Winkler, D., L. Wuester, and D. Knight. 2022b. "Russia's Global Value Chain Participation: Possible Implications of the Ukraine War for its Trade Partners and Key Value Chains." Updates from Trade, Investment and Competitiveness, World Bank, Washington, DC.

Wodon, Q., C. Tsimpo, P. Backiny-Yetna, G. Joseph, F. Adoho, and H. Coulombe. 2008. "Potential Impact of Higher Food Prices on Poverty: Summary Estimates for a Dozen West and Central African Countries." Policy Research Working Paper 4745, World Bank, Washington, DC.

Wodon, Q., and H. Zaman. 2008. "Rising Food Prices in Sub-Saharan Africa: Poverty Impact and Policy Responses." Working Paper 4738, World Bank, Washington, DC.

WFP (World Food Programme). 2022. "Food Security Implications of the Ukraine Conflict," World Food Programme, Rome.

World Bank. 2014. *Turn Down the Heat: Confronting the New Climate Normal.* Washington, DC: World Bank.

World Bank. 2017. *Global Economic Prospects: Weak Investment in Uncertain Times.* Washington, DC: World Bank.

World Bank. 2019. *Europe and Central Asia Economic Update: Financial Inclusion.* Spring. Washington, DC: World Bank.

World Bank. 2020. *Global Economic Prospects.* January. Washington, DC: World Bank.

World Bank. 2021a. *China Economic Update: Rebalancing Act—From Recovery to High-Quality Growth.* December. Washington, DC: World Bank.

World Bank. 2021b. *East Asia and Pacific Economic Update: Long Covid.* October. Washington, DC: World Bank.

World Bank. 2021c. *MENA Economic Update. Overconfident: How Economic and Health Fault Lines Left the Middle East and North Africa Ill-Prepared to Face COVID-19.* October. Washington, DC: World Bank.

World Bank. 2021d. *Global Economic Prospects.* January. Washington, DC: World Bank.

World Bank. 2022a. *East Asia and Pacific Economic Update: Braving the Storms.* October. Washington, DC: World Bank.

World Bank. 2022b. *Global Economic Prospects.* January. Washington, DC: World Bank.

World Bank. 2022c. "Consolidating the Recovery: Seizing Green Growth Opportunities." Semiannual Report for Latin America and the Caribbean. Washington, DC: World Bank.

World Bank. 2022d. *Commodity Markets Outlook: The Impact of the War in Ukraine on Commodity Markets.* April. Washington, DC: World Bank.

World Bank. 2022e. *Lebanon Economic Monitor: The Great Denial.* January. Washington, DC: World Bank.

World Bank. 2022f. *Pakistan Development Update.* April. Washington, DC: World Bank.

World Bank. 2022g. *South Asia Economic Focus: Reshaping Norms: A New Way Forward.* April. Washington, DC: World Bank.

World Bank. 2022h. *Afghanistan Development Update: Towards Economic Stabilization and Recovery.* April. Washington, DC: World Bank.

World Bank. 2022i. *Bhutan Development Update.* April. Washington, DC: World Bank.

World Bank. 2022j. *Nepal Development Update: Global Challenges and Domestic Revival.* April. Washington, DC: World Bank.

World Bank. 2022k. *Africa's Pulse. Boosting Resilience: The Future of Social Protection in Africa.* April. Washington, DC: World Bank.

World Bank. Forthcoming. *Under the Pandemic's Shadow: Growth in Emerging and Developing Economies.* Washington, DC: World Bank.

Real GDP growth

	Annual estimates and forecasts[1] (Percent change)						Quarterly estimates[2] (Percent change, year-on-year)					
	2019	2020	2021e	2022f	2023f	2024f	20Q4	21Q1	21Q2	21Q3	21Q4	22Q1e
World	2.6	-3.3	5.7	2.9	3.0	3.0	-0.9	3.2	12.1	4.7	..	..
Advanced economies	1.7	-4.6	5.1	2.6	2.2	1.9	-2.7	-0.2	12.6	4.2	4.6	..
United States	2.3	-3.4	5.7	2.5	2.4	2.0	-2.3	0.5	12.2	4.9	5.5	3.5
Euro area	1.6	-6.4	5.4	2.5	1.9	1.9	-4.3	-0.9	14.6	4.1	4.7	5.1
Japan	-0.2	-4.6	1.7	1.7	1.3	0.6	-0.9	-1.7	7.4	1.2	0.4	0.5
Emerging market and developing economies	3.8	-1.6	6.6	3.4	4.2	4.4	2.0	8.5	11.3	5.4	..	..
East Asia and Pacific	5.8	1.2	7.2	4.4	5.2	5.1	4.9	15.3	8.1	4.3	4.1	4.8
Cambodia	7.1	-3.1	3.0	4.5	5.8	6.6	..	..	..	..	..	..
China	6.0	2.2	8.1	4.3	5.2	5.1	6.4	18.3	7.9	4.9	4.0	4.8
Fiji	-0.4	-15.7	-4.1	6.3	7.7	5.6	..	..	..	..	..	..
Indonesia	5.0	-2.1	3.7	5.1	5.3	5.3	-2.2	-0.7	7.1	3.5	5.0	5.0
Kiribati	3.9	-0.5	1.5	1.8	2.5	2.3	..	..	..	..	..	..
Lao PDR	5.5	0.5	2.5	3.8	4.0	4.2	..	..	..	..	..	..
Malaysia	4.4	-5.6	3.1	5.5	4.5	4.4	-3.3	-0.5	15.9	-4.5	3.6	5.0
Marshall Islands[3]	6.6	-2.2	-2.5	3.0	2.4	2.6	..	..	..	..	..	..
Micronesia, Fed. Sts.[3]	1.2	-1.8	-3.2	0.4	3.2	1.9	..	..	..	..	..	..
Mongolia	5.0	-4.4	1.4	2.5	5.8	6.8	-0.2	15.1	-0.5	-1.2	-3.5	-3.8
Myanmar[3][6]	6.8	3.2	-18.0	..	..	..	..	..	..	..	..	..
Nauru[3]	1.0	1.1	1.5	0.9	2.6	2.4	..	..	..	..	..	..
Palau[3]	-1.8	-9.7	-17.1	7.2	16.2	4.5	..	..	..	..	..	..
Papua New Guinea	5.9	-3.5	1.0	4.0	2.7	2.5	..	..	..	..	..	..
Philippines	6.1	-9.6	5.6	5.7	5.6	5.6	-8.2	-3.8	12.1	7.0	7.8	8.3
Samoa[3]	4.4	-2.6	-8.1	-0.3	2.5	3.8	..	..	..	..	..	..
Solomon Islands	1.2	-4.3	0.1	-2.9	5.3	3.8	..	..	..	..	..	..
Thailand	2.2	-6.2	1.6	2.9	4.3	3.9	-4.2	-2.4	7.7	-0.2	1.8	2.2
Timor-Leste	1.8	-8.6	1.6	2.4	2.8	3.0	..	..	..	..	..	..
Tonga[3]	0.7	0.7	-2.7	-1.6	3.2	3.2	..	..	..	..	..	..
Tuvalu	13.9	4.4	2.5	3.5	3.8	4.0	..	..	..	..	..	..
Vanuatu	3.9	-6.8	1.2	2.0	4.1	3.7	..	..	..	..	..	..
Vietnam	7.0	2.9	2.6	5.8	6.5	6.5	4.6	4.7	6.7	-6.0	5.2	5.1
Europe and Central Asia	2.7	-1.9	6.5	-2.9	1.5	3.3	0.0	1.2	13.5	5.6	..	..
Albania	2.2	-3.5	8.5	3.2	3.5	3.5	2.9	4.3	17.7	6.8	5.5	..
Armenia	7.6	-7.2	5.7	3.5	4.6	4.9	-8.9	-1.7	9.0	2.3	11.5	8.6
Azerbaijan	2.5	-4.3	5.6	2.7	2.2	2.3	..	..	..	..	..	..
Belarus	1.4	-0.9	2.3	-6.5	1.5	1.6	-0.2	1.5	6.0	1.7	1.1	..
Bosnia and Herzegovina[5]	2.8	-3.1	7.1	2.7	3.1	3.5	-2.5	2.6	11.6	6.9	7.5	..
Bulgaria	4.0	-4.4	4.2	2.6	4.3	3.7	-4.1	0.2	6.5	3.9	5.6	..
Croatia	3.5	-8.1	10.4	3.8	3.4	3.1	-7.4	-0.6	16.4	15.1	9.7	7.0
Georgia	5.0	-6.8	10.6	5.5	5.5	5.0	-7.4	-4.1	28.9	9.1	8.8	..
Hungary	4.6	-4.5	7.1	4.6	3.8	3.4	-2.7	-1.9	17.8	6.2	7.1	8.2
Kazakhstan	4.5	-2.5	4.0	2.0	4.0	3.5	-2.1	-1.6	6.3	6.1	5.4	..
Kosovo	4.8	-5.3	9.1	3.9	4.3	4.2	..	..	..	..	..	..
Kyrgyz Republic	4.6	-8.4	3.6	-2.0	3.4	4.0	..	..	..	..	..	..
Moldova	3.7	-7.4	13.9	-0.4	2.7	4.2	-3.4	1.8	21.5	8.3	..	..
Montenegro	4.1	-15.3	12.4	3.6	4.7	3.7	..	..	..	..	..	..
North Macedonia	3.9	-6.1	4.0	2.7	3.1	3.2	-0.8	-1.8	13.4	3.0	2.3	..
Poland	4.7	-2.2	5.9	3.9	3.6	3.7	-2.1	-1.1	11.0	6.1	8.0	9.2
Romania	4.2	-3.7	5.9	2.9	3.7	3.9	-1.5	-0.1	15.4	6.9	2.4	6.5
Russian Federation	2.2	-2.7	4.7	-8.9	-2.0	2.2	-1.3	-0.3	10.5	4.0	5.0	3.5
Serbia	4.3	-0.9	7.4	3.2	2.7	2.8	-1.0	1.6	13.8	7.6	7.0	4.4
Tajikistan	7.4	4.4	9.2	-0.4	3.3	4.3	..	..	..	..	..	..
Turkey	0.9	1.8	11.0	2.3	3.2	4.0	6.2	7.3	21.9	7.5	9.1	7.3
Ukraine	3.2	-3.8	3.4	-45.1	2.1	5.8	-0.1	-2.2	6.0	2.8	6.1	..
Uzbekistan	5.7	1.9	7.4	4.3	5.3	5.5	..	..	..	..	..	..

Real GDP growth *(continued)*

	Annual estimates and forecasts[1] (Percent change)						Quarterly estimates[2] (Percent change, year-on-year)					
	2019	2020	2021e	2022f	2023f	2024f	20Q4	21Q1	21Q2	21Q3	21Q4	22Q1e
Latin America and the Caribbean	0.8	-6.4	6.7	2.5	1.9	2.4	-15.4	-6.9	-2.6	-0.1	4.0	..
Argentina	-2.0	-9.9	10.3	4.5	2.5	2.5	-4.3	2.9	17.9	11.9	8.6	..
Bahamas, The	0.7	-14.5	5.6	6.0	4.1	3.0	..	..	..	..	..	..
Barbados	-1.3	-13.7	1.4	11.2	4.9	3.0	..	..	..	..	..	..
Belize	2.0	-16.7	9.8	5.7	3.4	2.0	-16.2	-8.3	23.6	13.8	14.8	..
Bolivia	2.2	-8.7	6.1	3.9	2.8	2.7	1.0	-0.6	23.1	5.5	0.2	..
Brazil	1.2	-3.9	4.6	1.5	0.8	2.0	-0.9	1.3	12.3	4.0	1.6	1.7
Chile	0.8	-6.0	11.7	1.7	0.8	2.0	0.4	0.0	18.9	17.2	12.0	7.2
Colombia	3.2	-7.0	10.6	5.4	3.2	3.3	-3.6	0.9	18.3	13.7	10.8	8.5
Costa Rica	2.4	-4.1	7.6	3.4	3.2	3.2	-3.1	-0.7	10.4	12.8	9.3	6.0
Dominica	5.5	-11.0	3.7	6.8	5.0	4.6	..	..	..	..	..	..
Dominican Republic	5.1	-6.7	12.3	5.0	5.0	5.0	-2.9	3.1	25.4	11.5	11.2	..
Ecuador	0.0	-7.8	4.4	3.7	3.1	2.9	-6.4	-4.1	11.6	5.5	4.9	..
El Salvador	2.6	-8.0	10.7	2.7	1.9	2.0	-2.2	2.5	26.5	11.6	3.7	..
Grenada	0.7	-13.8	5.3	3.8	3.4	3.1	..	..	..	..	..	..
Guatemala	4.0	-1.8	8.0	3.4	3.4	3.5	2.1	4.5	15.4	8.1	4.7	..
Guyana	5.4	43.5	19.9	47.9	34.3	3.8	..	..	..	..	..	..
Haiti[3]	-1.7	-3.3	-1.8	-0.4	1.4	2.0	..	..	..	..	..	..
Honduras	2.7	-9.0	12.5	3.1	3.6	3.7	-7.8	1.9	27.2	12.8	11.2	..
Jamaica[2]	0.9	-10.0	4.6	3.2	2.3	1.2	-8.3	-6.6	14.2	5.9	6.7	..
Mexico	-0.2	-8.2	4.8	1.7	1.9	2.0	-4.3	-3.8	19.9	4.5	1.1	1.8
Nicaragua	-3.8	-1.8	10.3	2.9	2.3	2.5	-1.6	4.2	17.7	10.2	10.1	..
Panama	3.0	-17.9	15.3	6.3	5.0	5.0	-11.2	-8.4	40.0	25.5	16.4	..
Paraguay	-0.4	-0.8	4.2	0.7	4.7	3.8	1.1	0.7	13.9	2.9	0.6	..
Peru	2.2	-11.0	13.3	3.1	2.9	3.0	-1.6	4.5	41.8	11.4	3.2	3.8
St. Lucia	-0.1	-20.4	6.6	6.4	5.2	3.3	..	..	..	..	..	..
St. Vincent and the Grenadines	0.4	-5.3	-2.8	3.7	6.4	3.2	..	..	..	..	..	..
Suriname	1.1	-15.9	-3.5	1.8	2.1	2.7	..	..	..	..	..	..
Uruguay	0.4	-6.1	4.4	3.3	2.6	2.5	-2.9	-4.3	10.2	6.2	5.9	..
Middle East and North Africa	0.9	-3.7	3.4	5.3	3.6	3.2	-2.8	-0.9	5.2	6.7	6.2	..
Algeria	1.0	-5.1	3.9	3.2	1.3	1.4	-1.5	2.2	6.3	3.4	..	..
Bahrain	2.2	-4.9	2.2	3.5	3.1	3.1	-3.5	-2.8	5.5	2.1	4.3	..
Djibouti	7.8	0.5	4.3	3.3	5.2	6.2	..	..	..	..	..	..
Egypt, Arab Rep.[3]	5.6	3.6	3.3	6.1	4.8	5.0	2.0	2.9	7.7	9.8	8.3	..
Iran, Islamic Rep.[3]	-6.8	3.4	4.1	3.7	2.7	2.3	3.9	6.7	..	..	..	..
Iraq	5.5	-11.3	2.8	8.8	4.5	3.0	..	..	..	..	..	..
Jordan	2.0	-1.6	2.2	2.1	2.3	2.3	-1.6	0.3	3.2	2.7	2.6	..
Kuwait	-0.6	-8.9	2.3	5.7	3.6	2.5	-11.2	..	..	..	..	..
Lebanon[6]	-7.2	-21.4	-10.5	-6.5	..	..	..	..	..	..	..	..
Libya[6]	2.5	-31.3	99.3	..	..	..	..	..	..	..	..	..
Morocco	2.6	-6.3	7.4	1.1	4.3	3.6	-5.1	1.0	15.2	7.8	6.6	1.2
Oman	-0.8	-2.8	2.1	5.6	2.8	2.6	..	..	..	..	..	..
Qatar	0.8	-3.6	1.5	4.9	4.5	4.4	-3.9	-2.1	4.0	2.4	2.0	..
Saudi Arabia	0.3	-4.1	3.2	7.0	3.8	3.0	-3.8	-2.6	1.9	7.0	6.7	9.6
Syrian Arab Republic[6]	3.7	1.3	-2.1	-2.6	..	..	..	..	..	..	..	..
Tunisia	1.3	-8.7	3.1	3.0	3.5	3.3	-6.4	-2.2	15.2	0.3	1.8	2.7
United Arab Emirates	3.4	-6.1	2.8	4.7	3.4	3.6	..	..	..	..	..	..
West Bank and Gaza	1.4	-11.3	7.1	3.7	3.2	3.1	-12.1	-6.4	19.3	6.7	11.2	..
Yemen, Rep.[6]	1.4	-8.5	-2.1	0.8	2.5	..	..	..	..	..	..	..

Real GDP growth *(continued)*

	Annual estimates and forecasts[1] (Percent change)						Quarterly estimates[2] (Percent change, year-on-year)					
	2019	**2020**	**2021e**	**2022f**	**2023f**	**2024f**	**20Q4**	**21Q1**	**21Q2**	**21Q3**	**21Q4**	**22Q1e**
South Asia	**4.1**	**-4.5**	**7.6**	**6.8**	**5.8**	**6.5**	**0.7**	**2.6**	**19.9**	**8.2**	**5.3**	**..**
Afghanistan[6]	3.9	-1.9	..	..	..	..	..	..	..	..	..	..
Bangladesh[34]	7.9	3.4	6.9	6.4	6.7	6.9	..	..	..	..	..	..
Bhutan[34]	4.4	-2.4	-3.7	4.4	4.7	6.7	..	..	..	..	..	..
India[34]	3.7	-6.6	8.7	7.5	7.1	6.5	0.7	2.5	20.1	8.4	5.4	4.1
Maldives	6.9	-33.5	31.0	7.6	10.2	7.1	-32.8	-9.2	72.8	77.4	49.4	..
Nepal[34]	6.7	-2.1	1.8	3.7	4.1	5.8	..	..	..	..	..	..
Pakistan[34]	3.1	-0.9	5.7	4.3	4.0	4.2	..	..	..	..	..	..
Sri Lanka	2.3	-3.6	3.7	-7.8	-3.7	1.0	1.3	4.2	12.4	-1.5	1.8	..
Sub-Saharan Africa	**2.6**	**-2.0**	**4.2**	**3.7**	**3.8**	**4.0**	**-1.1**	**-0.1**	**11.5**	**4.3**	**..**	**..**
Angola	-0.7	-5.2	0.7	3.1	3.3	3.2	..	..	..	..	..	..
Benin	6.9	3.8	7.2	5.9	6.1	6.0	..	..	..	..	..	..
Botswana	3.0	-8.5	12.1	4.1	4.0	4.0	-4.6	0.8	37.1	8.4	5.6	..
Burkina Faso	5.7	1.9	7.0	4.8	5.4	5.3	..	..	..	..	..	..
Burundi	1.8	0.3	1.8	2.5	3.3	4.1	..	..	..	..	..	..
Cabo Verde	5.7	-14.8	7.1	5.5	6.1	6.0	..	..	..	..	..	..
Cameroon	3.7	0.5	3.5	4.0	4.3	4.4	..	..	..	..	..	..
Central African Republic	3.1	0.9	0.9	3.2	3.4	4.0	..	..	..	..	..	..
Chad	3.2	-1.6	-1.2	2.8	3.5	3.9	..	..	..	..	..	..
Comoros	1.8	-0.3	2.4	2.8	3.1	3.7	..	..	..	..	..	..
Congo, Dem. Rep.	4.4	1.7	5.7	6.0	6.4	6.1	..	..	..	..	..	..
Congo, Rep.	-0.1	-6.2	-3.5	3.5	3.0	4.5	..	..	..	..	..	..
Côte d'Ivoire	6.2	2.0	7.0	5.7	6.8	6.6	..	..	..	..	..	..
Equatorial Guinea	-6.0	-4.9	-1.6	1.8	-2.6	-2.1	..	..	..	..	..	..
Eritrea	3.8	-0.6	2.9	4.7	3.6	3.7	..	..	..	..	..	..
Eswatini	2.6	-1.9	3.1	2.0	1.8	1.8	..	..	..	..	..	..
Ethiopia[3]	9.0	6.1	6.3	3.3	5.2	5.9	..	..	..	..	..	..
Gabon	3.9	-1.8	1.5	3.3	2.6	3.0	..	..	..	..	..	..
Gambia, The	6.2	-0.2	5.6	5.6	6.2	6.5	..	..	..	..	..	..
Ghana	6.5	0.4	5.4	5.5	5.2	5.0	4.3	3.6	4.2	6.5	7.0	..
Guinea	5.6	4.6	3.1	4.3	5.9	5.8	..	..	..	..	..	..
Guinea-Bissau	4.5	1.5	3.8	3.5	4.5	4.5	..	..	..	..	..	..
Kenya	5.0	-0.3	7.5	5.5	5.0	5.3	2.3	2.7	11.0	9.3	7.4	..
Lesotho	2.6	-6.5	1.6	2.3	2.1	2.0	-12.0	-10.4	16.2	0.0	1.5	..
Liberia	-2.9	-3.0	4.0	4.4	4.8	5.2	..	..	..	..	..	..
Madagascar	4.4	-7.1	4.4	2.6	4.2	4.6	..	..	..	..	..	..
Malawi	5.4	0.8	2.8	2.1	4.3	4.2	..	..	..	..	..	..
Mali	4.8	-1.2	3.1	3.3	5.3	5.0	..	..	..	..	..	..
Mauritania	5.3	-0.9	2.4	4.5	5.3	7.7	..	..	..	..	..	..
Mauritius	3.0	-14.9	3.9	5.9	6.0	3.9	..	..	..	..	..	..
Mozambique	2.3	-1.2	2.2	3.6	6.0	5.8	-1.8	0.2	2.1	3.5	3.6	4.1
Namibia	-0.9	-8.5	0.8	2.9	2.1	2.0	-6.6	-6.8	3.0	2.4	..	..
Niger	5.9	3.6	1.4	5.2	7.1	10.4	..	..	..	..	..	..
Nigeria	2.2	-1.8	3.6	3.4	3.2	3.2	0.0	0.4	5.4	4.1	4.6	3.6
Rwanda	9.5	-3.4	10.9	6.8	7.2	7.4	-0.7	3.6	20.6	10.1	10.3	..
São Tomé and Príncipe	2.2	3.1	1.8	2.8	3.0	3.3	..	..	..	..	..	..
Senegal	4.6	1.3	6.1	4.4	8.5	10.6	..	..	..	..	..	..
Seychelles	2.0	-13.3	7.9	4.6	5.7	5.0	-4.7	-13.8	17.7	7.7	0.0	..
Sierra Leone	5.3	-2.0	3.1	3.9	4.4	4.8	..	..	..	..	..	..

Real GDP growth *(continued)*

	Annual estimates and forecasts[1]						Quarterly estimates[2]					
	2019	2020	2021e	2022f	2023f	2024f	20Q4	21Q1	21Q2	21Q3	21Q4	22Q1e
Sub-Saharan Africa (continued)												
South Africa	0.1	-6.4	4.9	2.1	1.5	1.8	-3.5	-2.4	19.6	2.9	1.7	..
South Sudan[3]	3.2	9.5	-5.1	-0.8	2.5	4.0	..	..	..	..	..	..
Sudan	-2.2	-3.6	0.1	0.7	2.0	2.5	..	..	..	..	..	..
Tanzania	5.8	2.0	4.3	5.3	5.7	6.1	..	..	..	..	..	..
Togo[7]	5.5	1.8	5.1	5.0	5.8	6.4	..	..	..	..	..	..
Uganda[3]	6.4	3.0	3.4	3.7	5.1	6.5	-0.4	2.8	13.2	3.5	5.2	..
Zambia	1.4	-3.0	3.6	3.3	3.6	4.0	-2.7	0.5	8.5	3.3	2.1	..
Zimbabwe	-6.1	-6.2	5.8	3.7	3.6	3.6	..	..	..	..	..	..

Sources: World Bank; Haver Analytics.

Note: e = estimate; f = forecast.

1. Aggregate growth rates calculated using GDP weights at average 2010-19 prices and market exchange rates.

2. Quarterly estimates are based on non-seasonally-adjusted real GDP, except for advanced economies, as well as Algeria, Ecuador, Morocco, Poland and Tunisia. In some instances, quarterly growth paths may not align to annual growth estimates, owing to the timing of GDP releases. Quarterly data for Jamaica are gross value added. Quarterly data for Montenegro are preliminary. Data for Timor-Leste represent non-oil GDP.

Regional averages are calculated based on data from the following economies:

East Asia and Pacific: China, Indonesia, Malaysia, Mongolia, the Philippines, Thailand, and Vietnam.

Europe and Central Asia: Albania, Armenia, Belarus, Bosnia and Herzegovina, Bulgaria, Croatia, Georgia, Hungary, Kazakhstan, Moldova, North Macedonia, Poland, Romania, the Russian Federation, Serbia, Turkey, and Ukraine.

Latin America and the Caribbean: Argentina, Belize, Bolivia, Brazil, Chile, Colombia, Costa Rica, the Dominican Republic, Ecuador, El Salvador, Guatemala, Honduras, Jamaica, Mexico, Nicaragua, Panama, Paraguay, Peru, and Uruguay.

Middle East and North Africa: Bahrain, the Arab Republic of Egypt, Jordan, Morocco, Qatar, Saudi Arabia, Tunisia, and West Bank and Gaza.

South Asia: India, Maldives, and Sri Lanka.

Sub-Saharan Africa: Botswana, Ghana, Kenya, Lesotho, Mozambique, Namibia, Nigeria, Rwanda, South Africa, Uganda, and Zambia.

3. Annual GDP is on fiscal year basis, as per reporting practice in the country.

4. GDP data for Pakistan are based on factor cost. For Bangladesh, Bhutan, Nepal, and Pakistan, the column labeled 2022 refers to FY2021/22. For India and the Islamic Republic of Iran, the column labeled 2022 refers to FY2022/23.

5. Data for Bosnia and Herzegovina are from the production approach.

6. Forecasts for Afghanistan (beyond 2020), Lebanon (beyond 2022), Libya (beyond 2021), Myanmar (beyond 2021), the Syrian Arab Republic (beyond 2022), and the Republic of Yemen (beyond 2023) are excluded because of a high degree of uncertainty.

7. For Togo, growth figure in 2019 is based on pre-2020 rebasing GDP estimates.

To download the data in this table, please visit www.worldbank.org/gep.

Data and Forecast Conventions

The macroeconomic forecasts presented in this report are prepared by staff of the Prospects Group of the Equitable Growth, Finance and Institutions Vice-Presidency, in coordination with staff from the Macroeconomics, Trade, and Investment Global Practice and from regional and country offices, and with input from regional Chief Economist offices. They are the result of an iterative process that incorporates data, macro-econometric models, and judgment.

Data. Data used to prepare country forecasts come from a variety of sources. National Income Accounts (NIA), Balance of Payments (BOP), and fiscal data are from Haver Analytics; the World Development Indicators by the World Bank; the World Economic Outlook, Balance of Payments Statistics, and International Financial Statistics by the International Monetary Fund. Population data and forecasts are from the United Nations World Population Prospects. Country- and lending-group classifications are from the World Bank. The Prospects Group's internal databases include high-frequency indicators such as industrial production, consumer price indexes, emerging markets bond index (EMBI), exchange rates, exports, imports, policy rates, and stock market indexes, based on data from Bloomberg, Haver Analytics, IMF Balance of Payments Statistics, IMF International Financial Statistics, and J. P. Morgan.

Aggregations. Aggregate growth for the world and all subgroups of countries (such as regions and income groups) is calculated using GDP weights at average 2010-19 prices and market exchange rates of country-specific growth rates. Income groups are defined as in the World Bank's classification of country groups.

Forecast process. The process starts with initial assumptions about advanced-economy growth and commodity price forecasts. These are used as conditioning assumptions for the first set of growth forecasts for EMDEs, which are produced using macroeconometric models, accounting frameworks to ensure national account identities and global consistency, estimates of spillovers from major economies, and high-frequency indicators. These forecasts are then evaluated to ensure consistency of treatment across similar EMDEs. This is followed by extensive discussions with World Bank country teams, who conduct continuous macroeconomic monitoring and dialogue with country authorities and finalize growth forecasts for EMDEs. The Prospects Group prepares advanced-economy and commodity price forecasts. Throughout the forecasting process, staff use macroeconometric models that allow the combination of judgement and consistency with model-based insights.

Global Economic Prospects: Selected Topics, 2015-22

Global Economic Prospects: Selected Topics, 2015-22

Growth and business cycles		
Cross-border spillovers		
	Who catches a cold when emerging markets sneeze?	January 2016, chapter 3
	Sources of the growth slowdown in BRICS	January 2016, box 3.1
	Understanding cross-border growth spillovers	January 2016, box 3.2
	Within-region spillovers	January 2016, box 3.3
	East Asia and Pacific	January 2016, box 2.1.1
	Europe and Central Asia	January 2016, box 2.2.1
	Latin America and the Caribbean	January 2016, box 2.3.1
	Middle East and North Africa	January 2016, box 2.4.1
	South Asia	January 2016, box 2.5.1
	Sub-Saharan Africa	January 2016, box 2.6.1
Productivity		
	How do disasters affect productivity?	June 2020, box 3.2
	Fading promise: How to rekindle productivity growth	January 2020, chapter 3
	EMDE regional productivity trends and bottlenecks	January 2020, box 3.1
	Sectoral sources of productivity growth	January 2020, box 3.2
	Patterns of total factor productivity: A firm perspective	January 2020, box 3.3
	Debt, financial crises, and productivity	January 2020, box 3.4
	Labor productivity in East Asia and Pacific: Trends and drivers	January 2020, box 2.1.1
	Labor productivity in Europe and Central Asia: Trends and drivers	January 2020, box 2.2.1
	Labor productivity in Latin America and the Caribbean: Trends and drivers	January 2020, box 2.3.1
	Labor productivity in Middle East and North Africa: Trends and drivers	January 2020, box 2.4.1
	Labor productivity in South Asia: Trends and drivers	January 2020, box 2.5.1
	Labor productivity in Sub-Saharan Africa: Trends and drivers	January 2020, box 2.6.1
Investment slowdown		
	Investment: Subdued prospects, strong needs	June 2019, Special Focus 11
	Weak investment in uncertain times: Causes, implications, and policy responses	January 2017, chapter 3
	Investment-less credit booms	January 2017, box 3.1
	Implications of rising uncertainty for investment in EMDEs	January 2017, box 3.2
	Investment slowdown in China	January 2017, box 3.3
	Interactions between public and private investment	January 2017, box 3.4
	East Asia and Pacific	January 2017, box 2.1.1
	Europe and Central Asia	January 2017, box 2.2.1
	Latin America and the Caribbean	January 2017, box 2.3.1
	Middle East and North Africa	January 2017, box 2.4.1
	South Asia	January 2016, box 2.5.1
	Sub-Saharan Africa	January 2016, box 2.6.1
Forecast uncertainty		
	Scenarios of possible global growth outcomes	June 2020, box 1.3
	Quantifying uncertainties in global growth forecasts	June 2016, Special Focus 2
Fiscal space		
	Having space and using it: Fiscal policy challenges and developing economies	January 2015, chapter 3
	Fiscal policy in low-income countries	January 2015, box 3.1
	What affects the size of fiscal multipliers?	January 2015, box 3.2
	Chile's fiscal rule—an example of success	January 2015, box 3.3
	Narrow fiscal space and the risk of a debt crisis	January 2015, box 3.4
	Revenue mobilization in South Asia: Policy challenges and recommendations	January 2015, box 2.3
Other topics		
	Impact of COVID-19 on global income inequality	January 2022, chapter 4
	Education demographics and global inequality	January 2018, Special Focus 2
	Recent developments in emerging and developing country labor markets	June 2015, box 1.3
	Linkages between China and Sub-Saharan Africa	June 2015, box 2.1
	What does weak growth mean for poverty in the future?	January 2015, box 1.1
	What does a slowdown in China mean for Latin America and the Caribbean?	January 2015, box 2.2

Global Economic Prospects: Selected Topics, 2015-22

Monetary and exchange rate policies	
Asset purchases in emerging markets: Unconventional policies, unconventional times	January 2021, chapter 4
The fourth wave: Rapid debt buildup	January 2020, chapter 4
Price controls: Good intentions, bad outcomes	January 2020, Special Focus 1
Low for how much longer? Inflation in low-income countries	January 2020, Special Focus 2
Currency depreciation, inflation, and central bank independence	June 2019, Special Focus 1.2
The great disinflation	January 2019, box 1.1
Corporate debt: Financial stability and investment implications	June 2018, Special Focus 2
Recent credit surge in historical context	June 2016, Special Focus 1
Peg and control? The links between exchange rate regimes and capital account policies	January 2016, chapter 4
Negative interest rates in Europe: A glance at their causes and implications	June 2015, box 1.1
Hoping for the best, preparing for the worst: Risks around U.S. rate liftoff and policy options	June 2015, Special Focus 1
Countercyclical monetary policy in emerging markets: Review and evidence	January 2015, box 1.2

Fiscal policies	
Resolving high debt after the pandemic: lessons from past episodes of debt relief	January 2022, Special Focus
How has the pandemic made the fourth wave of debt more dangerous?	January 2021, box 1.1
The fourth wave: Rapid debt buildup	January 2020, chapter 4
Debt: No free lunch	June 2019, box 1.1
Debt in low-income countries: Evolution, implications, and remedies	January 2019, chapter 4
Debt dynamics in emerging market and developing economies: Time to act?	June 2017, Special Focus 1
Having fiscal space and using it: FiscFal challenges in developing economies	January 2015, chapter 3
Revenue mobilization in South Asia: Policy challenges and recommendations	January 2015, box 2.3
Fiscal policy in low-income countries	January 2015, box 3.1
What affects the size of fiscal multipliers?	January 2015, box 3.2
Chile's fiscal rule—an example of success	January 2015, box 3.3
Narrow fiscal space and the risk of a debt crisis	January 2015, box 3.4

Commodity markets	
Russia's invasion of Ukraine: Implications for energy markets and activity	June 2022, Special Focus 2
Commodity price cycles: Underlying drivers and policy options	January 2022, chapter 3
Reforms after the 2014-16 oil price plunge	June 2020, box 4.1
Adding fuel to the fire: Cheap oil in the pandemic	June 2020, chapter 4
The role of major emerging markets in global commodity demand	June 2018, Special Focus 1
The role of the EM7 in commodity production	June 2018, SF1, box SF1.1
Commodity consumption: Implications of government policies	June 2018, SF1, box SF1.2
With the benefit of hindsight: The impact of the 2014–16 oil price collapse	January 2018, Special Focus 1
From commodity discovery to production: Vulnerabilities and policies in LICs	January 2016, Special Focus
After the commodities boom: What next for low-income countries?	June 2015, Special Focus 2
Low oil prices in perspective	June 2015, box 1.2
Understanding the plunge in oil prices: Sources and implications	January 2015, chapter 4
What do we know about the impact of oil prices on output and inflation? A brief survey	January 2015, box 4.1

Globalization of trade and financial flows	
High trade costs: causes and remedies	June 2021, chapter 3
The impact of COVID-19 on global value chains	June 2020, box SF1
Poverty impact of food price shocks and policies	January 2019, chapter 4
Arm's-length trade: A source of post-crisis trade weakness	June 2017, Special Focus 2
The U.S. economy and the world	January 2017, Special Focus
Potential macroeconomic implications of the Trans-Pacific Partnership Agreement	January 2016, chapter 4
Regulatory convergence in mega-regional trade agreements	January 2016, box 4.1.1
China's integration in global supply chains: Review and implications	January 2015, box 2.1
Can remittances help promote consumption stability?	January 2015, chapter 4
What lies behind the global trade slowdown?	January 2015, chapter 4

Prospects Group:
Selected Other Publications on the Global Economy, 2015-22

Commodity Markets Outlook	
Causes and consequences of metal price shocks	April 2021
Persistence of commodity shocks	October 2020
Food price shocks: Channels and implications	April 2019
The implications of tariffs for commodity markets	October 2018, box
The changing of the guard: Shifts in industrial commodity demand	October 2018
Oil exporters: Policies and challenges	April 2018
Investment weakness in commodity exporters	January 2017
OPEC in historical context: Commodity agreements and market fundamentals	October 2016
From energy prices to food prices: Moving in tandem?	July 2016
Resource development in an era of cheap commodities	April 2016
Weak growth in emerging market economies: What does it imply for commodity markets?	January 2016
Understanding El Niño: What does it mean for commodity markets?	October 2015
How important are China and India in global commodity consumption?	July 2015
Anatomy of the last four oil price crashes	April 2015
Putting the recent plunge in oil prices in perspective	January 2015

Inflation in Emerging and Developing Economies: Evolution, Drivers, and Policies	
Inflation: Concepts, evolution, and correlates	Chapter 1
Understanding global inflation synchronization	Chapter 2
Sources of inflation: Global and domestic drivers	Chapter 3
Inflation expectations: Review and evidence	Chapter 4
Inflation and exchange rate pass-through	Chapter 5
Inflation in low-income countries	Chapter 6
Poverty impact of food price shocks and policies	Chapter 7

A Decade After the Global Recession: Lessons and Challenges for Emerging and Developing Economies	
A decade after the global recession: Lessons and challenges	Chapter 1
What happens during global recessions?	Chapter 2
Macroeconomic developments	Chapter 3
Financial market developments	Chapter 4
Macroeconomic and financial sector policies	Chapter 5
Prospects, risks, and vulnerabilities	Chapter 6
Policy challenges	Chapter 7
The role of the World Bank Group	Chapter 8

Global Waves of Debt: Causes and Consequences	
Debt: Evolution, causes, and consequences	Chapter 1
Benefits and costs of debt: The dose makes the poison	Chapter 2
Global waves of debt: What goes up must come down?	Chapter 3
The fourth wave: Ripple or tsunami?	Chapter 4
Debt and financial crises: From euphoria to distress	Chapter 5
Policies: Turning mistakes into experience	Chapter 6

Prospects Group:
Selected Other Publications on the Global Economy, 2015-22

Global Productivity: Trends, Drivers, and Policies	
Global productivity trends	Chapter 1
What explains productivity growth	Chapter 2
What happens to productivity during major adverse events?	Chapter 3
Productivity convergence: Is anyone catching up?	Chapter 4
Regional dimensions of productivity: Trends, explanations, and policies	Chapter 5
Productivity: Technology, demand, and employment trade-offs	Chapter 6
Sectoral sources of productivity growth	Chapter 7

The Long Shadow of Informality: Challenges and Policies	
Overview	Chapter 1
Understanding the informal economy: Concepts and trends	Chapter 2
Growing apart or moving together? Synchronization of informal- and formal-economy business cycles	Chapter 3
Lagging behind: informality and development	Chapter 4
Informality in emerging market and developing economies: Regional dimensions	Chapter 5
Tackling informality: Policy options	Chapter 6

Commodity Markets : Evolution, Challenges and Policies	
The evolution of commodity markets over the past century	Chapter 1
Commodity demand: Drivers, outlook, and implications	Chapter 2
The nature and drivers of commodity price cycles	Chapter 3
Causes and consequences of industrial commodity price shocks	Chapter 4

High-frequency monitoring	
Global Monthly newsletter	

www.ingramcontent.com/pod-product-compliance
Lightning Source LLC
Chambersburg PA
CBHW041707210326
41598CB00007B/566

* 9 7 8 1 4 6 4 8 1 8 4 3 1 *